Welcome to the *EVERYTHING*® series!

These handy, accessible books give you all you need to tackle a difficult project, gain a new hobby, comprehend a fascinating topic, prepare for an exam, or even brush up on something you learned back in school but have since forgotten.

You can read an *EVERYTHING*® book from cover-to-cover or just pick out the information you want from our four useful boxes: e-facts, e-ssentials, e-alerts, and e-questions. We literally give you everything you need to know on the subject, but throw in a lot of fun stuff along the way, too.

We now have well over 100 *EVERYTHING*® books in print, spanning such wide-ranging topics as weddings, pregnancy, wine, learning guitar, one-pot cooking, managing people, and so much more. When you're done reading them all, you can finally say you know *EVERYTHING*®!

FACTS

Important sound bytes of information

Quick handy tips

ALERT

Urgent warnings

QUESTIONS?

Solutions to common problems

Dear Reader,

Anyone can be rich. That's the driving conviction behind this book.

People who fail to grow rich often do so because they lack a few surprisingly simple tools and an understanding of the fundamental financial values that turn income and investments into wealth. We wrote this book to offer you an easy-to-follow road map toward your wealth goals.

This book is backed by years of experience, and can help you create and control what we call your "wealth plan." In it, we take a holistic view of generating riches, because your wealth plan is greater than the sum of its parts. We cover the technicalities of such things as investments and insurance, as you might expect. But we also make suggestions that will prompt you to assess your financial values and your attitudes toward money.

Besides equipping you with the tools you need to grow wealthy, we want to inspire you to remain focused on your financial goals and to believe that you, too, can be rich.

Sincerely,

Jennifer Lane

Bill Lane

THE
EVERYTHING®
GET RICH
BOOK

Surefire techniques to
increase your wealth

Jennifer Lane, CFP, with Bill Lane

Adams Media Corporation
Avon, Massachusetts

Dedication:
To William Cecil Lane, for opening the doors

EDITORIAL
Publishing Director: Gary M. Krebs
Managing Editor: Kate McBride
Copy Chief: Laura MacLaughlin
Acquisitions Editor: Bethany Brown
Development Editor: Micheal Paydos
　　　　　Lynn Northup

PRODUCTION
Production Director: Susan Beale
Production Manager: Michelle Roy Kelly
Series Designer: Daria Perreault
Cover Design: Paul Beatrice and Frank Rivera
Layout and Graphics: Brooke Camfield,
Colleen Cunningham, Michelle Roy Kelly,
Daria Perreault

An Everything® Series Book.
Everything® is a registered trademark of Adams Media Corporation.

Published by Adams Media Corporation
57 Littlefield Street, Avon, MA 02322 U.S.A.
www.adamsmedia.com

ISBN: 1-58062-670-X
Printed in the United States of America.

J   I   H   G   F   E   D   C   B   A

Library of Congress Cataloging-in-Publication Data
available from publisher.

This publication is designed to provide accurate and authoritative information with regard to the subject matter covered. It is sold with the understanding that the publisher is not engaged in rendering legal, accounting, or other professional advice. If legal advice or other expert assistance is required, the services of a competent professional person should be sought.
　　　　　—From a *Declaration of Principles* jointly adopted by a Committee of the American Bar Association and a Committee of Publishers and Associations

Illustrations by Barry Littmann.

This book is available at quantity discounts for bulk purchases.
For information, call 1-800-872-5627.

Visit the entire Everything® series at everything.com

Contents

Acknowledgments

We'd like to thank the following wonderful people for their support and feedback during the writing of this book: Kathy Dollard, C.F.P., Sharon Burke, C.P.A., Jan Cannon, Sandy LeDuc, C.P.A., Adelaide Aiken, C.F.P., Terry Blanchette, C.P.A., and Asa Phillips, Esq., who all gave us the benefit of their experience with clients and colleagues in developing their personal visions of what it means to get rich and be rich, and their relationships with money. We thank Gail Shapiro and Ann Smith, of Womankind Educational and Resource Center Inc., who gave Jennifer her first chance at writing about wealth. We are grateful to Nancy Cherico, Ph.D., who helped us develop our thoughts about how people feel about money and its role in their lives. And we are indebted to Carolyn Ehrman, who has been an invaluable resource and expert on insurance, and who helped develop the chapters on risk management.

A special thank you to Gina Ghioldi, Esq., and Paige Stover Hague, my wonderful radio partners, for numerous lunches and on-air shows spent listening to my trials and tribulations as the book developed. To Jean Sifleet, Esq., for her legal suggestions, feedback, and support.

Special thanks to my business partner Cindy Sechrest, C.P.A., who shares my vision of empowering individuals to take control of their money and to get rich, and who was endlessly forgiving of the time and attention this book demanded of our practice. And thanks to my special friend, Nancy Sartanowicz, who provided the emotional support through a summer's worth of weekends spent writing and thinking about money. And, of course, to my family whose love and encouragement has always helped me to grow.

Introduction

Everybody wants to be rich. Late-night television shows, day traders on the Internet, books that tell you how to make a million by working part-time from your home, or doing extra work on weekends—the message is everywhere: Anybody can be rich, something for nothing, a gimmick without a plan.

These snake oil salesmen have got it partly right—virtually anybody can become rich. And although not literally overnight, it can happen faster than you think, and true wealth builders have a plan, albeit a simple one. Building wealth is not rocket science, but it must be a way of life. No matter who you are, how much money you make, or where you live, you can be wealthy. In fact, who the real wealthy are may surprise you—it can be anybody. You probably talk to them everyday. They repair your car, do your taxes, cut your hair, and work near you in the next cubicle. They're salespeople, engineers, hairdressers, doctors, managers, and teachers. Understanding who the successful and wealthy among us are, and how you can fit into that elite group, is an important part of building wealth.

Wealth building is a process. First, you must understand what wealth looks like to you. Then you can define your wealth goal in a specific and quantifiable way. This quantifiable goal can be broken down into the steps that become your plan. We'll talk about these steps and the planning and steering process throughout this book, but first we need to understand who is rich and how they got there.

There's no doubt about it, there are some megawealthy people around us—movie stars, business tycoons, and the like. But they are the exception among the wealthy. Many wealthy people tend to be frugally minded, and are more focused on accumulating assets than displaying their wealth. They tend to buy modest homes in middle-class neighborhoods—even if their net-worth statement shows they can afford to move to more expensive digs—and have been saving a healthy portion of their income for as long as they can remember. They don't spend much of their money on extras like expensive cars, swimming pools, or designer clothes for their kids. They do spend it on education, though. Many of today's wealthy worked hard for their money. The self-employed wealthy started small, but worked hard and always made room in their budgets to "pay themselves first." The wealthy who worked as employees started day one at their job saving a large part of their paychecks in order to start building savings, and then investments.

Does this mean that in order to be wealthy you need to pinch pennies and clip coupons? Not if you don't want to. In fact, one common thread among today's wealthy is their focus and control. People who are able to build wealth understand what wealth means to them, and are focused on achieving it. They understand where their money goes, and deliberately channel it toward the things that will help them reach their life and wealth goals. Not surprisingly, their life and wealth goals often become so intertwined that it's difficult to tell where one leaves off and the other starts. Their life goal becomes wealth, financial stability, and long-term security. They have defined that goal and have single-mindedly gone after it.

The lesson is, you can still become rich, even if you've decided on a job, career, or vocation that will pay only a moderate income. You may not have a lot of control over the supply side of the equation—your income—but you can control the demand side, and this book will help you learn how.

CHAPTER 1

What's Your Definition of Wealthy?

Everyone feels differently about money: Some love it, some hate it, some are afraid of it, and others are comforted by it. Some people are savers; others are spenders. Some see money as a tool; others see it as a problem to be managed. Recognizing how you feel about money will help you gain control over this most elusive of our personality characteristics.

Money Types:
Are You a Saver or a Spender?

Anyone can be rich! You've reached true wealth when your deepest desires meet your means. But, like other parts of our lives, it takes personal awareness and reflection, and technical know-how, to achieve. The importance of money and wealth, and the role money plays in our lives, is not the same for everyone. Some fortunate people seem to attract money; others seem to repel it. Cash-strapped people always seem to be cash-strapped—well-off people always seem to be well-off, even after financially hard times. How do you treat the money in your life? How does it treat you?

Building wealth is a lifelong process, and part of that process requires that you develop a familiarity with the role of money and wealth in your life. Understanding the different financial personalities—or what we call "money types"—can teach you about your own, and others', relationship with money and will help create the money awareness you need to create wealth. This doesn't necessarily mean that you'll be able to change your internal feelings about money, but, by understanding your own money type, and the money types of those around you, you'll be better able to change your money behavior and, ultimately, to get rich.

FACTS

You and your spouse or partner may feel very differently about money and wealth. Time spent understanding your own approach to money is only well-spent if you extend that reflection to include other money decision makers in your household.

We have classified four basic money types: saver/attracter, spender/attracter, saver/repeller, and spender/repeller. Like other personality traits, most people will not fall cleanly into one type but instead will find degrees of these money types within their own personalities. We're looking for the concentration here—"Where you live," you might say. Accept that sometimes, or for some things, you'll be more of a saver than other times and more of a money attracter than others.

To better explain what we mean, take the following quiz. After you've scored the quiz, we'll talk more about each money type, and you'll get a better idea of how you and your money relate to each other.

These questions will help you discover more about your financial personality—your "money type." Answer each as honestly as you can on a scale of 1 to 5: **1** is very untrue, **2** is usually untrue, **3** is neither true nor untrue, **4** is usually true, and **5** is very true.

There are no right or wrong answers, but there is a neutral answer—number 3—if you feel that the question doesn't apply to you. However, there should be very little about wealth that you feel neutral about. If you find yourself tempted to answer 3, then maybe you are not being as honest with yourself as you could be. Before marking a 3, think more about whether you have some bias toward the question. If it's a little true, or sometimes true, answer 4. If the question is usually untrue, answer 2. This quiz is your path to financial self-discovery. Be honest with yourself—it's for your eyes only.

MONEY QUIZ

1. Are you concerned about accumulating money for long-term goals? __4__

2. More than others around you, do you try to give up short-term extras in order to build your bank account? __1__

3. Are you the last to buy the new "thing" that everyone is buying—in-fact, you skip many fads altogether? __2__

4. Does having extra money stashed in an account somewhere makes you feel good? __1__

5. Do you try to always have enough cash in your account(s) to cover any unexpected expenses? __2__

6. Do you try to maximize all available tax-deductible savings plans available to you? __5__

7. Does money always seems to "appear," through gifts or other windfalls, or from jobs, when you need it? __4__

8. Are you seldom forced to avoid an expense for lack of money? __3__

9. If you lost your source of income today, do you feel certain that you would land on your feet? __5__

10. Do you have a good job or career that pays enough to cover your needs? __1__

To add up your score, give yourself 1 point for every "1" answer, 2 points for every "2" answer, and so on.

Total your score on questions 1 through 6 here: ___15___.

Total your score on questions 7 through 10 here: ___13___.

SSENTIALS

Your history with money has a lot to do with the way you treat money today. If you find this quiz difficult, consider discussing money and your relationship with it with a qualified mental health counselor.

- If you scored higher than 18 on questions 1 through 6, you are a **saver**. Savers generally prefer to set aside their money rather than spend it. They enjoy feeling in control of their money. They usually have an easier time reaching their wealth goals than their spender neighbors, because they are willing to forego some immediate gratification to reach their goals.

  Savers can have difficulty, though, if they behave too miserly and don't allow themselves some enjoyment of their money. They can become convinced that they are not saving enough, though their advisors may be assuring them that they are. They can be troubled by changes in the value of their savings and investment accounts, leading them to invest more conservatively than they should. This can result in them having to work harder to achieve their goals than a less risk-averse investor who is willing to take more risk and let their money work harder for them.

- If you scored lower than 18 on questions 1 through 6, you are a **spender**. Spenders like to use their money to buy things now. They typically have difficulty reaching their long-term wealth goals because they have difficulty delaying the gratification they receive from spending their money. They may feel that it's more important to live in the present—to enjoy the here and now—and worry about the future later.

  Some spenders find themselves trying to show others how successful they are by buying the trappings of wealth. Ironically, the new cars, electronic gadgets, big houses, and lavish vacations work to sap the very wealth they are trying to convey. Some spenders use their participation in the financial markets as a "wealth indicator" to impress their friends. Whether their accounts are large or small, they will often talk about their market wins to their friends and others, looking for acceptance.

Spenders are often driven to earn a high salary to support their spending habits. When they land well-paying jobs, they often do well with forced-savings programs like employer-sponsored retirement plans or other direct-deposit devices that invest their money directly from their paycheck.

- If you scored higher than 12 on 7 through 10 you are a **money attracter**. Like a cat, money attracters always seem to land on their financial feet. They seem to have money when they need it—sometimes from their own savings, sometimes not. Some attracters work hard and have successful careers or businesses, some marry well, some receive inheritances or financial assistance from family or friends, some are big "deal makers" on a success streak of get-rich-quick schemes. No matter the source, attracters must guard against the end of their streak. They must not be distracted from building a strong financial foundation. The money may not always be there.

   For some attracters, the precariousness of their income leads them to take unreasonable risks, while others become overly miserly. Attracters that depend on funds from outside sources can have difficulty developing financial independence. They can remain dependent on this outside wealth source, beyond the source's ability to support them. Attracters who create their own opportunities can be very successful wealth builders if they are able to manage their success and strike a balance between their money-attracting activities and the rest of their life.

- If you scored lower than 12 on 7 through 10 you are a **money repeller**. Money repellers always seem to be short of cash. They often have great difficulty reaching long-term financial goals because they're forced to focus on making short-term ends meet. While many money repellers have well-paying jobs, they seem to experience a lack of control over their money that always leaves them strapped. Generally poor forward thinkers, they're forever trying to recover from the latest financial calamity.

Saver/attracters seem to have the best of both financial worlds. They naturally enjoy saving money and they have a relatively steady stream of it coming in.

Most people will find that they resemble some combination of spender or saver and attracter or repeller. Saver/attracters have the fortitude to accumulate funds for future wealth goals, and they have sufficient cash available to reach those goals. Saver/attracters should guard against being overly conservative or miserly with their money. Like the other money types, they should seek a balance in their financial life that allows them to both save and spend their money. They should try not to be overly conservative with their investments and should develop a wealth plan that will let them move towards their long-term wealth goals while reducing the anxiety of taking financial risks and spending some money to enjoy today.

FACTS

It's never too early to start your kids on the track to building wealth. While they may not be old enough to take this quiz themselves, you should still try to recognize their normal tendencies about money and work to help them moderate their behaviors so that they'll grow into deliberate managers of their money.

Spender/attracters are walking a tightrope of financial security. Because they enjoy spending the money they're pulling in, they can get caught in a cycle of over-reliance on their income stream. Spender/attracters sometimes find it difficult to reach wealth goals, even thought they have a strong income stream. They may discover after a lifetime of earning and spending that they haven't saved enough to retire. They may have difficulty recovering from a financial disaster that jeopardizes, or even stops, that income stream. Spender/attracters must work on moderating their spending habits, and should develop a plan to reach both their long-term and short-term financial goals. Regardless of the security of their income stream, they should still plan against the possibility of losing that income.

Saver/repellers find themselves caught in a frustrating circle of working hard to build assets while constantly trying to manage wealth-robbing situations. The holes that their money seems to disappear into may vary, but it usually seems like they have no choice but to spend it: The grown children need financial help, the car needs repairs, or a friend needs a loan. Sometimes the money stream is simply taken away from them: They're laid off, their business has a down season, or their investments lose value. Saver/repellers have got half the equation working in their favor—they tend to save money. Through planning, they can get control of the other side of the equation and reduce the flow of money away from them. By looking forward to possible wealth-robbing events and planning to avoid, or at least minimize them, saver/repellers can work to build wealth. Saver/repellers should pay extra attention to building emergency funds, perfecting insurance plans, and diversifying their income streams. Emergency funds should be in safe investments such as savings or money market accounts. Insurance plans should be funded to protect income and the financial stability of the family through economic disasters. Income streams should come from more than one source, if possible, or expenses should be reduced to ensure that the one income source is adequate regardless of the situation. If both partners are not working—or can't work—the budget should be trimmed to allow for the family's lifestyle, insurance premiums, and savings to fit within the means of the one worker.

Spender/repellers have a tough row to hoe. Their natural tendency is to spend their money while they're also subject to the wealth-draining problems that confront money repellers. Spender/repellers must work hard to plan for wealth-robbing events such as car repairs, long-term medical bills, or the loss of a wage earner. They should pay particular attention to building an emergency fund and having a strong insurance program—both things spenders usually hate to do. Spender/repellers with kids should work to help them develop financial independence. They should try to avoid the temptation to encourage their kids to overspend, as well, and should avoid supporting them financially longer than is absolutely necessary. Spender/repellers should spend extra time tracking expenses, and should be sure to develop and follow a strict wealth plan to accumulate assets for the long term.

Spending the extra time to analyze the extent of your money type will help you to better track your progress toward a controlled balance between saving and spending, attracting and repelling.

Developing a Positive View of Your Money

Whether you're mostly a saver or a spender, a money attracter or a money repeller, understanding your default behavior and managing money deliberately is an important part of building wealth. Managing assets is both a technical pursuit full of account statements and calculations of future money values and an emotional pursuit. This book will help you develop the skills used to build wealth. It's up to you to look within to understand the internal obstacles you face.

There is no right way or wrong way to think about money. Understanding your preference—and that of your spouse, partner, and other loved ones—will help you find a common ground in your relationships from which to work.

It's important to begin to understand your relationship with money and to make that relationship as positive as you can. Money is purely a tool under our control. We are the ones who choose to save it, spend it, or give it away. We choose to invest it or put it under the mattress. Because it's the tool through which we provide ourselves with what we desire and need in life, the decisions we make about money are very important.

Your Wealth Mission Statement

Your wealth mission statement is an outline of where you want to go financially—what your ultimate goals are. These goals are both life and financial goals and, at first, should not be limited by what you think is achievable or not. Your wealth mission statement is going to help you stay on course to your wealth goals by providing an outline of your destination that you will refer to when making a financial decision. Many people have career goals, or educational goals, or goals for their kids that they refer to when met with decisions to make that affect those goals.

A wealth mission statement is just as important. You can start with a rough draft and refine it as you read through this book.

Start by writing about your financial goals, without being concerned about the immediate feasibility of reaching them. What do you want to accomplish from here? Regardless of where you have been, what would you like to do next? The particulars of your wealth mission statement will be tailored to your needs, but it might sound like this: "My primary financial goal is to have enough financial security to be able to spend more time with my family while my kids are young. I would like to accumulate enough wealth for retirement so my husband and I can make choices about where we work and we're not working as hard at age fifty as we are now."

As you read through this book, you can refine your wealth plan to make it fit your means and any changes to your goals. As you learn more about budgeting, investing, insurance, retirement planning, and the like, you can refine your wealth mission statement to outline what your goals are and how you are going to reach them.

You've become rich when your desires meet your means. Understanding the desires, and then working to build or create the means, is a mature way to maintain financial security while moving towards your goals.

Revisit the rough draft of your statement regularly as you read this book. Make changes when you feel they're necessary, then put the mission statement aside. After a month or two, go back to it and make changes based on how you feel about what you have learned. Once you have what you think is a finished statement, post it in a place where you're bound to see it often, preferably daily. When you are ready to make a financial decision—pay for a vacation, make an investment, or take out a loan—go back to your statement to see if your decision helps you reach your goals. Reflecting on your original goals will help you avoid short-term temptation and keep you on track to wealth.

The Wealthy—and Their Debts

Wealthy people seldom have any significant debt. If they are still young, they may have a mortgage on their home (which they are focused on paying down), but they generally will try to avoid the extra cost of financing anything else. They will generally concoct a plan to accumulate most, if not all, of the cost of a car, vacation, home-improvement project, or other such expense ahead of time so that the extra costs of financing can be minimized.

People who are focused on accumulating wealth also avoid late charges and bank fees on bills, credit cards, ATM withdrawals, and the like. Late charges and extra fees are often invisible depleters of wealth. Who ever thinks that a $1 ATM fee or a $5 late charge on a utility bill will ever amount to anything? Wealthy people do. They know that $10 per month in extra fees from the time you start work (let's say at age twenty-three) until you retire at age sixty-five can amount to over $30,000!

Using debt is not an absolute no-no for wealth builders, but be sure you keep track of your total cost, not just the monthly payments— these can add up to much more than one would expect.

In fact, just about the only time a rich person will use debt is when the convenience or leverage it provides has the ability to increase their wealth. Wealthy business owners will borrow money to start or grow businesses in order to increase their return on invested money, as the interest on the loan is a deductible business expense. Other wealthy folks will use debt over a short time to take advantage of an investment opportunity, or in order to purchase something now at a more convenient price. They will seldom carry the debt for long, however, and are very careful to calculate the added financing cost into the total cost of their purchase.

Not everyone, especially new wealth builders, will be able to avoid all debt all the time, but the discussions later in this book will help you to assess your own debt, the cost of that debt, and what adjustments need to be made to build wealth.

The Wealth Formula

Most wealthy people are frugal—to some degree—but not all are penny pinchers. Frugality is the natural byproduct of being focused on a goal, almost like the successful dieter who can avoid overdoing it on the treats they used to crave. The successful wealth builder has learned to direct their money toward what they truly value. Wealth building has two sides to it—the supply side—your ability to make money—and the demand side—your expenses. We call this the "wealth formula." The wealth formula is the key to building wealth. Anybody can become rich by discovering their own wealth formula, and managing both the supply and demand side of their finances. Once you know where your control lies, you will be able to create your plan for wealth.

Managing the Demand Side—Strengths and Pitfalls

Many wealth builders are rich, despite (or because of) modest incomes by becoming expert demand-side managers. They understand the wealth formula, and have taken control of the demand side. They have control over their budget, expenses, and the outflow of money. They work mostly in cash, as a way of limiting spending to what they have, and keep a very close record of it. Their chosen profession often provides a modest income so, to compensate, they have become masters of the demand side—they live within their means and save their money.

ESSENTIALS

Building wealth must become a lifestyle if you are to become successful. Like the dieter who loses weight on a new fad diet, only to gain it back when he returns to regular eating habits, wealth building should be a lifestyle change if it's going to succeed.

As you might expect, would-be demand-siders can get sidetracked before they even get started by trying to appear more successful than they are, or by taking shortcuts to wealth accumulation. Like their counterparts the supply-siders, whom we'll look at next, off-course demand-siders might be tempted to spend money on things that will make them appear more successful—bigger cars or houses, more vacations—or carry a lot of cash just to flash a full wallet to their friends. If they succumb to the temptation, the cash could get spent without them knowing where it went.

Managing the Supply Side—Strengths and Pitfalls

Some folks who are rich are expert supply-side managers. They're engineers, computer programmers, chemists, doctors, and business owners. They've excelled in their professions and are paid a high income. They make a lot of money on the supply side, but have still prioritized the demand side.

Not all strong supply-siders are rich, though. They've managed to master only half the equation: They make a lot of money but they spend a lot, too. They figure that since they have successful jobs, they must appear successful. In doing so, they spend more than they earn. Without being aware of their life and wealth goals, they can get trapped in having to endlessly prop up the supply side without realizing that a few changes on the demand side could solve their wealth-building problem.

If you have succeeded in creating a strong inflow of money, but don't feel rich, you can become so by taking a closer look at the demand side. Are you spending money on things that aren't important? Are you neglecting to pay yourself first—meaning pumping money every month into your investments—or is your savings program a neglected part of your overall budget? (Yes, successful supply-siders need a budget, too.) Are you spending time away from additional money-making pursuits by trying to pinch a few pennies on the demand side?

Assessing Your "Work Value"

Wealthy people can be found in all vocations: They sell cars, practice medicine, broker stocks, and teach school. Successful wealth builders have mastered their wealth formula and have balanced the demand and supply sides of their finances. Successful wealth builders also understand the value of their time—we call it their "work value." They know the maximum that they can generate over time, and they manage their expenses accordingly.

Many financial planners and life coaches have wrestled with the concept of a "life value" or "real hourly wage" to help people understand how to balance their home and work lives with their life goals. Consider a person who wants to have free time to spend more time with their family. In a perfect world, this person could choose not to work at all, and also hire help at home so that they were not distracted with the extra chores and could focus on family. The life goals of this person are shared by many of us. But, how does one quantify the balance that they need to make between their supply and demand sides to avoid ruining both their work life and their relationship with their family, and themselves by running themselves ragged trying to have both? How do they find the balance?

Too many people get drawn away from their well-laid wealth-building plans by the temptation to "keep up with the Joneses." Remember, buying a new car every year only shows that you own a new car—not that you can afford it.

Figuring a "work value" might help. We'll briefly explain it here, then later we'll introduce a wealth journal that will help you look deeper into your life and wealth goals and clarify your priorities. In its simplest form, your "work value" is the amount per hour you can make during your workweek. This kind of measure is a way to better quantify the supply side of your wealth formula as a way to get a better handle on the demand side. If you know how much you can generate per hour of work, you can better assess how many hours you have to work for everything you want or need to buy to support your lifestyle.

People who are paid by the hour will be well aware of this number. But people paid by salary will need to calculate this by dividing their salary by 2,000 hours. (Two thousand hours is the number of work hours in a fifty-two-week year, minus two weeks vacation, forty hours per week.) For example, if you make $50,000 per year, your "work value" is $25 per hour (50,000 divided by 2,000).

Beyond your monthly budget, which we'll discuss in Chapter 4, understanding your real hourly wage will help you better value the things you spend your money on. For example, if you make $50,000 per year:

- Spending an extra $10,000 on a new luxury car, over the price of a regular auto, costs an extra 400 hours of work.
- A meal out each Friday costing $75 costs 3 hours of work every month.
- Weekly daycare for a child costing $500 per week costs 10 hours of work.
- Spending an additional $100,000 on a home closer to work to cut down on the commute could cost (at 6.5 percent annual mortgage interest) just under 13 hours per month.
- A two-week vacation costing $3,000 costs 120 hours of work.

If you have a long commute to work, consider adding the time that you commute to your total work day when figuring your work value. If you commute two hours each day (one hour to and from work) add 500 hours to your work year. If you make $50,000 per year, then your work value, including the commute, is $20 per hour instead of $25.

Thinking in terms of "work value," you can look at your expenses in terms of time worked. This might help you set spending priorities and gain better control of your demand side. Understanding the value of the money you create and your expenses, and by psychologically placing the familiar trappings of wealth into a subordinate category behind creating legitimate wealth, everyday people can build the habit of becoming and being wealthy.

Chapter 2

Setting Goals: Who Needs a Plan?

Most every successful wealth-builder maintains an accurate, thoughtful wealth plan. Not all wealth plans must be formal, though highly structured ones work best. They need only be structured in a way that enables you to put it to work quickly, and be capable of modification and fine-tuning as you grow rich.

The Wealth Plan: Your Key to Riches

Flexibility is a quality that all wealth plans have in common. Suppose you have been saving toward retirement ever since you began working after college. Your retirement savings might be accumulating nicely, but now you have young children and you realize the time has come to start investing for college. With a flexible wealth plan, the shift from retirement planning to college investment should be simple and painless. By the same token, when the college fund is fully stocked or the kids graduate from college and are living on their own, a carefully charted wealth plan will simplify the process of stepping back onto the retirement track, or to take a new direction entirely, depending on your priorities.

QUESTIONS?

Must I hire a financial advisor to help me get rich?
A competent financial planner is almost essential in guiding you toward wealth. Your financial planner should be a partner and an educator, not someone to whom you turn over your entire life.

The virtue of a wealth plan is very similar to the virtue of a reliable road map. When you begin a journey, your priorities might be "Get from my home to my vacation cabin as quickly as possible." Before starting out on your trip, you will examine the map and select the route that best suits your needs, taking into consideration any construction roadblocks or traffic delays. But somewhere en route, your priorities may change. Now, instead of a route selected for speed, you decide you'd prefer a trip that permits you to enjoy beautiful scenery at a leisurely pace.

Thanks to a good road map, you'll be able to restructure your route to meet your new goals. The comparison to a wealth plan is virtually identical. An accurate assessment of your wealth goals, and a clear understanding of the various means you can take to reach them, helps ensure a successful journey.

Maximize Your Contributions

How formal must a wealth plan be if it is to be successful? See if this example sounds like a wealth plan:

When you first started working during high school, your family opens an Individual Retirement Account and expects you to invest $1,000 of your pay in the account. As an incentive, your family matches the money, helping you reach the maximum annual contribution to an IRA. Thanks to good savings habits, you continue to fully fund your retirement account every year since. Once you're out of college and embarking on your career, you participate in your employer's 401(k) retirement plan to the maximum amount each year. Later, with years of expertise on your resume, you open a consulting practice that flourishes, and you're able to put money toward a self-employed retirement plan. Like all your other retirement investments since high school, you fund this one to the full allowable amount, too.

In effect, your strategy has been to "max out" your retirement savings to the maximum allowable limit at every stage in your working life. Is that a wealth plan? You bet it is, and a terrific one. Wealth plans need not be complex, and this example is very simple—maximize your contribution to your retirement savings program each and every year. As long as this is a plan that is compatible with your financial goals, it can be put into action simply and with a minimum of interruptions.

A plan like this one, as simple as it is, can be a very powerful wealth builder. Would you be satisfied with the same choices? Perhaps, but it ignores some important financial goals many people share, such as saving for a home and saving for college. Each person's choice, like each person's wealth plan, is unique.

Invest Your Bonuses

Other plans, equally simple, can be enormously successful at building wealth. But each must be tailored to the individual. For example, assume you're a salesperson who has built a career on your ability to sell almost any product because you have a natural gift for selling. But despite selling everything from computers to copiers at one time or another, you worry about job security because you know that sales jobs are never guaranteed.

Because you're good at your job, you usually post yearly sales high enough above quota to earn bonuses, so you incorporate this extra income into your wealth plan. Early in your career, you develop a plan in which, in addition to contributing the maximum amount to your retirement plan, you also invest your bonuses. This last part is the key. Rather than allowing your lifestyle and expenses to expand with each bonus so that you grow dependent on them, you invest the bonuses first toward your home mortgage, and then into an investment account. For people who earn regular bonuses, a plan like this can help pay off a mortgage, fund a college account, provide a comfortable emergency account in the event of a layoff, and provide peace of mind in a career like sales that can be fraught with uncertainty.

Don't like the selection of investment choices offered by your employer's retirement plan? Ask your company to add a self-directed brokerage account option so you can pick your own investments. But beware of the costs; read all the fine print.

Why People Fail to Get Rich

Why do people fail to get rich? Usually because they have failed to plan. More often than not, failure to get rich can be blamed on people allowing happenstance to get the better of their finances. People often focus on the day-to-day responsibilities of career and family rather than the long-term view that includes buying homes, planning for children's educations, and retirement, to mention just a few of the life events you'll encounter as you build wealth.

In other cases, people are compelled to flaunt their high earnings by buying expensive houses, luxury cars, and other trappings of wealth. They've managed their careers wonderfully, because that's where their focus is, but their wealth plans take a back seat to conspicuous displays of apparent wealth. They've neglected to look to the long term, to plan where they want to be financially in five, ten, or twenty years.

We call these people "high-income paupers." They earn very high—often six-figure—paychecks, but are still unable to get rich. They may project all the outward appearances of wealth, but they are often dealing with feelings of frustration, fear, and loss of control over their finances. If high-income paupers don't put a stop to the financial chaos in their lives and design a rational, practical wealth plan, their hopes of wealth will evaporate and they can only look ahead to a money-troubled future.

A High-Income Pauper

High-income paupers might appear where you'd least expect them. Surprisingly, young professionals are among the most likely to be high-income paupers, thanks to the high expense of their schooling, generally low pay during the first several years of their "apprenticeship," and social myths of the prosperous young doctor or lawyer that many professionals emulate.

Many people who are content in comfortable, high-income lifestyles fail to get rich despite their affluence simply because they enjoy a sense of invulnerability. It may take a family tragedy or a financial disaster to shake their complacency and, unfortunately, by then it might be too late.

Take a typical situation, that of a young woman attorney a few years out of law school, who is working hard to earn a promotion to partner in her firm after years of grueling work and long hours. Perhaps married to a career man and with a couple of kids, she may believe her career requires a live-in nanny, a housekeeper, a pair of leased luxury cars, and a new home in an affluent suburban neighborhood. With a couple of expensive vacations each year and plans for a lavish European trip when she is named partner, the young professional, from all appearances, has a successful career, a well-provided-for family, and wealth.

Yet, a startling number of such apparently affluent professionals simply can't make ends meet! How can someone like this step off the treadmill of high-income poverty?

Stepping Off the Treadmill

First, you have to ask, do people fall into high-income poverty because they failed to plan? Not necessarily. In this example, the young attorney might be exactly on her timeline for promotion to partner in her law firm, certainly a ticket to potential wealth.

But a wealth plan can't stop there. For example, an expensive vacation might seem like a well-deserved break from the pressure of a busy law practice. Leased luxury cars might seem to project the appropriate image of a successful career. And the extra expense of a new, lavishly appointed home in an affluent neighborhood might seem like a reasonable investment for a hard-charging young attorney and her executive husband. But the expense of this lifestyle can rapidly outstrip the family's income, and the young couple could quickly find themselves overworked, exhausted, and desperate for a plan that will help them find their way to wealth.

FACTS

According to the IRS, 70 percent of taxpayers in 2001 received refunds averaging $1,751. Refunds can be fun to spend, but they represent lost wealth and unearned interest. Consult with your tax accountant to help modify your W-4 or estimated tax payments to trim your monthly withholding, which can help make you—not Uncle Sam—rich.

Refining Your Wealth Plan

When it's time to refine your wealth plan, where do you start? Refining your plan, or creating a new one from scratch, is possible at any time and at any age. You don't have to earn as much money as an attorney with a flourishing practice; for the most part, income isn't the most relevant factor in becoming rich, as long as you have at least a moderate income and sufficiently frugal spending habits. Far more important is a process for getting rich and measurable and achievable goals.

Perhaps the most important habit of successful wealth builders is to review the wealth plan at least once a year. This doesn't mean simply taking it off the shelf for a quick read. Set up an appointment with your financial advisors and spend a few hours updating your wealth plan based on the changes in your life and fortunes in the past twelve months.

FACTS

Parents of children born in 2001 could have a jaw-dropping surprise in store when those kids go off to a private college. According to one estimate, the cost of sending a child to a private college in 2019 will be a mind-boggling $275,000.

In Chapter 1, you crafted your own wealth mission statement. Does yours mention a desire to be seen by friends behind the wheel of an expensive car or to live in an expensive house? If not, and a lifestyle inventory reveals that your life includes such things, you should do one of two things: Rewrite your wealth mission statement to include these wealth-robbing extras and others like them, or trim the costly extras from your life. If you elect to rewrite your wealth mission statement to include expensive luxuries in your life, you must be prepared to significantly postpone the date when you'll reach your wealth goal, and that could be a warning signal that your spending and investing discipline is not up to the task of getting rich.

Measurable and Achievable Goals

Once you have made sure your wealth mission statement accurately reflects your lifestyle, the next step in reworking your financial plan is to write down measurable and achievable financial goals. These goals must be clearly measurable if you are to map out an objective plan for achieving them. You might also plot intermediate goals as measurable steps toward your primary goal to give you a clearer picture of your progress.

Let's look at three examples:

- **Preliminary financial goal:** to retire with financial security. Specific and measurable financial goal: to retire at age sixty-five with $50,000 per year of inflation-adjusted income from investments.
- **Preliminary financial goal:** to send the kids to college. Specific and measurable financial goal: to save $120,000 per child by the time they reach eighteen.
- **Preliminary financial goal:** to purchase a home. Specific and measurable financial goal: to save $30,000 as a down payment on a home within the next four years.

Write It Down!

It's important that your goals be in writing. By committing your goals to paper you are able to spend time reviewing each one and fleshing it out in your mind. When you write down your goal, you think about it and refine it until it matches your desires. Some people also find it helpful to recite their goal aloud on a regular basis. The whole process makes your wealth mission statement more real to you and will help you build ownership of your goals. By doing so, you will be better able to recall them from memory whenever you're tempted to stray from your wealth mission.

FACTS

According to the Society for Human Resource Management, 21 percent of the companies they queried in 2001 offer financial planning services to their employees. If your company offers financial planning through a competent and qualified advisor, this could be an excellent start toward your wealth goals.

Keeping It Real

Of course, your goals must be realistic and achievable so you're not frustrated by failure. You'll read in Chapter 7 how to gauge and adjust your goals to make them realistic and achievable. There, you'll find the tools you need to craft your financial goals and calculate the amount of wealth you'll need to achieve them.

Your financial goals are not written in stone and they can change over time. Once you've had the chance to fully develop your goals and outline your plan it's important that you allow yourself the flexibility to adjust your plan to make it achievable. Consider implementing your plan in stages so that you have accomplished a number of short-term goals that will help you build steadily toward your final goal.

In later chapters you'll learn how to calculate the nest egg required to support your desired income in retirement or to satisfy other financial goals. You'll also be supplied with the tools you'll need to develop a savings plan that you can implement today to start building toward your wealth target.

How can a few hundred dollars a month invested now turn into millions in a few decades? Thank "compounding," the phenomenon that accelerates your investment growth thanks to the interest earned on your principal plus the interest earned on your interest!

In the space below or on a separate piece of paper, write down your specific, measurable financial goals as you imagine them now. Later in the book you'll have an opportunity to review these goals and make revisions.

_____

_____

_____

_____

_____

_____

_____

Self-Help: Your Wealth Organizer

Part of building a financial plan is organizing your financial information, thoughts, and goals. The following Wealth Organizer worksheet can help you simplify the process. This worksheet can be a very helpful planning tool because it can become the warehouse for your financial information. By keeping a complete financial worksheet and updating it regularly, you will always have your financial information at your fingertips. You may want to photocopy it or create something similar that you find easy to use so you can have it in front of you as you read the rest of the book. In the next chapter, you'll collect and organize the financial records you'll need to complete the first part of this worksheet.

WEALTH ORGANIZER WORKSHEET

Date completed: _____

Name _____   Name _____

Social security # _____   Social security # _____

Date of birth _____   Date of birth _____

1. **Dependents and/or Beneficiaries** (list name, relationship, date of birth, social security number)

Name _____   Name _____

Social security # _____   Social security # _____

Date of birth _____   Date of birth _____

2. **Income** (list income from all sources and their origination)

Salary/wages/self-employment income:

$_____, _____ $_____, _____

$_____, _____ $_____, _____

$_____, _____ $_____, _____

Investment income that is not reinvested:

$_____, _____ $_____, _____

$_____, _____ $_____, _____

Other income:

$_____, _____ $_____, _____

$_____, _____ $_____, _____

3. **Assets** (list everything you own, and the owner)
Cash and Cash Equivalents
Cash in checking account(s):

$_____, _____ $_____, _____

Credit union:

$_____, _____ $_____, _____

Money market fund(s):

$_____, _____ $_____, _____

Certificate of Deposit:

$_____, _____ $_____, _____

Fixed annuities:

$_____, _____ $_____, _____

Life insurance cash value (whole life/universal life):

$_____, _____ $_____, _____

Investments (stocks, bonds, mutual funds, exchange traded shares, variable life insurance cash value, etc.; list value, ownership, and original cost):

$_____, _____, $_____

$_____, _____, $_____

$_____, _____, $_____

$_____, _____, $_____

Retirement Accounts (list the value, the type of account—IRA, 401(k), 403(b), Roth IRA, etc. and the owner):

$_____, _____, _____

$_____, _____, _____

Personal Property (list the approximate value of your personal property, and the owner)
Home furnishings:

$_____, _____ $_____, _____

Automobiles:

$_____, _____ $_____, _____

Boat, trailer, airplane:

$_____, _____ $_____, _____

Clothing, furs:

$_____, _____ $_____, _____

Jewelry, silver:

$_____, _____ $_____, _____

Antiques:

$_____, _____ $_____, _____

Coins, collections, etc.:

$_____, _____ $_____, _____

Other (specify):

$_____, _____ $_____, _____

Personal Real Estate

Market value of personal residence $_____

Original cost $_____ Date purchased _____

Remaining mortgage principal _____ Interest _____

Term_____ Monthly payment _____

Owner(s) _____

Market value of second home $_____

Original cost $_____ Date purchased _____

Remaining mortgage principal _____ Interest _____

Term _____ Monthly payment _____

Owner(s) _____

Investment Real Estate (list the owner, address, purchase price, and market value)

Owner: _____ Address _____

Purchase price: $_____ Market value $_____

Owner: _____ Address _____

Purchase price: $_____ Market value $_____

Business Interests (list owner, address, type of business, market value, and income)

_____

_____

_____

Plan for business continuation or dissolution in event of owner death or disability

_____

_____

_____

4. Liabilities (list creditor, what you OWE, remaining balance, payment, and interest)

_____, $_____, $_____, _____%

_____, $_____, $_____, _____%

_____, $_____, $_____, _____%

_____, $_____, $_____, _____%

5. Insurance

Life Insurance (list policy owner, insured, beneficiary, insurance company, face amount, and type of policy, i.e. whole life, universal life, term life, variable life, group term life)

_____

_____

_____

_____

_____

_____

Homeowner's and Business Insurance (list the property covered, liability amount covered, property coverage, and deductible)

_____

_____

_____

Health Insurance (list policy owner, insured, insurance company, major medical coverage, hospital daily benefit, co-pay information)

_____

_____

_____

Disability Insurance (list policy owner, insured, insurance company, monthly benefit, waiting period, benefit period)

_____

_____

_____

_____

_____

In the event of your long-term disability, how much annual income would you and your family

need to maintain your present standard of living in today's dollars? $_____

Other Insurance

Insurance last reviewed: _____   Next review due: _____

Personal excess liability coverage (umbrella liability) amount: $_____

6. Estate Information

Wills, power-of-attorney, health care proxy, living will (as appropriate):

Owner: _____ Date signed/completed _____

Owner: _____ Date signed/completed _____

Trusts:

Owner: _____ Date signed/completed _____

Trustee: _____

Owner: _____ Date signed/completed _____

Trustee: _____

7. Financial Objectives

How do you feel about your current income?

_____

_____

_____

What are your financial goals?

_____

_____

_____

Rank the following financial objectives in their order of importance to you.

(1 = most important, 8 = least important):

_____ Conserving capital for heirs   _____ Increase current income

_____ Reduce current income taxes   _____ Children's education

_____ Growth of capital   _____ Retirement income

_____ Reduce estate taxes   _____ Other _____

8. Retirement

At what age do you want to be financially independent? _____

How much annual income will you want at retirement? $_____

9. Survivor's Income

If you or your partner died today, how much annual income would your family need to maintain their standard of living? $_____

After your children become financially independent, how much annual income would your partner need? $_____

10. Education

Estimated future college or education expenses in today's dollars:

$_____, year expected to start _____

$_____, year expected to start _____

$_____, year expected to start _____

11. Investment Temperament and Financial Objectives

How do you feel about your investments and the amount of risk you are willing to take?

_____% Very conservative investments; capital conservation is most important.

_____% Conservative investments; capital appreciation with relatively safe, *high-quality* investments is most important.

_____% Investments with moderate risk, capital growth is most important.

_____% Investments with high risk; aggressive capital growth is most important.

100 % Total

Are there any particular investments for which you have either a preference or objection?

_____

_____

_____

What is your primary financial concern?

_____

_____

_____

12. **Your Professional Advisors and Contact Information**

Accountant/firm/phone number/e-mail:

_____

_____

_____

Attorney/firm/phone number/e-mail:

_____

_____

_____

Stockbroker/firm/phone number/e-mail:

_____

_____

_____

Portfolio Manager(s)/firm(s)/phone number(s)/e-mail(s):

_____

_____

_____

Banker/bank/phone number/e-mail:

_____

_____

_____

Other professional advisors:

_____

_____

_____

CHAPTER 3

Assets and Liabilities: The Net Worth Statement

The net worth statement serves as an overview of your financial position. Basically, a net worth statement is a list of your assets—what you own—compared to a list of your liabilities—what you owe. A net worth statement enables you to determine your basic financial health.

Collecting Data:
Building a Net Worth Statement

Here's a blank net worth statement to help get you started. As you fill in the details of your assets and liabilities, be sure they all reflect the same time frame. The most recent month for which you have complete financial records will work just fine. As you move toward your wealth goals, you'll want to create fresh and updated net worth statements to track your progress. Once you've collected a series of net worth statements over a period of years, you'll be able to view a kind of "photo album" that records your journey to wealth.

QUESTIONS?

Do I really need a net worth statement?
Absolutely. The net worth statement, combined with the cash flow statement, is your map to riches. Without both, your odds of reaching your financial destination would be only slightly better than random chance.

The following sample net worth statement can help you complete your own, which you'll do later in this chapter. When compiling your statement, pick a recent date on which you're certain you can determine the value of your assets. For example, if you only receive some of your account statements on a quarterly basis, use the end of the last quarter for which you have complete records. If you use the Internet to download daily account information, you could choose to use the end of the most recent month. Be certain that you compile a complete "snapshot" of your finances at a specific moment in time.

Like everything else in your wealth plan, this statement is for your own use and is only as accurate as the information you put into it. Try to be as accurate as you can so that you don't build your wealth fortress on a foundation of sand. Trying to "fudge" your net worth statement in hopes of painting a falsely flattering picture won't impress anyone, because a net worth statement is meant to be something you discuss only with your spouse, family, and financial advisor.

FIGURE 3-1a:

Blank
Net Worth
Statement

ASSETS

Cash/Cash Equivalents

    Checking account   _____

    Money market account   _____

    Bank A Certificate of Deposit
      (7% interest)   _____

    Total Cash/Cash Equivalents   _____

Invested Assets

    _____   _____

    _____   _____

    _____   _____

    _____   _____

    _____   _____

    Total Invested Assets   _____

Retirement Plans

    _____   _____

    _____   _____

    _____   _____

    Total Retirement Plans   _____

Use Assets

    Residence   _____

    Automobiles   _____

    Personal property   _____

    Total Use Assets   _____

TOTAL ASSETS   _____

LIABILITIES

Liabilities

    Mortgage   _____

    Home equity loan   _____

    Credit cards   _____

    TOTAL LIABILITIES   _____

NET WORTH   _____

**TOTAL LIABILITIES
AND NET WORTH**   _____

FIGURE 3-1b:
Sample
Net Worth
Statement

Nick and Nora Rich
Statement of Financial Position
As of June 30, 2002

ASSETS[1]		LIABILITIES[2]	
Cash/Cash Equivalents		Liabilities	
Checking account	5,000	Mortgage	175,000
Money market account	1,000	Home equity loan	200,000
Bank A Certificate of Deposit		Credit cards	35,000
(7% interest)	10,000		
Total Cash/Cash Equivalents	**16,000**	**TOTAL LIABILITIES**	**410,000**
Invested Assets			
ABC mutual fund (Nora)	4,000		
ABC mutual fund (Nick)	6,000		
XXX Brokerage account	125,000		
XYZ Stock (1032 shares)	8,000		
FNMA Agency Bond	10,000		
Home town state municipal bond	10,000		
Total Invested Assets	**163,000**	**NET WORTH**	**582,000**
Retirement Plans			
Nora–Roth IRA	2,000		
Nora–401(k)	92,000		
Nora–IRA	9,000		
Total Retirement Plans	**103,000**		
Use Assets			
Residence	650,000		
Automobiles	20,000		
Personal property	40,000		
Total Use Assets	**710,000**		
		TOTAL LIABILITIES	
TOTAL ASSETS	**992,000**	**AND NET WORTH**	**992,000**

[1]Presented at estimated fair market value; all assets held in joint tenancy with right of
survivorship, except as noted
[2]Principal only

Collect Your Raw Data

Let's look at this important tool in more detail using a sample net
worth statement as a guide. You should compile your net worth statement

as we compile the sample, so before beginning, you'll need to gather your financial information, including:

- life insurance policies
- bank statements
- mutual fund statements or brokerage account statements
- stock certificates or statements detailing the number and value of your shares
- the value of your home
- appraisals, or your own estimates, of the value of your personal property and collectibles

SSENTIALS

When trying to estimate your home's value, use the purchase price if you bought it recently, the price of a comparable home that was recently sold in your neighborhood, a real estate agent's assessment of value, or a formal appraisal.

You may spend a day or two collecting documents and contacting professionals for some information. There's no reason why you shouldn't read on, but be sure to return to this chapter and complete your net worth statement once you've collected your data.

We can't emphasize this point enough: The net worth statement is one of the two most important tools, along with the cash flow statement, in helping you determine your starting point on the route to wealth. You must not omit this step!

Put Your Records in Order

Once you've collected the information needed to compile your net worth statement, we'll sort it into the following categories:

- **Cash and cash equivalents.** Examples of these are savings, checking, money market accounts, and cash value of traditional life insurance.
- **Invested assets.** These assets, also called semi-liquid investments, which usually include stocks, bonds, mutual funds, and the cash

value of variable life insurance can be sold and converted to cash in a few days but are not as liquid as cash because they may fluctuate in value. They are held in taxable accounts as opposed to your tax-deferred retirement accounts and will usually be directly in your name; for example, Mary Smith Brokerage account or Elizabeth and Kate Joint Tenants with Rights of Survivorship, as opposed to Mary Smith IRA.

- **Retirement accounts.** These are the tax-deferred "baskets" written into tax law into which we can deposit some of the same type of investments (mutual funds, stocks, etc.) seen in the previous category. They deserve their own category in your net worth statement to clearly signify the tax limitations of withdrawing the money. These accounts are often called IRAs, 401(k)s, employee savings plans, or 403(b)s. You'll learn about these accounts in more detail in Chapter 13. For now, you simply need to collect the statements and record the balances on your net worth worksheet.

- **Use assets.** These are the assets that you use every day; for example, your personal property, home, and automobile. These assets have cash value but would take some effort to sell. List the price at which you believe you could realistically sell the asset on your net worth statement.

- **Liabilities.** Simply put, these are the debts you owe. List the principal balance, or "pay-off balance," of all your debts separately on your net worth statement. There is no need to include future interest on the balance due that you report.

The Lowdown on Your Assets

Let's review some of the asset components of your net worth in more detail.

Life Insurance Policies

As you'll learn in Chapter 6, a life insurance policy can possess more value than simply the amount of money that would be paid at the insured person's death. Some policies provide a savings feature by charging a premium greater than the pure cost of the insurance, then applying the additional amount to a cash account within the policy. This "cash value" is separate from the death benefit and is usually available during the insured person's lifetime. Depending on the policy, the cash value may or may not increase the death benefit paid when the insured person dies.

Because this extra cash value may be available while the insured person is still alive, this amount will usually be reflected on periodic statements from your insurance company. Contact them for your current balance if you haven't received a statement from them in some time. Their phone number and address is often listed on the policy or on a past statement. If you can't find your policy and don't have an agent to call, your state's insurance commission will have contact information about the companies licensed to do business in your state.

If you own a traditional life policy, its cash value should be listed under the "cash and equivalents" section of your net worth statement because it's money that's available for you to use right away, without risk of loss of principal. If you own a variable life policy, whose cash value fluctuates, you should list the value under the invested assets category that we discuss next.

Invested Assets

Invested assets are typically stocks, bonds, mutual funds, and other holdings that can fluctuate in value over short periods of time. The money in these accounts can be withdrawn at any time without the tax penalties that typically accompany a retirement account. Cashing out these investments also typically does not involve the expenses incurred by selling an illiquid asset like real estate, but invested assets are not as readily available or as liquid as basic cash because at any moment in time the account may be worth less than its original value.

Retirement Accounts

When completing your net worth statement, retirement plans should be listed separately from your other investments because there are often tax consequences to withdrawing the money from the accounts. By organizing your net worth statement with your tax-sensitive retirement accounts segregated from other assets, you or your financial advisor can more readily visualize how much money is set aside for the future and is not readily available for short-term expenses before retirement.

Use Assets

Real estate and other use assets, such as automobiles, vacation homes, and boats, are "illiquid," meaning there are greater expenses involved in their sale and it can take months—even years—to find a buyer. The complications involved in liquidating use assets create a potentially large fluctuation in their value. By organizing these in the "use assets" segment of the net worth statement, you can quickly see the money that is locked up in these assets.

Cash and Cash Equivalents

Here you should list the value of all your accounts that can be immediately turned into cash, including your savings accounts, checking accounts, and money market accounts. If your life insurance has a cash value invested with the insurance company at interest, you would also list the value here.

If your checking account balance is unusually high at the time you compile your net worth statement, use a typical average balance to avoid overstating your realistic net worth. List each account separately (this might also be a good time to look for ways to simplify your life by organizing your accounts under one or two service providers). By listing each account separately on the net worth statement—perhaps with a brief notation indicating the amount of interest that each account earns—you may see ways that you can consolidate your accounts and earn more interest on your money.

Bonds and Fixed Assets

List your bonds' principal value, or "face value," in this section. The financial strength, or creditworthiness, of the company, government, or government agency that issued the bond will affect the certainty that you'll be able to redeem it when it matures. If you have any doubts that your bonds or other fixed assets could fail to pay you back your full principal when they mature, you may need to list a reduced value on your net worth statement.

It's dangerous to try to go it alone when trying to place a value on a bond that's threatening to default. Call your personal broker and ask what he or she would pay you for the bond if you were to sell it. Or consider depositing the bond in your brokerage account; the brokerage will value the bond when you do.

Certificates of deposit, or CDs, with maturities greater than six months should be listed with bonds as a fixed asset because they are not readily redeemable without a penalty until they fully mature. Conversely, if the fixed asset will mature in the next couple of months, you might list its value in the cash and cash equivalent portion of the statement, as it is mature enough to be regarded as highly liquid.

Market Securities

Most of us associate market securities with the stock markets, namely mutual funds, stocks, exchange-traded funds, unit investment trusts, and other closed-end funds. We'll go into more detail about these types of investments in Chapters 9 and 11, but for now we'll briefly outline each to help you pull together the information you need for your net worth statement:

- **Mutual funds** are pooled investment accounts that enable an investor with relatively little cash to purchase a diversified portfolio of investments. Mutual funds can invest in a wide variety of investments, as outlined in their informational literature called a prospectus, but generally they invest in portfolios of stocks and/or bonds. They are managed by professional money managers who are paid from the assets of the mutual fund.

- **Stocks** represent individual shares of ownership in a specific company. The value of those shares will fluctuate with the investing public's perceived value of the company.
- **Exchange-traded funds**, or ETFs, are pooled investments that seek to mirror a particular market or index. These funds are traded among individuals, unlike mutual funds that provide a "continuous market" for their shares by offering to buy or sell them—meaning to permit deposits or withdrawals—on demand. ETFs are becoming popular because they offer the advantage of investment diversification without the cost and tax consequences associated with professional management.
- **Unit investment trusts** are fixed baskets of investments whose shares are sold among individual investors. Many exchange-traded funds are organized as unit investment trusts.
- **Closed-end mutual funds** are a type of unit investment trust. These fixed baskets of securities are traded among individual investors and are professionally managed.

FACTS

Mutual funds are among the most popular investments because they offer simple and convenient access to a diverse investing universe, automatic reinvestment of returns for accelerated investment growth, and the peace of mind of professional management. Of course, all mutual funds are not created equal, so do your homework before investing in one.

It's helpful to list equity investments in a net worth statement by account. For example, if you have a selection of mutual funds and stock holdings in an ABC Brokerage Co. account, and a selection of other stocks in an XYZ Brokerage Co. account, you should list the total value of each account, no matter how many individual securities contained in each. Equity values are typically reported each month by the firm that holds the account, and you should have little difficulty in finding the value of these investment accounts. (We'll explain the ins and outs of investment accounts in Chapter 9.)

It's also a good idea to organize your accounts by owner, for example your investments or your partner's. This extra step will be helpful when you do estate planning in which ownership of each asset is important. We talk more about estate planning in Chapter 18. You might also list the amount you paid for the investments, or what is called the "cost basis," either on your net worth statement or on a separate note that you'll keep among your financial records. This information will help you calculate the tax consequences of selling your investment. We'll talk more about cost basis later in this chapter and in Chapter 16.

Retirement Plans

All of the assets we've discussed so far could also be found within a retirement account. If you have these types of accounts, list each separately in the "retirement assets" portion of the net worth statement. Retirement account statements are often mailed on a monthly basis, but daily values might also be available through brokerages that provide Internet access to your accounts. But beware: Some employers and insurance companies only issue statements on a quarterly basis. If so, you'll need to list all of your assets in your net worth statement as of the end of a quarter so that they match the retirement accounts.

Real Estate, Personal Property, and Collectibles

Unfortunately—or perhaps fortunately, depending on what you own!— you usually don't receive a monthly statement in the mail valuing your home and personal property. If you did, perhaps you would fret as much about the depreciation of a new car as you do about the ups and downs of your stocks and mutual funds.

Use caution when valuing hard assets like real estate, collectibles, and jewelry. As always, consider the source. Should you rely on a real estate agent's appraisal of your house's market value? Real estate professionals will often analyze the value of your home for you without a charge. But consider how their interests might conflict with yours. Does the real estate agent hope to win your listing by (perhaps unconsciously) over-estimating the price your home might command in the local market?

Have comparable houses in your neighborhood actually sold for similar amounts? And does the jeweler who just gave you that appraisal of your grandmother's heirloom ring hope to buy it from you, meaning that his appraisal could be on the low side?

To help you weed through the maze of appraisals, it's important to seek out the opinions of several professionals. And by educating yourself you'll be better equipped to weigh and evaluate an appraisal of your belongings.

Get It Right!

The trouble you go to and the precision you require in placing a value on your use assets is determined by how you intend to use your net worth statement. Rough estimates will do the trick if you're just starting to chart your financial course. But if you might sell your use asset, such as a valuable collection, in the near future as part of reaching your financial goals, it's important to get a professional appraisal and to consider sales costs and taxes against the value that you list in your net worth statement. It wouldn't be smart to base your net worth on the hope of raising $200,000 from your deceased uncle's stamp collection when, in fact, a professional appraisal might show that it's worth only $10,000.

In the final analysis, and professional appraisal notwithstanding, use assets—including real estate—are worth only what a buyer will actually pay for them, and it's best not to count your chickens—or your stamp collections!—before they're hatched.

Barriers to Wealth: Assessing Your Liabilities

On the other side of your personal balance sheet are your liabilities—what you owe. These are typically loans or lump-sum payments that you must pay on a specific future date. In most cases, it's sufficient to list each debt on your net worth statement simply in terms of the principal you owe, or what the "payoff" amount would be if you were to pay the full balance tomorrow. It's not generally necessary to include future interest due on your net worth statement.

Mortgage

The bank that holds the mortgage on your home may note on your monthly account statement the principal balance due. If you're making payments from a payment booklet you should find a contact phone number in the booklet that you can call for balance information.

Home equity loans and home equity lines can be treated the same way: List the balance owed on the net worth statement on a separate line from the mortgage, even if the mortgage and home equity line happen to be borrowed from the same lender.

Credit Cards

Credit card lenders include principal balance due information on most statements. List this amount on the net worth statement along with a notation about the annual percentage interest rate, or APR, charged by the lender. If you make a similar interest rate notation for all your liabilities, your net worth statement will become a powerful tool to help you organize, and possibly consolidate, your debts to save on interest payments.

Loans and Other Liabilities

Balances due on auto loans, school loans, and other loans by banks, loan companies, friends, family, as well as tax payments you owe should also be listed in the liability section with a notation as to the term over which the liability is due. This will help in Chapter 12 when we look more closely at interest payments and how to create wealth by "paying yourself first."

Interpreting Your Financial Records

Most of the financial records needed for a personal net worth statement—including mutual fund, brokerage, bank, and loan statements—will arrive in the mail, fresh and updated, on a regular basis, usually monthly. Life insurance statements often arrive only quarterly or annually.

Some financial services companies now provide access to your accounts over the Internet. Check with your company: You may find that, in addition to checking your balance, you can make deposits, choose investments, and even pay your liabilities online.

Each statement, whether for an asset or liability, will note the statement's date or the time period it covers. For the purposes of your net worth statement you should use the final or closing date. For instance, your mortgage statement might detail the account activity since the last month, along with the change in your principal balance since the previous statement. You'll also often see your last mortgage payment, the amount applied toward principal and the amount applied toward interest. Many statements will also show the principal balance remaining after adding in the amount of your last payment. Use this amount, the principal balance remaining, on your net worth statement.

Mortgage Statements

Your mortgage statement might also indicate the interest rate and the period remaining on the loan. This is helpful information to note parenthetically on your net worth statement to help assess the amount of interest you are paying each month. (This also could help you decide whether to refinance your mortgage, something we'll discuss in detail in Chapter 4.)

Investment Accounts

Investment statements often take a little more analysis than simple bank and liability statements. Most mutual fund companies post the value of your shares on your monthly statement. But, some statements of your mutual fund and stock holdings show only the number of shares you own as of the statement date, leaving you to calculate the value of your account. Of course, the calculation is a simple one, being the product of the number of shares and the share value. The key, though, is to locate the closing value of your stocks and mutual funds on the statement date, which could be a week or more in the past.

Individual Stocks

For stocks, unless you happen to keep back copies of the *Wall Street Journal* around your house, we recommend turning to the Internet. Point your browser to ✐*http://finance.yahoo.com* or a similar site, type in the ticker symbol of your stock or mutual fund, then scan the Web page for the link to "historical quotes." From there it's simple to find the price of an equity on a specific date. If you're still unsure of the value of your shares on a specific date, contact the company directly for historical or current prices.

Brokerage Accounts

If you are using a brokerage firm to hold your securities, you'll be faced with a somewhat more complicated account statement. However, with practice you'll come to rely on the extra information these accounts provide. For example, many brokers' statements include an introductory summary that lists the value of all your accounts held by them. This can be very helpful, as the balances can simply be transferred to the net worth statement. But it's also important to review the statement for other important information on your investments.

SSENTIALS

Brokers can simplify the gathering of your financial information. Your broker can place a value on your bonds, supply cost basis information, and, if you hold all your accounts with one broker, all your account values with a single phone call. There's a cost, of course, but how much is your time worth?

In addition to the value of your account at month's end, your brokerage's statement will usually list the account's value at the end of the previous month and a calculation of your investment gains or losses during the last thirty days. The statement will generally list any transactions during the statement period and the results of those transactions. For example, the statement might note that you sold 500 shares of ABC stock at $25 per share, and that your broker's commission on your $12,500 transaction was $50. The statement will also show, in this case, that the cash resulting from this sale was placed in your core cash account.

While this doesn't apply directly to creating your net worth statement, this is a good time to look closely at the brokerage statement and review the commission you paid and the value in your core cash account. Think of your core cash account as your investment cash register. Proceeds from the sale of securities, interest payments on your bonds, and any other investment earnings can be funneled into your cash account, where it can then be used to purchase other investments or even to write personal checks. Core cash accounts earn only moderate interest, so don't let money idle here. If you're not planning to make a new investment right away, you might contact the brokerage firm to transfer that money into a money market account that pays higher interest.

Cash

Depending on the amount of cash being held in your brokerage account, you might list it as a separate item in your cash and equivalents category instead of including it in the investments section. But if you do, be careful: Don't duplicate the value by including your core-account cash that you listed under cash and equivalents when you list the brokerage account in the investment section of your net worth statement.

Cash in retirement accounts should not be separated from the account as a whole. Because that cash is not available without paying some tax consequences related to this type of account, it should not be listed with the liquid assets of cash and equivalents.

Cost Basis

Some investment account statements will also list your average cost per share, also known as your "cost basis" or "tax basis" per share. This cost basis represents your total investment in the account to date. It includes your initial deposit plus any dividends or interest that you have reinvested but paid taxes on already.

This is useful information, because when you sell your equities, you may owe capital gains tax on the profits your investments have earned. Accurate record keeping is important to avoid repaying tax on these reinvested dividends and interest payments upon which you have already been taxed once. Many statements will list this amount in the detail section of the statement; in the case of a mutual fund statement, look near the bottom of the report.

If this cost basis information is not available on your statement, you should contact the investment company directly to ask if they have these records. Many companies don't, so it's important to keep previous statements to avoid overpaying capital gains taxes when you sell your investment. We'll talk more about this and other issues relating to taxes and wealth in Chapter 16.

The amount of time you should store your various financial records can vary. Account statements showing activity in both asset and liability accounts should be kept for each month of the year. If the final December statement shows a summary of all activity, or if the company sends a year-end summary statement, you can discard the eleven previous year statements. It's important to retain records of investment transactions so you can track tax-basis information.

If you haven't retained these records, some investment companies will send you past year-end statements to help you calculate your tax basis and, in a pinch, the schedule B of your past tax returns will also list income, dividends, and capital gains received from your investments. It's a good rule of thumb to store these annual records either with your tax preparation information or in a separate file for each year.

Using the Sample Net Worth Statement

Now that you have all your financial information laid out in front of you, it's time to get to work completing your net worth statement. Using the blank net worth statement earlier in this chapter, or a similar one that you can easily draft, list each asset value on one side of the statement—in their respective categories—and each liability on the other. Remember, your net worth is the sum of your assets less the sum of your liabilities.

Refer to the sample net worth statement for Nick and Nora Rich earlier in this chapter for help in completing your own statement. It indicates assets of $992,000: $16,000 in cash and cash equivalents, $163,000 in invested assets, $103,000 in retirement accounts, and $710,000 in use assets. Liabilities, which total $410,000, consist of a mortgage of $175,000, a home equity loan of $200,000, and credit card debt of $35,000. Subtracting liabilities from assets, the Richs' net worth is $582,000.

How did you do at completing your net worth statement? Are you in good financial shape? No matter what your answer, by the end of this book you'll know exactly what you need to do to chart your course toward wealth. But for now, let's take a closer look at the Richs' net worth statement and see what kind of financial condition it indicates.

Cash Issues

One characteristic that stands out is that 3 percent of the Richs' total net worth, $16,000, is in cash. This is money that is readily available without the risk of losing value or paying penalties to withdraw. Depending on expenses, this may be too little. Some planners recommend that clients maintain three to six months' worth of expenses in the form of cash and cash equivalents.

The percentage itself is not the only important factor. It's also important to have an adequate amount of cash relative to your monthly budget. We will examine this more closely in the next chapter.

Proper Balance

27 percent of the Richs' total assets is in the form of invested assets and retirement plans, versus 75 percent in use assets—primarily real estate. This imbalance, known as being "house heavy," is common for many couples who are focused on providing a comfortable home for themselves and their children. Although this is not necessarily a bad situation during a couple's working years, it often limits their choices when they arrive at retirement and are reluctant to sell the house in order to reinvest the cash locked up in the form of home equity. Planning ahead and seeking a balance between liquid investments, retirement assets, and real estate can mitigate this situation. And in later chapters, we'll show you how.

Home

The Richs' net worth statement shows a home with 42 percent equity. This is comfortably above the 20 percent minimum we strive for in order to avoid mortgage insurance premiums. Mortgage insurance is required by the lender to protect their investment in the residence. It is not expensive, but it's an expense that diverts cash that could be producing returns in an investment account, and it doesn't necessarily benefit you as the homeowner and premium payer—it benefits the mortgage company.

When homeowners commit less than 20 percent of a house's value from their own pockets, lenders see them as a greater risk than those homeowners who commit more than 20 percent. By requiring the homeowner to carry and pay for homeowner's insurance, the bank ensures that the mortgage will be paid if the homeowner defaults.

ALERT

Mortgage insurance is a benefit to the lender and a wealth-robbing cost to the borrower. Contact your bank as soon as your equity reaches 20 percent so that you no longer are required to carry the insurance; the lender will keep expecting the premium payments until you do.

Whenever possible, wealth builders strive to maintain at least a 20 percent equity position in their homes. And it's a good wealth-building idea to pay extra money toward principal each month—and even seek a new appraisal if you feel that your home's value has grown enough to warrant the expense—to reach 20 percent equity. This important strategy is especially effective in a fast-growing real estate market.

Let's say you purchase a home for $100,000 and make a down payment of 5 percent, or $5,000. Because you have less then 20 percent equity you will be required to pay mortgage insurance premiums. You strive to pay extra principal each month to hasten the day when the value of your home, minus your mortgage, is 20 percent.

But your extra payments are only one way to widen this gap between value and mortgage—your house may also appreciate in market value faster than you can make extra payments. Your mortgage company will not send you a report listing the appreciation of your home, and unless you stay alert you may be unaware that your $100,000 house has appreciated to $118,750. This new value, minus your mortgage of $95,000, achieves the coveted 20 percent goal even without your extra principal payments.

By staying aware of the local real estate market, and by paying for an appraisal to prove that you now have 20 percent equity, you can save the premiums on this extra insurance and boost the amount of money each month that can be turned toward other wealth goals.

Credit Card Debt

Six percent of the Richs' net worth is tied up in credit card debt. Credit cards are among the worst wealth-robbers we encounter in day-to-day living. For example, if you were to pay only the 2 percent minimum payment on a $1,000 original balance, after twenty years you would have paid $2,920 with $335 balance remaining on your account. There's a reason credit card lenders encourage low minimum payments!

Depending on their income and credit approval, a family with a net worth statement like the one in the example could fold their credit card debt balance into their home equity loan to trade non–tax deductible interest for deductible interest. If they do this, they need to realize that they would have to offer their home as collateral against those debts. They should look back at their budget to be sure that they would be able to pay off that part of the home equity loan more quickly than the part that went toward the home improvement.

It's a sure wealth killer to refinance short-term debt like business or entertainment expenses on a ten-year home equity loan or a thirty-year mortgage. This strategy appears to save on interest expenses in the short term because the card payments are reduced. But by rolling these costs into longer-term mortgage or home equity lines, these temporary expenses ultimately cost many times their value in interest.

We'll look more closely at net worth and financial condition, and offer more suggestions for improving your own, after completing the financial picture by compiling a cash flow statement in the next chapter.

CHAPTER 4

Tracking Your Money: The Cash Flow Statement

This tool provides a gauge of the money going into and out of your pocket. As such, it is your most potent wealth-building weapon. Unlike other elements of your finances, your cash flow is something you can directly control. By tracking your spending, and focusing primarily on things you value—what we call "spending deliberately"—you can increase your financial security and build wealth.

Where Does the Money Go?

Unfortunately, measuring cash flow often generates great anxiety. Many a household argument has ensued when a couple finds they have "too much month at the end of the money." It's important to not let the gathering of cash flow information degrade into a "he spent/she spent" argument. If this happens to your family as you compile your cash flow statement, try backing up a bit to examine your purpose for creating this important document. Do you want to work together to create wealth? What are your goals?

Often, couples can work through their conflicting spending priorities by discussing their financial goals with each other. Once their goals are defined, couples can then budget money toward achieving them.

SSENTIALS

If you can't finish a discussion about money with your partner or spouse without it erupting into an argument, consider talking to a counselor who specializes in this area. Relationship strife caused by money is so common that many financial advisors are working closely with counselors to offer services to money-troubled couples.

The most important elements of a personal cash flow statement are accuracy and usability. We will suggest the process that we have found useful in building a cash flow statement. As with any of the exercises in this book, you should adjust our suggestions to fit your situation.

Tracking Your Expenses

The first step in creating a cash flow statement, as with developing a net worth statement, is to collect the raw data. Listed in the following sections are some techniques we've found particularly helpful. The key to any of these approaches is how simple they are to use. Many people have purchased an expensive bookkeeping software program only to grow frustrated over its complexity, or have allowed it to go unused in the box. Create a system that is easy to use and provides enough flexibility to allow changes if it doesn't suit your needs. (If you like the idea of using your computer to help you construct your net worth and cash flow statements, Intuit's Quicken and Microsoft's Money can help you build these reports. But remember, computer software is not essential, and every dollar you save on software is a dollar that can be invested in getting rich!)

Drafting an accurate, useful, and simple record of income and expenses doesn't have to be rocket science; simply spend a little time and diligence, and your cash flow statement will become a valuable tool in your plan to get rich.

Money Diary

Rich people often get that way, in part, with the help of what is called a "money diary," and you're going to learn how to keep one and how it can help you reach your goal of getting rich. There is no expensive booklet you must buy, no single method that has any advantages over another. We recommend you keep the process simple by buying a small, inexpensive spiral-bound notebook at your local store. After all, frugality is a key ingredient to getting rich, why not incorporate it into the process of your wealth-building money diary?

The first order of business as you begin your money diary is to begin tracking your expenses. Jot down every cash purchase for eight weeks, no exceptions. Depending on your spending habits, you might even want to keep the diary for twelve weeks, giving you enough points of information to compile an accurate picture of your spending.

We can't overemphasize the importance of keeping a money diary for at least three weeks. Everyone in the family who spends household cash—including Junior's lawn-mowing proceeds and Sis' babysitting earnings—must keep a diary if it is to be a useful tool in planning for wealth.

After a while, you'll have compiled a list of cash purchases that might surprise you. For folks who spend a lot of cash, this process can serve as an eye-opener to uncovering how much spending goes unnoticed. At the end of eight weeks, you'll be prepared to combine the knowledge of your cash transactions with other financial information to create a personal cash flow statement.

And cheating is strictly forbidden! The whole point of a money diary is to find the holes in the pockets where cash simply seems to disappear unnoticed. No one's going to tell you that you should deprive yourself of your latté fix on the way to work, but the sheer size of the annual cost of a premium coffee habit just might shock you into voluntarily switching to a more inexpensive cup of java from the neighborhood doughnut shop.

ALERT

If you've got a pack-and-a-half a day cigarette habit or a premium coffee vice, the cost and the lost investment opportunity can be staggering. The $5.25 per day you'd pay for these habits costs you $19,163 in ten years—money that could have compounded to $27,748 if invested at 7 percent.

Go back and look at your wealth mission statement from Chapter 1. It may sound like an absurd question, but was "To have a great cup of gourmet coffee every morning" one of your financial goals? If it wasn't, then you might want to reallocate your spending toward your goal of getting rich. Of course, we don't advocate that you begin to live the self-depriving life of a monk, but you should begin to compare your spending habits to your wealth goals, and see just how much value you place in individually small, but cumulatively costly pleasures.

Cigarettes, pulp paperbacks, the occasional cigar, a few cocktails at the neighborhood watering hole—they're all part of our lives, and without them, we'd be less content. The point of a money diary is not to identify expenses to cut, but merely to note the direction our money is flowing each month, then be able to sit down with our wealth plan at our side and consciously decide where our priorities lie. Comparing our cash spending to the wealth mission statement we crafted in Chapter 1 can be a valuable exercise in goal-setting.

Bank and Credit Card Statements

Bank credit card statements carry a wealth of information about your financial condition, especially if your lender reports the locations at which you use your debit card for cash purchases. By pulling together your bank and credit card statements for the previous three months, you can begin to form a picture of your spending patterns. Your goal is to account for the money that isn't spent on regular bills—mortgage, rent, utilities and such—so that the expense categories listed below can be accurately tracked.

Fixed Expenses

Each expense should be recorded on a monthly basis. You may want to add or subtract categories as your situation warrants, but be sure to have enough separate designations so that you can identify money that's being spent elsewhere than on building wealth and reaching your financial goals.

Here are some common cash flow categories:

- Income taxes, real estate taxes, and other taxes
- Mortgage or rent payment
- Homeowners' association fees
- Utilities—telephone, electric, gas, oil, cable, Internet services
- Personal insurance—health, life, disability
- Homeowner or renter's insurance and umbrella liability
- Auto insurance
- Alimony or child support
- Commuting expenses—train fare, taxi fare, gas, automobile maintenance
- Day care expenses
- Tuition and educational costs
- School loans
- Medical and dental expenses, including prescriptions
- Debt payments (other than mortgage)
- Home equity loan or line
- Auto loans
- Credit card debt
- Loans from parents and friends

Variable Expenses

These are expenses that you have some control over. They might include:

- Savings and investments
- Retirement account contributions
- Home and yard maintenance
- Household cleaning services
- Groceries, including personal care items
- Entertainment—dining out, movies, lessons, books, subscriptions, toys, videos, and so on
- Recreation—sporting equipment, sporting events, club memberships, golf green fees, vacations, and so on
- Gifts
- Clothing and accessories
- Cell phone expenses
- Charitable giving and donations
- Miscellaneous expenses—marina fees for your boat, rental costs for your storage locker, and so on

By pulling together your money diary, your bank and credit card transactions, and your monthly bills, you should be able to arrive at a monthly amount for each of these categories. Add or subtract categories as needed with the object of visualizing where your money goes each month.

Tallying the Income

Now that you have the expense portion of your cash flow statement completed, you need to gather the information for the income side. Collect all the paperwork reflecting the money you bring in, including:

- **Pay stubs from employers.** You may use the gross amount before taxes and other deductions (for example, health, disability, life insurance, and other pre-tax payroll deductions) as long as you remember to include those items in the expense portion of your balance sheet. For simplicity, though, many people opt to start with net income, or take-home pay, and then not bother with listing expenses withheld from the paycheck.

- **Non–W-2 income.** Collect 1099 forms (reports of interest, dividend, and self-employment income, among other types) and invoices from self-employment income.
- **Investment returns.** Compile reports of interest or dividend earnings from investments.
- **Other non-business income.** This includes records of cash gifts and other regular allowances or income like child support or alimony payments.
- **Other business income.** This includes royalties or rents received.

FACTS

If you typically reinvest interest and dividends from your investments, don't include that income in your cash flow statement. Include only the money you regularly receive that you're able to use each month to pay expenses and set aside to build wealth. You can break out each income stream according to the person in the household who earns it or by the type of income.

Deciphering Your Cash Flow

Finally, subtract your total expenses from your total income. The resulting sum will be your discretionary income, and will provide a telling glimpse into your financial health.

What does it mean if the remainder is less than zero? This is certainly a vexing problem, though you might take comfort in knowing you are not alone. Of course a sub-zero balance at the bottom of your cash flow statement is an alarm that you are spending beyond your means. But the prognosis is not entirely dire in every case.

Still, one thing is sure: Something has to give if you intend to get rich, and wealth is still possible even if you find you're now spending more than you earn—if you're willing to take drastic action. Whether caused by excessive credit card debt or too little savings, an unbalanced cash flow statement, if left unresolved, can keep you from achieving your wealth goals.

Check It for Accuracy

If your cash flow statement surprises you with how little discretionary income remains each month, you might need to check your figures for accuracy. Have you correctly noted each expense in its monthly—not annual—amount? Have you double-counted something, such as listing your after-tax take-home pay, but also including payroll taxes in the expense column?

Trim Expenses

Once you've checked for accuracy, revisit your cash flow statement with an eye for expenses that can be reduced. Look at where you are spending your money and determine if you are spending it on what is truly important to you, or rather on mere luxuries that sap wealth rather than help create it. Review your wealth mission statement from Chapter 1 and your financial goals from Chapter 2 and flag the parts of your cash flow statement where money is being diverted from those things you value. Is your goal to retire with a secure income but your cash flow statement reveals you spend more money on entertainment than on retirement savings? Do you want to help pay for your kids' college expenses, but your cash flow statement discloses that you spend more money on the children's games and toys than on college savings?

Budgeting and Cash Flow: Pay Yourself First

The concept of paying yourself first is an old one among financial advisors, but one that is often ignored by families as the financial pressures and temptations of the present intrude on a disciplined pursuit of future goals. Simply put, paying yourself first means that before you spend a dime of your salary or income on expenses, you make a regular contribution to your future. Depending on your situation, that could mean funding your personal or employer-provided retirement plan, an automatic deposit to savings or investment accounts, or even the purchase of government savings bonds.

Thumb through Chapter 1 again, if necessary, and remember how we described the behavior and spending habits of the wealthy. Most wealthy folks have earned their money rather than inheriting it, and have kept that money in their own pockets by paying themselves first, rather than paying for luxury cars, custom homes, and many of the other wealth-robbing temptations of modern life.

With that kind of wealth-building behavior in mind, reflect on your own cash flow statement and decide: Are you controlling your spending, or is your spending controlling you?

Hitting Your Budgeting Targets

We've found that it's helpful to rely on a few budgeting rules of thumb. These provide some general limits on how your budget should be allocated, but they alone are no guarantees of financial success. If your cash flow is on the high end of the range in one category, it will need to be on the low side of another to provide balance. Look back at your financial goals to remind yourself which part of your budget you'll want to emphasize. Each of these guidelines is based on gross income before taxes:

- **Housing expense: 30–35 percent.** This includes mortgage or rent, homeowner's insurance, home equity loan payments, utilities, home repair, cleaning services, property tax, and any other costs of living in your home.
- **Income taxes: 20–25 percent.** Taxes are difficult to manage, but with the help of a good accountant and our suggestions in Chapter 16, your may glean some tips that will help to drive down the tax percentage of your cash flow.
- **Living expenses other than housing: 20–25 percent.** This includes groceries, clothing, medical expenses, childcare, commuting expenses, miscellaneous taxes, entertainment, recreation, and any other expenses that don't fall under the other categories.

- **Retirement, mid-term savings, and emergency savings: 10–15 percent.** This is the money that you budget for meeting your wealth goals—the money that will make you rich!
- **Charitable giving: 10 percent.** This is the money you spend on causes that you value and to support those less fortunate. We are firm believers in the power of charity: Keep the money flowing to noble causes and it will flow back to you!
- **Debt payment: 5 percent.** This includes auto loans, school loans, installment loans, and other debts.

To test your wealth success, separate your cash flow statement into these categories and examine where your spending places you in each range. It's likely that, in some categories, you'll find that your spending places you in the lower portion of the range. That means you'll be able to comfortably spend in the high portions of the range in other categories. What if your cash flow statement shows you're breaking some of the guidelines we've described here? Remember, the goal of this exercise is not to scold yourself but to piece together a portrait of your spending that can serve as a starting point on the journey toward wealth.

FACTS

You may choose to spend extra money on your home and less on your savings because of your personal financial goals. By spending deliberately you will focus your resources on achieving your long-term goals. You will begin rejecting short-term treats in favor of long-term financial security—and you'll stop wasting money!

From Poor Money Management to Sensible Budget

Now let's look at a sample cash flow statement and see how Nick and Nora Rich decided to manage their budget for wealth.

FIGURE 4-1:

Sample
Cash Flow
Statement

Nick and Nora Rich
Cash Flow Statement
June 30, 2002

Monthly Income

Nora salary	5,167
Nick self-employment income (after expenses, before taxes)	10,417
TOTAL MONTHLY INCOME	**15,584**

Monthly Expenses

Income taxes—Nora	1,550
Income taxes including self-employment taxes—Nick	3,333
Pre-tax deductions from Nora's paycheck	
(health insurance, pre-paid medical, disability insurance)	200
Nora's 401(k) (15% contribution)	775
Savings	0
Mortgage (30 year note at 6%)	1,049
Home equity line (10 year note at 8.5%)	2,480
Credit card payment	350
Real estate taxes	975
Homeowner's insurance (incl. umbrella liability)	200
Auto insurance	300
Life insurance	167
Groceries, etc.	700
Utilities	700
Nick's car lease	440
Entertainment	1,300
Recreation	0
Medical (other than health insurance)	200
Kid's things (piano, dance, hockey)	600
Charitable	50
Vacation	680
TOTAL MONTHLY EXPENSES	**$16,049**
Net per month	**-$465**

Housing expenses	$5,404	33.7%
Debt	$350	2.2%
Savings	$775	4.8%
Charitable	$50	0.3%
Living expenses	$4,587	28.6%
Taxes	$4,883	30.4%
	$16,049	100%

For the sake of our example, we'll assume that the Rich family is spending more money each month than they bring in in salary and other income. A tendency to overspend is often reflected in high credit card balances when regular income is spent on ordinary living expenses. An overspent budget can also place stress on a marriage and create a feeling that no matter how hard you work you still can't save money and are seemingly always in a cash crunch.

It appears that overspending is not the only problem the Rich family has. Two important elements are missing from their cash flow statement— disability insurance, and credit card payments above the minimum 1 percent most credit lenders require each month. If the top wage earner is disabled, the family will find it almost impossible to get by without that income. As we'll see in Chapter 6, disability insurance can be expensive, but it is a necessary part of a family's financial security. What's more, if the Rich family continues to make only the minimum payments on their credit card debt, the extra interest they pay will continue to hamper their quest for wealth.

These problems can seem overwhelming, but we can offer some suggestions. Because the top wage earner in our example is self-employed, the family's taxes will tend toward the high side of the cash flow statement guidelines we outlined earlier. It's probable that the Rich family pays more than 31 percent of their gross income in taxes because a self-employed worker must pay the employer's share of his payroll taxes. (If someone employs you, you pay half the payroll taxes and the employer pays half. Self-employed folks pay both halves of this tax, which is applied towards their social security and Medicare credits.) This extra tax burden puts a pinch on the rest of a family's budget.

Lighten the Tax Load

To lighten the tax load, the self-employed wage earner in our example can choose to open a retirement savings plan. After looking at his cash flow and net worth statements, it doesn't appear that he has taken advantage of this option. In our example, the spouse contributes to her 401(k) retirement plan at work, but that only provides the family with a total savings ratio of 5 percent. If the lead wage earner were to contribute to a Self-Employed Pension plan, or SEP, he could help raise his family's savings percentage to 15 percent and save about $6,000 a year in taxes at the same time.

We'll look closer at managing taxes and retirement planning in later chapters, but for now let's go back to our sample cash flow statement and see how the Rich family are doing on their other expenses.

Match Lifestyle to Income

According to their cash flow statement, they spend $5,404 a month, or 33.7 percent of their income, on housing expenses. While a big home addition they completed last year may at first glance seem expensive, the cost of the work was still within what we would consider a normal range. But the home-equity loan to finance the addition has added $2,480 to the bottom-line monthly expenses. This may have been money that they had been saving or using to pay other expenses; now it serves to put them into the red. By maintaining their "pre-addition" lifestyle and the related expenses, rather than paring down their spending to match the added cost of the home-equity loan payment, the family has veered off the course to their financial goals by overextending their budget.

Invest Windfalls

The Rich family purchased a new van two years ago with money inherited from a relative. This gift has been very helpful because now the family has no car payment. The lead wage earner leases a luxury car, so we'll categorize that expense under living expenses.

Failure to invest windfalls such as an inheritance is a financial vice that threatens to keep many families from getting rich. Remember your priorities when deciding what to do with "found money."

Was the van purchase the best use of the modest inheritance? Perhaps, if the car will last for a long time and the family invests an amount equal to the car payment they are saving. But many families wouldn't do this, and in three years—roughly the time they'd be ready to replace the van—the value of the inheritance would be gone and they would once again have a car payment in their budget while having failed to invest any money toward their long-term goals.

Make Larger Payments on Credit Cards

The Rich family has no college loans or debts to friends and family, so their only loan payment is their credit card, to which they pay $350 per month. This may look good at first glance, because they are spending only 2.2 percent of their gross income on debt. But by using the net worth statement to see the broader picture, we see that they are wasting money on interest payments by only making the minimum payment and carrying the credit card balance far longer then they should. They should consider paying extra toward the balance of the card each month to reduce the term of repayment.

Roll Debts into Home Equity Loans—with Caution

The Riches could also consider folding the credit card balance into their home equity loan. This may make the interest they pay on the home equity loan a deductible expense, saving them future dollars in taxes. But they must be very careful: It isn't always prudent to put up your home as collateral for what should be short-term credit card debt. Also, if the Rich family chooses not to pay more than the minimum monthly home equity loan payment after transferring the credit card debt, they could actually end up financing what should have been a short-term expense over a much longer period of time, costing them money—and future wealth—in the meantime.

Check True Values

A glance at the sample cash flow statement shows the Rich family spending 28.6 percent of their gross income on living expenses. Because other categories, such as taxes, tend to be high, they should go back through their living expenses and look for places where they're spending money away from their wealth goals. Could the Rich family save money by cutting down on how often they dine out? Could the kids take either dance or piano lessons rather than both? Could they lease a less expensive car than the luxury model they're using now, or buy a low-mileage used one? These questions can only be answered by the parents themselves. What are their priorities? It's ultimately up to the family to complete their financial plan, and then revisit this budget with more information and the big picture in mind.

FACTS

After graduating from high school, a trip to Europe or across the United States marks a rite of passage for many college-bound teenagers. Start investing now by trimming your cable television to basic service during the summer when the extra selection of premium programming is unnecessary to keep the kids entertained. Saving $20 per month for six months a year will fund a graduation gift worth more than $4,000 in eighteen years.

Other Paths Toward Wealth

Here are some other tips to help the Rich family balance their budget:

- They could refinance their home to pay off the home equity line under a new mortgage that's financed over thirty years. Monthly savings: $1,280.
- The lead wage earner could open a retirement savings plan. Monthly cost, based on a maximum contribution: $1,562. Monthly tax savings: $500, making net monthly cost of fully funding a retirement plan = $1,062 (based on the lead wager earner's $125,000 gross income, a 15 percent retirement plan contribution, and 32 percent taxes).
- The family could try reallocating expenses as their lives change. For example, they might reduce their expensive nights out by volunteering at the local library or other charities. Activities like these help families save money on expensive restaurant dinners and movie nights, and enable them to contribute to their community at the same time.

These tips for spending frugally can help you redirect your money toward your wealth goals. The possible methods to economize are limited only by your imagination. We don't urge you to become misers; our hope is that you will use our tools and techniques to gain a clearer view of your spending, then learn to spend deliberately on those things that will make you rich. The key for couples and families who are committed to growing wealthy is to communicate with each other and keep an open mind about new spending habits. And above all, stay focused on your wealth goals!

With some creativity, investing for college can be effortless by simply reallocating your day care expenses to a college fund. For example, if a child were to leave day care at age six, and the $350 per week cost were invested at 7 percent annual return, it would yield $340,000 at age eighteen.

CHAPTER 5

Insure Your Belongings

I nsurance is a key component of any plan to become, and stay, wealthy. After all, the work you do building wealth could be for naught if you're struck by some costly financial disaster that destroys the wealth you've built.

Are You Overinsured?

Property and casualty policies are those that protect your assets, such as your home, your vehicles, or your business, against damage or destruction caused by natural disasters and manmade perils. Property and casualty (P & C) insurance is intended to restore you to the original financial state you enjoyed before suffering a loss covered by one of your policies.

When building wealth, it's important to fine-tune your insurance coverage so you're not spending dollars on unneeded insurance that could be multiplying in your investment accounts. The theory of insurance is based on two fundamental concepts: the law of large numbers and insurable risk. Let's take a closer look at each, and how they affect your coverage.

Law of Large Numbers

According to the law of large numbers, it's impossible to predict who will experience a loss of some kind, say an auto accident, but it is possible to predict how many losses will occur within a group. For example, no one can predict whether you'll be in a fender bender during rush hour tomorrow morning. But an insurance company could gather statistics on past driving and accident patterns in a particular region that would help it predict how many fender benders are likely to occur in a particular year.

By predicting how many individuals in a group will experience a loss, and what the cumulative cost of those losses will be, an insurer can calculate how large a premium to charge each participant in exchange for assuming the risk, for example, of auto damage and personal injury in a car accident.

Also, by measuring each participant's similarity, or dissimilarity, to the average group member, the company can calculate how much more or less than average a person should pay for their insurance. For example, the insurance company's actuaries calculate that, statistically, a teenage driver is more likely to be involved in an accident than an older driver, so the teen driver must pay a higher premium to offset the increased likelihood of a claim.

By the same token, actuaries may predict that a driver who has driven for a number of years without incident uses driving habits that make her less likely to be in an accident in the future. The insurer can offer the safe driver a lower premium in order to attract her business without being unduly worried they'll have to pay a claim. Without a sufficiently large group of policyholders, or "insureds" as the insurance industry sometimes calls them, an insurance policy cannot be written because the risk can't be predicted with enough statistical certainty.

FACTS

Actuaries are the statistical analysts who study broad demographic trends for insurance companies, pension plans, and other organizations that depend on reliable risk predictions. The information actuaries gather about the statistical likelihood of an event is compiled into "actuarial tables" that enable these companies to estimate risk and offset potential losses.

That's why an average four-person family might find it very risky to self-insure against the possibility that one of them might need major surgery or long-term medical treatment. The family could, if they were daring, estimate their total expected medical costs and develop a savings plan to accumulate enough money to pay those bills. But if an illness or an accident were to strike unexpectedly—and what illnesses or accidents *are* expected?—the account may not have grown large enough to cover the expenses. (Not to mention the fact that it's possible to pile up medical expenses in the millions of dollars!)

If they were self-insured, the family would be the only financial resource, and there would be no unaffected individuals to continue paying premiums to replenish the account as the family withdrew from it. As individuals, we can't tell when we will suffer a loss or an expense, so we benefit by transferring portions of our risk to an insurance company.

The insurance company, on the other hand, owes a duty to shareholders and policyholders to manage their business prudently, and that means, in part, underwriting only those risks that can be measured and safely assumed. It must calculate and collect enough premiums to cover claims as well as its operating overhead, and it does this by employing the law of large numbers and only providing coverage for insurable risks.

Insurable Risk

Insurable risks have three basic characteristics: The policyholders are independent enough from each other so that only a small number will experience a loss at any given time; the risks are accidental in nature and beyond the control of the insured; and the risk or loss can be determined and measured. By understanding these basic insurance concepts, and keeping them in mind through this chapter and the next, you'll be better able to manage the threats to your own wealth and decide which risks to retain and which to transfer to the insurance company. Because they are so important, let's look more closely at these three basic characteristics.

QUESTIONS?

How should I select my insurance agent?
Word of mouth references are often the best. Talk to friends and business associates whose circumstances closely mirror your own. When interviewing an agent, look for credentials that show advanced training, including Life Underwriter Training Council Fellow (LUTCF); Certified Life Underwriter (CLU); Licensed Insurance Advisor (LIA); Certified Insurance Counselor (CIC); and Licensed Insurance Counselor (LIC).

- **Random chance.** For insurance to operate effectively, the risk of loss must be random enough as to limit the number of folks who could experience a loss simultaneously. You sometimes hear of government subsidies to insurance companies and individuals in areas hard hit by major natural disasters such as hurricanes, earthquakes, or floods. It's expensive to provide coverage for these risks because of the large geographical areas that can be affected. And often, insurance companies need help from each other and from government agencies to reinsure and share the burden of these geographically broad emergencies that affect sometimes millions of people.
- **Beyond control.** The loss must be an accident that is beyond the policyholder's control. Insurance is meant to return policyholders to their original financial position—replacing what was lost—not to provide a windfall. If the policyholder could artificially create a loss, the

randomness that drives the law of large numbers would vanish, enabling some to be enriched by insurance claims.

- **Getting real.** An insurance company must be able to verify that a loss has taken place and measure the value of that loss. Without this limit, the risk assumed by the insurance company could, in theory, be infinite. This is why companies carefully note in their policies which risks they are assuming or which they aren't.

The Bottom Line on Insurable Risk

What does insurable risk mean to us, the policyholders? An insurable risk is one that we are willing to pay a premium to cover. If the insurance company feels it can't either measure the risk, determine extent of the loss—or even that it happened at all—and if it can't rely on the randomness of the loss, it will charge a premium so high that few consumers will consider it cost-effective to transfer the risk.

To use an extreme example, if you were to build a $100,000 house in a flood plain on the bank of a river that floods every spring, the only insurance you might be able to buy could come with a premium very close to $100,000—and in reality, there's probably no insurance company who'd be willing to write such a policy. When the loss is certain it's more appropriate to manage it through some other means—like moving away in this example!—than to transfer it to the insurance company.

FACTS

A helpful gauge of the likelihood of a particular loss is the relative cost of the premium the company charges in order to insure it. If it's a low premium, the loss is probably unlikely to occur; a high premium may indicate that a loss is more likely. Balance the premium against the loss's potential devastation on your own wealth plan, then decide whether to purchase insurance or self-insure.

As consumers, we need to feel that the value of being insured against loss is greater than the value of the premium. We must be willing to exchange the unknown expense of a loss for the known expense of a premium payment.

Homeowner's Insurance

Modern homeowner's insurance can be written to cover both the loss of your property as well as the legal responsibility you assume when you're a homeowner. This insurance may include coverage for injury to others, additional medical expense coverage, and additional living-expense coverage in case you have to vacate your home as a result of one of the covered disasters.

Homeowner's coverage is categorized as either "all-risk" or "named-peril" coverage. An all-risk policy, as its name suggests, covers all perils except for those that are specifically excluded, while a named-peril policy covers only those risks that are specifically listed in the policy. For many individuals, their home is their greatest asset, so it is important to seek the advice of your personal insurance agent as to the amount and type of coverage you need.

Ask the Right Questions

Here are some common concerns a wealth builder should discuss with the insurance agent.

Replacement Cost Versus Actual Cash Value

Replacement cost versus actual cash value coverage carries important distinctions when purchasing homeowner's insurance. Replacement cost coverage provides enough compensation to bring your property back to its original state, even if building and construction costs have risen relative to the cash value of your home. Cash value coverage, while sometimes carrying a lower premium, will only pay the cash value of the structure, even if the value is lower than when you first bought it. It's important to review your homeowner's insurance with your agent on a regular basis to be sure that your coverage is keeping pace with inflation. Nothing robs wealth faster than an insurance claim that pays only a portion of your property's value.

Tenant's Insurance

If you don't own a home, tenant's insurance (also called renter's insurance) is available to cover the personal property in your apartment and the liability you incur there. Although the coverage doesn't typically include the exterior of your building, the similarities between homeowner's and tenant's insurance are plentiful enough to make the rest of our discussion germane to both situations.

Don't send your child off to college without tenant's insurance. Check with the dorm administration and your personal insurance agent to be sure the expensive computer and other belongings your child took to college has coverage.

Scheduling Your Coverage

Homeowner and tenant policies provide limited coverage for some special items like jewelry, valuable silver, and home office equipment. Scheduling these items, which means listing them separately in your policy, could increase these limits and eliminate your policy deductible on these special items. This is an important consideration if you have a home office filled with valuable computer and office equipment or if you have a special collection of antiques or other such valuables.

Adding on the Extras

Homeowner's insurance is usually moderately priced insurance that should be an integral part of your home purchasing budget. In fact, if you have a mortgage, your bank will likely require you to maintain a minimum of coverage to protect their interest in the property. Ask your insurance agent to review the features of your policy and the related premiums. Decide whether you could provide your own coverage for some of the extra features and compare the premium savings for doing so.

Fine-Tuning the Deductible

A deductible is an agreement by the policyholder to pay the first portion of their claim, shielding the insurance company from part of the cost. It offers policyholders a method of reducing insurance costs because insurance companies will reduce premiums in return for not having to cover the entire loss. Consider increasing your deductible if you feel you could afford to pay a higher share of a loss. But be sure you are not carrying a deductible that doesn't save you a proportional amount of premium expense.

An insurance agent colleague of ours once related her frustration over a client who asked to carry an additional $100 deductible on her auto glass coverage in exchange for a savings of only $9 in annual premium. The average replacement cost of a car windshield in her area was only about $100, so she was effectively guaranteeing that if she needed a new windshield, she would have to pay the full cost. A better alternative might have been to not carry the auto glass replacement coverage at all, saving her $75 per year on the cost of the policy, rather than paying $66 per year for coverage that was all but useless because of the high deductible.

SSENTIALS

If your car is old and ready to be replaced, why pay for the same coverage you purchased when it was new? Reduce or drop your collision coverage and invest the amount you save on insurance premiums into an account to buy a new car (or, like most people who know how to get rich, a late-model used car).

Check Your Intentions

It's important to cover only the things you intend to replace if they are lost, and not pay higher premiums to insure property you no longer need. An insurance colleague tells of a client who maintains expensive coverage on her antique furniture collection, which she collected overseas as keepsakes of her travels. The furniture is irreplaceable, and the owner admits that if it were lost, it would be impractical to replace most of the pieces. She would probably visit a local furniture store to replace the most important pieces—after all, she'd need a kitchen table even if it weren't an antique—but she insists nonetheless on paying for more expensive scheduled coverage of the costly antiques!

Recognize Legitimate Risks

It's important to purchase adequate coverage when you have a legitimate risk, especially one that could be financially devastating. After all, losses can happen anytime. Our insurance colleague tells us of the time her agency recommended to an auto insurance customer that she also buy tenant's insurance to cover the personal belongings in her apartment. The customer demurred, saying her budget was tight and she'd like to think it over before making a decision—usually, a fairly sound way of making financial decisions. But as bad luck would have it, when the client returned home from the insurance agent's office, she found her apartment had been burglarized. As it turned out, the thieves had been in her apartment at the very moment she was declining the tenant's insurance that would have helped her pay to replace what was stolen.

Don't Go Overboard

Insurance should not be so expensive as to be a wealth robber if you are careful to only cover the risks that you can't afford to keep yourself. For example, a full homeowner or tenant's policy may be more comprehensive than you need. We know a newly married couple that saves a good deal of money on their tenant's insurance by scheduling all their valuables—meaning adding specific valuables to the policy on an item-by-item basis—and leaving a high deductible on the overall policy. They don't want to waste money covering the valueless furniture they've owned since college and are planning to replace anyway, but they wanted coverage for the expensive silver, crystal, and consumer electronics gifts they received at their wedding. By scheduling their most valuable belongings on the policy, their insurance deductible on those items
was automatically waived and the valuables received the higher coverage warranted, while the couple avoided coverage on items they wouldn't replace anyway. The money they save can be invested toward wealth, and at their young age, our friends can turn insurance savings into riches.

If you're considering scheduling some valuables on your policy, talk to your agent about the paperwork you'll need. If an item was purchased recently, a bill of sale may be all that's required as proof of value. In other cases, the insurance company may demand a professional appraisal.

ALERT

Extended warranties, the coverage that's often available to stretch manufacturers' warranties, are often nothing more than overpriced insurance policies. Consider the wisdom of paying $30 to extend the ninety-day warranty on a $100 personal stereo for an additional nine months when the $30 can be invested instead.

Auto Insurance

Automobile insurance, which is required by law in most states, comprises four basic components: liability, medical payments, uninsured/underinsured motorist, and collision/comprehensive.

Liability insurance covers your cost if another person sues you over an accident. It's a very important part of your coverage, on both your auto and home policies, especially if you have significant financial assets or value your future ability to earn an income. Merely because you have few assets doesn't necessarily mean you should forego liability insurance. Your automobile and homeowner coverage offers the foundation of your liability coverage with something like the familiar $100,000/$300,000 coverage package or the increasingly popular $250,000/$500,000 package. These numbers state your coverage per person over your coverage per incident.

Will such insurance shelter you from all potential lawsuits? No. But if you intend to get rich, you must protect yourself adequately against liability claims that could sap your wealth. Consult with your insurance agent about maximizing your liability coverage. Once you've done that, you might consider adding relatively inexpensive additional coverage called umbrella liability, which we'll explain shortly.

Medical payments insurance could provide extra coverage beyond that of your own policy to pay medical costs. Uninsured/underinsured insurance reimburses you if your accident is with someone without adequate coverage.

Finally, collision/comprehensive insurance pays some of the costs if your car is damaged in a collision or is stolen or burglarized. In deciding whether to carry collision/comprehensive insurance, which reimburses you for damage or loss of your vehicle, it's important to weigh the cost of replacing your vehicle against the cost of the insurance.

For example, we own a small boat trailer that we recently insured. The trailer cost about $700 and is so small and light that any collision with another vehicle will probably destroy the trailer and force us to replace it. We decided to carry only liability insurance on the trailer, and our reasoning went like this: If we are in an accident and the trailer causes potentially costly damage to another person's property, we need adequate liability coverage. But if the trailer is damaged, we can replace it for only $700. We can preserve wealth by retaining that risk and self-insuring against it rather than paying to transfer the risk to an insurance company.

Home-Office Liability

If you run a business from your home, you should pay extra attention to your agent's recommendations for liability coverage. The neighbor you invite into your home for a cup of tea is covered by your home-owner's liability coverage. But that same friend coming into your home as an employee or customer could expose you to liability risks outside the scope of your homeowner's policy. True, the icy stoop or the fallen limb might cause the same injury or auto damage in both cases, but when her visit is for business purposes, your homeowner's policy may fall short.

Some homeowner's polices can be expanded to cover this type of situation and might be more appropriate and more affordable than an extra business policy, unless your business is one that enjoys frequent customer visits, such as a hair salon or a pet grooming service. An extra business policy may also more affordably cover your home office equipment. In any case, it's worth discussing with your agent.

Personal Liability: Covering Your Assets

Umbrella liability insurance can offer important coverage in today's litigious world. Umbrella liability policies provide money to cover court judgments—and in some cases legal fees—over and above the liability limits on your homeowner's and automobile policies. Some insurers will write your auto and homeowner liability up to $500,000, then offer umbrella liability up to $1 million or more.

Discuss these costs with your agent. You may find that leaving your automobile and homeowner's coverage at $300,000 and adding umbrella coverage up to $2 or $3 million is less costly than auto and home policies totaling $500,000 before adding umbrella coverage. You could still enjoy the same amount of total liability protection, while preserving wealth thanks to lower premiums.

In trying umbrella coverage on for size, have your agent compare premiums of progressively higher liability limits. And remember, potential court judgments against you, and possibly the legal costs of defending yourself in court, could be very high and blow a catastrophic hole in your wealth plan. Consult a reputable insurance professional to be sure you're properly insured.

SSENTIALS Liability can creep up where you least expect it. For example, negligence, one of the most common triggers of liability claims, need not be intentional. Purchase enough liability coverage to safeguard your assets without factoring in your opinion of the unlikelihood of a loss.

In some regions of the country, five times more umbrella coverage costs only about two and a half times more money. Compared to the potential risk, premiums of $250–$300 per year for $1 million of umbrella liability coverage are comparatively inexpensive. True, the risk of a claim is low, but consider the damage to your wealth plan if a car accident costs you a $2 million damages judgment that $600 in annual umbrella liability premiums could have shielded you from.

CHAPTER 6
Insure Yourself

There are four basic types of personal coverage: life, health, disability, and long-term care, all of which can reduce the degree of financial risk you personally assume. Each can also be partly or fully self-insured, meaning you can choose to set aside funds in your own accounts to pay for potential losses without involving an insurance company. But without proper planning, this could quickly destroy wealth that took years to build.

Life Insurance

Life insurance protects your wealth and your financial plan across the breadth of the wealth-building spectrum. If you're a beginning wealth builder, life insurance can provide money to your family in case you don't survive to complete your savings goals. If you're already wealthy, you might use life insurance to provide liquidity to your estate, to pay taxes after your death, or to make the transfer of wealth to your family more equitable. This last point often arises when owners of a family business hope to leave the business to the child or children who have shown the most interest in it and have been groomed to carry it on. A life insurance policy can be used to provide a monetary inheritance to other children who won't be receiving the business, thereby providing fairness and equality to all heirs.

FACTS

The same "law of large numbers" that we discussed in Chapter 5 holds true in our discussion of personal coverage: While we can't predict the likelihood of any single person dying at a particular age, or becoming unable to work, or needing long-term medical care, we can predict the number of people in a large group that will suffer one of these personal tragedies.

Death Benefit and Cash Value

Every life insurance policy consists of two basic components: the death benefit and the cash value. The death benefit is the most straightforward, comprising the amount of money your beneficiaries would receive if you die while the policy is in force. The cash value is a little more complex and we will use that characteristic to distinguish between types of policies in our later discussion.

Insurability

Life insurance companies seek to create a group of policyholders who are of similar age, with similar—or at least somewhat predictable—health issues. This is the basic information that they use to calculate the risk they assume in insuring the group and, therefore, the premium they will charge each member of the group. If your health puts you into a higher risk group (as the insurance company sees it) because of smoking, for example, the insurance company will charge you a higher premium. Some policies will also raise your premium as you age, so it's important to analyze the premium schedule of your policy to be sure that it will remain affordable for the entire time that you will need it.

Different physical ailments create a higher risk under some insurance policies; it's important that you purchase the policy not only before you find it necessary to make a claim but also before you experience one of these life events. For example, a disability insurance company considering whether to issue you a policy would be concerned about a back injury that you recently suffered, and would probably charge you a higher premium, or even deny coverage altogether, because the injury puts you at higher risk for a disability claim than someone with a healthy back. But a life insurance company wouldn't necessarily be as concerned about a prior back injury because it wouldn't necessarily shorten your life expectancy.

The main point here is to avoid jeopardizing your wealth plans by failing to cover risks that may seem remote but that could be financially devastating.

Term Life: Insurance in Its Simplest Form

Let's start our discussion of the basic life insurance policies with the simplest of all—the no-cash value term life policy. Term life insurance policies pay a specific death benefit if you die during the term the policy is in effect—hence the name, term life insurance. They don't accumulate cash within the policy. Like auto or homeowner's insurance, your premium payments cover the cost of insuring you for a specific period of time, with a little profit left over (insurance companies also earn returns by investing part of your premium fees in securities and elsewhere).

Term life insurance is provided in two ways: privately and through an employer or other group. In almost every case, group insurance is less expensive, leaving you more money to invest toward wealth, but you give up the control over the policy that can be gained through direct policy ownership.

Group Life

Private insurance can be purchased through an insurance agent or directly from the insurance company. Employers and associations often pool their resources to persuade insurers to offer term life insurance at "wholesale" prices. But beware: Special caution should be used when relying solely on coverage through an employer or association because that coverage may not be "portable," meaning you may not be able to bring it with you when you leave one employer or association for another. If you're between jobs when you die, the group term life coverage that covered you during your previous job will no longer be in force and you won't be able to collect a death benefit. By the same token, if you're no longer insurable after leaving the group—for example, if you got sick or were injured during your previous job—you may have difficulty finding replacement coverage. We suggest you maintain your base life insurance coverage personally so that you have better control over it. Employers will often offer group life insurance with a death benefit equal to a multiple of your annual salary for a very low cost. It's difficult to turn down such an offer and you may decide to carry extra coverage when you are working. Consult with a financial advisor to pinpoint the exact amount of term life you need so you're not over- or underinsured.

ESSENTIALS

To save money on comparable insurance coverage, consider consulting an independent agent who can offer insurance through several different companies. Some insurers look for "prime policyholders" and offer coverage to only the healthiest applicants. This coverage is sometimes more expensive without offering a comparable value to the consumer.

Private term life insurance is available in a variety of terms, including the most common "yearly renewable term," or YRT; ten-year level; twenty-year level; and thirty-year level term. YRT is the policy most often provided by employers. This type covers you for one year and is renewable each consecutive year, though at a higher premium each year as you age. Depending on the policy, it may be renewable for life or it may completely expire—or more commonly become unaffordable because of increasing premiums—at a certain year. YRT premiums are usually lower than those of "level-premium" policies for the first few years, and then become more costly each year. YRT coverage is often the best choice when affordability of premiums is an issue and you want the cheapest coverage possible for a short period of time.

A Better Mousetrap: Level-Premium Insurance

Level-premium term life policies came into vogue because consumers were asking for premiums whose cost they could depend on for a longer time. Level-premium policies are designed to pay a guaranteed benefit in exchange for premiums that are guaranteed not to rise for a set number of years. This means that if you opt for a level-premium policy, your premium may initially be higher than that of your friend of the same age who purchased a YRT policy. The difference is that your premiums will stay level for the entire ten-, twenty-, or thirty-year term of the policy, depending on which you chose, while your friend's premiums will gradually increase.

Level-premium policies are very helpful for covering a fixed term need, such as paying for a child's college education or paying off a thirty-year mortgage. For example, you plan to accumulate $120,000 dollars for your child to go to college in eighteen years. If you don't live to accumulate this money through savings and investments, you would still like your son or daughter to be able to get a college education, so you might purchase a twenty-year level-premium term life policy with a death benefit of $120,000. If you die the year after you buy the policy, the child's college fund is covered by the insurance. If you accumulate the $120,000 before the term expires, you can choose to cancel the policy or leave it in effect for its term so it can provide coverage for another need.

Permanent Life Insurance

For those who need life insurance on a more permanent basis, a "permanent insurance" policy that offers a cash-accumulation option might be the right choice. Permanent insurance policies are designed for extra premiums paid in at the beginning of the policy to offset the increased cost of insurance as you age. Term life insurance is often very expensive past retirement age but permanent insurance is usually designed to maintain a level premium throughout your life. There are several types of permanent life insurance, including whole life, universal life, and variable life. Your insurance agent can provide details about the various types and what is best for your situation. It's important that you review you life insurance at least once a year and consult with a professional for more information about which coverage is best for you.

How Much Life Insurance Is Enough?

Rules of thumb can be misleading when it comes to life insurance. We've heard it said that the sum of your life insurance death benefits should equal five times your annual salary. We find it's better (and less wasteful of premium dollars) to spend a little time looking at your insurance needs before buying.

Life insurance on your kids to pay for their burial expenses may seem like a good idea, but be careful not to overdo it. The small dependent coverage offered by many employers is usually plenty to cover this tragic but unlikely event. You can better serve your kids by investing the premiums on their behalf elsewhere.

Review your financial goals and note which ones require your income to achieve. Are you planning to save for a child's education? Are you and your partner saving and investing for retirement? Are you responsible for the well-being and support of a family or business? How much money would you like to contribute to these goals if you don't live long enough to see them reached? How much money would be needed by your family or your business to carry on without you? Add up these numbers and decide how much insurance death benefit to purchase based on this direct need, plus a few adjustments. For example, you'll need to factor in inflation if the need for your death benefit will carry on for some time; level-premium policies don't typically increase their death benefit with inflation. Keep in mind, too, that an extra $250,000 of death benefit might cost only a fractional additional premium.

FACTS

Underwriting is the process insurance companies undergo to decide if a policy will be issued, and at what price. The process often includes medical exams by an insurance company employee called an underwriter. If your health is good enough to pass muster, the policy is underwritten. Should red flags appear in your medical records, the policy might be offered at a higher price or with specified exceptions.

Health Insurance: A Prescription for the Right Coverage

Health insurance, which provides coverage for medical expenses, is often provided as an employment benefit. As such, many people either take it for granted or ignore the details of their policies until they need them. Privately purchased policies for the self-employed or for people without such an employee benefit can be terrible wealth-robbers, so we're going to cover a few points that could help you fine-tune your health-care insurance.

Health insurance falls into one of four basic categories. Ranked in order of lowest premium and patient cost, they are: health maintenance organization, or HMO; preferred provider organization, or PPO; point-of-service plan, or POS; and indemnity plan.

The Indemnity Plan: Simple and Old-Fashioned

The once-widespread plan that you might already be familiar with is the indemnity plan. Under this type of plan the patient visits the doctor of their choice, pays the doctor after receiving services, and then submits claims paperwork to the insurance company for partial reimbursement. Many patients enjoyed this type of coverage because it gave them control over the doctors they chose, but they often struggled with paperwork and, although insurers generally paid 80 percent of covered medical expenses, there were occasional surprises when certain treatments were only partially covered. Under this type of plan, patients were essentially spending the insurance companies' money, and insurance companies eventually decided that they needed to do something to better manage costs.

Enter managed care. Under managed care the insurance company charges a premium and a type of deductible called a "co-pay" in exchange for a policy that will essentially cover all the medical care a patient may need. Without arguing over the controversies of managed care, essentially the patient benefits because almost all the medical risk is transferred to the insurance company. The insurance company also benefits, because they are part of the decision-making process before a medical service is provided. The only expense most patients should be required to pay is the premium and the patient's percentage of each covered service, or co-pay. In turn, the insurance company is permitted to build a network of doctors who agree to charge a standard price for their services. In theory, the insurance company is better able to calculate what premiums to charge its policyholders once it can better predict what its claims will be. By compensating the doctors in the network on a per-patient basis, insurance companies can contract with providers to manage costs.

The type of managed care plan you choose is predicated on the physicians network you prefer and the balance of premiums, co-pays, and deductibles you want to pay. Many plans are hybrids of the three basic plans we'll discuss next.

Health Maintenance Organization

Under a true HMO, you will pay the lowest premiums and will receive care from a closely controlled network of doctors. Often this network is even conveniently housed in a single building. The doctors who treat you may vary with each visit, but some folks prefer the convenience of the one-stop shopping and controlled costs that an HMO provides.

Preferred Provider Organization

Under a PPO, you will be offered a network of doctors through whom you may receive medical care. These doctors are overseen by the insurance company and have agreed to charge a certain amount for their services. You are asked to choose a primary care physician who is compensated for your subscription because they are responsible for overseeing your program of care. If you need to see a specialist, you first contact your primary care physician, who will issue you a formal referral to the specialist. Many PPO customers enjoy their freedom to select among a wide variety of physicians with whom they can establish long-term medical relationships, a feature most HMOs don't offer.

Point-of-Service Plan

The POS plan is a hybrid of the indemnity plan and the PPO. Through a POS plan, patients can choose whether to seek treatment from inside or outside a network of physicians and health-care professionals. If your choice of professionals come from within the network then, like a PPO, you consult your primary care physician. If you choose service outside the network, you are reimbursed for a fixed percentage of cost.

Key Questions

Regardless of the type of plan you choose, here are a few important questions to ask about your policy:

- Does the policy feature an unlimited lifetime benefit, or is the total benefit the insurance company will pay capped at some specific amount—commonly $2 million? If you have a choice, buy a policy that has an unlimited benefit.
- What is your policy's deductible and co-pay? You can pay lower premiums by retaining a greater share of health-care risk yourself by agreeing to pay a higher deductible and a higher per-visit co-pay. Be sure when comparing policies that both have the same deductible and co-pay, and be aware of the deductible/co-pay when planning your emergency fund or when funding your employer's prepaid medical account.
- What is the patient's out-of-pocket cap? When does the policy start covering you at 100 percent without co-pay or deductible? A policy that covers 100 percent after the first $3,000 out of pocket will be

more expensive than one that pays after $5,000. In either case, be sure your emergency fund is large enough to cover the risk of your portion of the first $3,000, for example.

Disability Insurance: It Works When You Can't

Disability insurance coverage replaces your income when you can't work because of illness or injury. It doesn't matter whether the injury or sickness is work-related—the coverage is in effect twenty-four hours a day, seven days a week.

Employers sometimes offer group disability insurance as an employee benefit; otherwise, workers must purchase their coverage privately. (Remember, when you hear "group insurance," think "low wholesale prices." But group insurance is often not portable between jobs.)

FACTS

If you're lucky, your employer will provide an account into which you can deposit pre-tax money towards your expected annual medical costs. If you have regular, predictable medical costs these accounts enable you to avoid the tax that you pay on the income that pays some of those expenses. But be careful: Money put into these accounts is often not refundable if not used by year's end.

Disability coverage insures one of your family's biggest assets—your ability to bring home a paycheck. Without an income, disability can be a wealth-robbing drain on your money. For this reason it is one of your most important coverages. Most disability policies will replace up to 66 percent of the income you were receiving before you were disabled. If your income has increased since you last reviewed your policy, you should amend the policy to reflect your higher pay. If you have retired and are still paying disability premiums, you should probably drop the coverage because most policies cover only the earned income you were making immediately before the disability. Of course, check with an insurance professional or financial advisor before canceling any insurance; canceling a policy could have unintended effects.

Disability policies are complex and should be reviewed with the help of an insurance agent or other competent financial advisor. Here are some of the characteristics you should look for.

Definition of Disability

How does the policy define disability? Is it the inability to earn the money you were previously earning due to any illness or injury, or are there limitations on the types of illnesses or injuries the policy recognizes? Some policies—the more expensive ones—will have better, more liberal definitions of disability.

Waiting Period

How long after a disability must you wait before benefits begin? It's to your cost advantage to purchase a policy that begins paying after you've been disabled for ninety days. You might be able to further reduce your premiums by self-insuring the period starting ninety days after the disability to 180 days. Premiums will be much lower if the insurance company doesn't have to cover the claim until you have been disabled for six months because they know workers are less likely to be disabled for that long. If you self-insure like this, be sure to hold resources aside in your emergency fund or elsewhere for the additional retained risk.

Benefit Period

How long will the company continue making payments to you? If you remain disabled to age sixty-five, will the policy continue to pay benefits? Depending on your occupation, or the premium you are willing to pay, you may need to choose a policy with a shorter benefit period. Many insurance companies will offer a five-year or shorter benefit period to workers in riskier occupations, like carpenters and roofers.

Benefit Amount

Disability insurance typically pays a benefit as high as 66 percent of your working income. You may choose to purchase this maximum benefit or, in order to cut premiums, a lower percentage, if your personal assets are high enough to enable you to self-insure a portion of your working income. Obviously, this strategy leaves you with some risk, and you must plan accordingly.

Cancellation

Can the insurance company cancel your policy for any reason besides your failure to pay your premiums? We recommend you steer clear of any policy the insurance company can cancel for any other reason.

Occupation

Will the policy pay a benefit even if you can work at a different type of job that's not limited by your disability? Many will, at least for a little while. After a specific period of time, though, most policies require that, if you are able, you seek employment in a job that suits your experience and education. The insurer may even help pay for rehabilitation!

Residual Benefit

Does the policy pay a partial benefit if you are able to work but at a reduced earning capacity? This is an important benefit because many people who are disabled choose to return to work but are unable to keep the same hours or work the same high-paying job that they did before their disability.

Long-Term Care Insurance: Staying Wealthy for Life

Long-term care insurance pays a daily benefit for as long as you are receiving long-term medical services. Most people think of this as nursing home insurance, but it is much more sophisticated.

Beyond age eighty-five, an individual has a 40 percent chance of requiring some kind of long-term care, experts say. Long-term care can be devastating to your wealth plan and place a tremendous burden on your family. To meet the costs of long-term care, like anything else, you have two choices: pay for it yourself or transfer the risk to the insurance company. There's also a third choice that seems obvious but often gets overlooked and is important to people building wealth—do a little of both.

The federal Medicare health-care system for the elderly provides medical coverage for people over sixty-two, but its long-term care benefits are very limited. To receive Medicare coverage in a nursing home, for example, you must first have spent three days in a hospital, and even then Medicare will only cover 100 days of nursing-home services. Medicare often won't pay for most home health services or for assisted-living services.

Apply for life, disability, or long-term care insurance *before* you visit the doctor. If your latest physicals have been healthy, the time to buy insurance is now. Don't go back to the doctor for a routine checkup until after your policy has been underwritten. A nasty surprise on a physical can mean higher premiums or even denial of coverage.

Medicare coverage is meant to cover the costs of making you well again; long-term care services help you maintain your dignity and your lifestyle when you are not going to get better.

What Will Care Cost You?

Ask your local long-term care facilities what the average per-day cost of care in their facility is, or contact your state insurance commissioner's office for information. Then assess whether you have enough assets to cover your potential long-term care expenses. If you decide to supplement your own resources with a long-term care insurance policy, you should pay particular attention to the following concerns.

Activities of Daily Living, or ADL

Insurance companies have categorized our basic living skills into as many as six activities, including eating, dressing, transferring from bed to chair, toileting, continence, and bathing. Most policies will pay a benefit if, for either mental or physical reasons, you cannot perform two or three of these activities of daily living. Because bathing is often the first thing people have difficulty with as they age, pay particular attention to this part of the policy and be sure that the policy you buy lists six ADLs and pays a benefit when you can't perform any two of them.

Waiting Period

How long does the policy require you to pay for all of your care before the insurance company starts paying? Policies with a "time deductible" of 30 to 100 days are most common.

Benefit Period

How long does the policy pay a benefit? Three years? Five years? The rest of your life? The longer the benefit period, the higher the premium, so review your assets with your advisor and decide how much care you want the insurance company to pay for and how much you are able to cover through self-insurance.

Benefit Amount

Daily expenses for long-term care vary widely across the country. Some regions average $150 per day, while others average $250 or more. Decide how much of this you are willing to self-insure and how much of the risk you want to transfer to the insurance company. Remember, the higher the insurance company's risk the higher the premium.

Pool-of-Money Versus Flat-Payment Plan

Some policies reimburse you for the cost of care that you received, up to your daily benefit amount, while other policies simply mail you a check for your daily benefit amount, even if the care you received was less expensive. The first of these styles uses a "pool-of-money" approach, meaning that, if your daily expenses are lower, your benefit period could extend longer than you had anticipated. For example, if you bought a policy to pay you $200 per day for five years, your total pool of money would be $365,000. If you only had expenses of $150 per day, the pool of money would last one and a half years longer. Because they wouldn't be reimbursed from the pool of money if they didn't use it, some folks prefer the type of policy that pays a flat benefit regardless of the actual expense of care. If their costs of care are lower than their daily benefit, they invest the difference.

Long-term care insurance has very stringent insurability expectations. That means it's very important that you purchase your policy *before* you've suffered a heart attack, a stroke, or some other debilitating illness. Many companies won't offer you coverage if you've already suffered a major illness; others will insure you, but only in exchange for a very high premium.

Inflation Protection

If you are buying your policy at a young age (in the case of long-term care insurance, that means age sixty-five or younger) you should carefully consider inflation protection. Without this protection your benefit will stay level for the life of the policy, meaning the benefit payments will be the same in twenty years as they would be today, without increasing to reflect the fact that many more dollars will be required in twenty years to pay the inflated cost of care. Be sure you have the option to accept benefit increases (and are willing to accept premium increases, of course) without proof of insurability throughout the life of your policy.

Summing It Up

Your decision whether to buy insurance is a crucial part of getting rich. In fact, other than the lifestyle decision to live frugally and spend deliberately, no decision is more important. An insurance policy that balances your wealth-building goals with your personal risks could help you maintain a better standard of living if you get sick, maintain your family in their own home if you die, or pay for the urgent medical care that you need. For that reason, it's important to get good advice when designing your plan.

You should purchase policies only from insurance companies with high ratings from the independent rating companies listed in Appendix A, and you should review your plan with your agent or advisor at least once a year.

But beware: The potential conflicts of interest between you and your advisors are many. Insurance professionals are often compensated for the number of policies they sell, and they might not have your best interests at heart. In some cases, the policy that earns the highest commission might be one that carries unnecessarily high premiums and robs you of wealth while failing to provide the best protection from risk. Ask several professionals for their opinions, and be critical of their advice. Above all, ask many questions.

CHAPTER 7

Building a Successful Investment Plan

T hrough prudent and methodical management, your money can start working for you with power and efficiency. Investment management also helps you recognize your intentions, directing your focus beyond the short-term, wealth-robbing luxuries and toward the ultimate long-term wealth goals.

Coming to Grips with Risk

All investments are a balance of risk and reward. Here are just a few of the risks your investments face (we'll talk about rewards in the next chapter):

- **Market risk.** Any investor runs the risk that the price a new buyer is willing to pay for his securities is lower than his original price. What's more, when companies go bankrupt, their stock usually plunges in value or even becomes worthless. Your investment could all but vanish.
- **Inflation risk.** An investor could find himself behind the inflation curve when the prices of goods and services go up faster than the value of his investment. This risk could sneak up on him; it's never noted on account statements. Moreover, investments could languish in low-interest holdings, while inflation drives up the return on current issues.
- **Default risk.** Investors in bonds could learn that the company, government, or agency to which they loaned their money when they bought the bond refuses to make its interest payment or to repay the principal, or "face value." Bonds with this kind of risk will typically pay higher returns than safer ones.

Investments that promise higher rewards carry greater risks, and vice versa. Investors perform a delicate balancing act in combining the right mix of investments while maintaining acceptable levels of risk.

Starting and stopping your wealth plan can lead to buying investments at high prices, an investing vice known as "chasing the winners," and then selling them when their prices disappoint, called "dumping the losers." The sure cure for such wealth-robbing misbehavior is to build a strong investment plan and stick to it.

Rating Your Risk Tolerance

Like deliberate spenders, deliberate investors determine the amount of risk they're willing to tolerate, outline that tolerance in an investor profile, and then build their portfolio around this risk/reward balance.

A person's investment risk tolerance is not always obvious, and behavior can be a false indicator. A self-employed business owner who seems to invite entrepreneurial business risks may prefer more conservative investments, while a secure middle-manager at a large corporation who appears to court job and income stability may choose investments that are very risky. The following quiz will help you determine your own investment risk tolerance. Rate your answer to each question on a scale of 1 to 4: **1** is absolutely not/never; **2** is no/sometimes; **3** is maybe/frequently; and **4** is absolutely/always.

Think of your answers in concrete financial terms, as though your hard-earned dollars were at stake. And remember, these answers are for your eyes only, so be candid!

RISK TOLERANCE QUIZ

1. Are you flustered by month-to-month fluctuations in your investments?_____

2. Would you consider three or more consecutive "down months," in which your investments lost value, to be cause to sell? _____

3. Would you consider six or more consecutive "down months" to be cause to sell? _____

4. Would you consider twelve or more consecutive "down months" to be cause to sell? _____

5. Are you intimidated by the idea of researching and selecting your own investments? _____

6. Do you fret about choosing the right investments to help you meet your financial goals? _____

7. Would you liquidate an investment if it declined in value 5 percent in one year? _____

8. Would you liquidate an investment if it declined in value 10 percent in one year? _____

9. Would you liquidate an investment if it declined in value 20 percent in one year? _____

10. Do you find it difficult to maintain an adequate cash reserve in case of emergencies so that your long-term investments needn't be liquidated to meet short-term needs? _____

To add up your score, give yourself 1 point for every "1" answer, 2 points for every "2" answer, and so on. Add up your total and see how you rank on the risk tolerance scale:

- 20 or below: Willing to take risks, aggressive investor
- 21–29: Willing to take a modest risk, but slightly uncomfortable with too much uncertainty, moderate investor
- 30 or above: Demands safe investments that don't fluctuate wildly, conservative investor

Going beyond the three numerical categories, there are shades of risk tolerance. Where you fall within each numerical range will indicate your degree of risk tolerance. For example, if you scored in the high 30s, or even reached the maximum score of 40, you are very conservative.

Write your score here, along with the date and your assessment of your risk tolerance:

> My risk tolerance score: _____
> Date: _____
> I am a _____ investor.

Revisit this quiz as part of your annual investment program review. You may find that as you become more familiar with investing and feel more empowered by your wealth plan your risk tolerance will change and your score will decrease slightly. If it doesn't change over time, your risk tolerance has plateaued, and that, too, is important for you to understand.

FACTS

Don't look at your investment accounts every day. You should review your account statements monthly, but beware of knee-jerk buying or selling decisions. If you've thoughtfully constructed a sound investment portfolio and nothing relevant has changed in them, there's no reason to make adjustments on a month-to-month basis.

You may find that you and your partner have different risk tolerance. This is not unusual, and could even be turned to your advantage.

Complete the risk tolerance quiz together and try to negotiate a middle ground. Revisit the quiz every quarter to see if your views are converging.

Wealth Horizon

Once your risk tolerance is measured and understood, the next step in developing your investment plan is to determine your "wealth horizon," the future date when your wealth goals will be reached.

In Chapter 2, we discussed developing measurable and achievable goals. We gave some examples of how these goals should read on paper, such as "Save $120,000 per child by the time they reach eighteen." But we left until this chapter the discussion of how to determine whether our goals are achievable, or excessively optimistic. After all, a goal like "Save $60 million to buy a personal jet by age fifty-five" certainly meets our criteria of measurable, but few of us would consider that kind of goal achievable.

Constructing Achievable Goals

Achievable wealth goals are made up of three elements:

- The dollar amount of the goal
- The time frame over which the goal will be reached
- The planned periodic investment

An achievable goal is one that balances all three of these components. But remember, all three must remain flexible and may change over time as your priorities change. And, if a goal as you initially construct it turns out to be unachievable, you may need to adjust one or two of the components to make the third, and thus the overall goal, achievable.

Let's say our goal is "Save $30,000 to go on a round-the-world vacation next year, by setting aside $1,000 per month to achieve the goal." The first element in determining the achievability of our goals, the dollar amount, is a clear $30,000 in this example. The time frame is one year, and the planned periodic investment is $1,000 per month.

Unless there has already been some money saved toward this goal, $1,000 per month will only accumulate $12,222.46 in one year (at 4 percent annualized interest with monthly payments made at the end of the month—more on how we calculate this in a moment), not quite half the goal of $30,000. To make this wealth goal achievable, we must alter one of the three factors:

- We can alter the *size* of our goal and plan a less expensive trip that costs only the $12,222 that we'll have accumulated in twelve months.
- We can alter the *term* of our goal, meaning we would plan on departing on our original vacation in thirty-two months, after there's been sufficient time to accumulate the money.
- We can alter the *amount we invest* each month, increasing our monthly set-aside to $2,455 in order to take the full trip on time—a decision that will probably force us to trim our expenses in other aspects of our lives.

Many wealth goals can be treated as simply and directly as this example, as long as we measure each of our financial goals to the same three "achievability" benchmarks.

Long-Term Complications

Long-term retirement goals are a bit more complicated than mid-term fixed goals like the vacation example. That's because the first factor and second factors—the size of our retirement goal, or the "nest egg," and the term, or time until retirement—have powerful reciprocal effects on each other. Simply stated, the longer you postpone retirement, the more years you can spend investing and the smaller your effective nest egg must be, if we assume your lifespan remains unchanged.

For example, assume you are age forty and expect to live until age ninety-five (financial planners know this is somewhat optimistic, but they prefer to assume you'll live longer than you probably will so that it's less likely you'll outlive your retirement nest egg). Retiring at seventy gives you thirty years to accumulate a nest egg that will support you for twenty-five years.

If you change your retirement target to age fifty, you have only ten years from now to accumulate a fund that must support you for forty-five years! (Because retirement planning is complex, we have set aside Chapters 12 and 13 to cover it in detail.)

Time Value of Money

The concept of the time value of money is central to wealth planning because it recognizes the effect that compounding and time have in growing your savings and investments. You work hard to earn your money but, given time, your investments may earn more by simple compounding than you earn in salary! Indeed, if you've planned your retirement properly, your investments will replace your salary by the time you collect your gold watch—perhaps with some extra dollars to spare. Let's look more closely at how this works.

Use conservative growth and inflation assumptions when calculating the time value of money. Hypothetical time value of money examples don't leave any room for the negative rates of return that are possible in the real world. Many financial planners use a conservative 6 percent compound growth rate and 4 percent as the average rate of inflation.

Reconciling the Goals

Earlier in this chapter we said that the $1,000 per month we were saving towards our vacation would grow to $12,222.46 after twelve months if it earned 4 percent annualized interest, the type of rate you might earn in a savings or money market account. The extra $222.46, above and beyond the $12,000 principal, is the interest that would be earned if the payments were made each month and the interest of 0.333 percent per month were compounded monthly. This compounding is the key to investing; it turns the earning table around and makes your money work for you.

The Leverage of Time

With enough time, even a small sum of money could grow to a great sum. Let's see how.

- **Goal:** accumulate money for a bar mitzvah in thirteen years (cost of a similar celebration this year: $5,000)

- **Savings needed:** $8,400 in thirteen years
- **Savings plan:** $505 per year

How did we figure that? Unfortunately, the time value of money doesn't just work for us, it works against us, too, in the form of inflated prices over time. So, the first thing we must do is calculate the effect of thirteen years of inflation on the $5,000 that the bar mitzvah would cost today. Let's assume that inflation will average 4 percent per year, a conservative assumption made by many financial planners because it's slightly higher than the average inflation rate over the last twenty years. To calculate the effect of inflation, refer to the Future Value Factors—Chart A in Appendix B to project the future value of $5,000.

By following down the left-hand "Periods" column to year thirteen—to represent the number of years the $5,000 will inflate in cost—and by tracking the rate across to the 4 percent column—to represent the annual amount by which the cost will go up with inflation—we find that the inflation factor is 1.6651. Multiply the original $5,000 by the inflation factor to arrive at $8,326, the inflation-adjusted cost of the bar mitzvah in thirteen years.

Not all inflation is the same. While overall inflation has averaged less than 4 percent over the past twenty years, college expenses are expected to increase 6 percent per year for the next twenty years.

So the new, restated goal is to accumulate $8,400 for the bar mitzvah in thirteen years. (To keep the calculation neat, and to add a small level of conservatism, we decided to round up a bit from $8,326.)

Next, we need to calculate the amount of money we'll need to save each year to reach this goal. For this we use the Future Value of Annuity Factors—Chart C in Appendix B. If we assume that the investment or savings account keeps pace with the 4 percent inflation rate, here's how we calculate the required monthly savings.

Drop down the left "Periods" column to year thirteen, the number of years left to save before bar mitzvah day. Then track across to the 4 percent column, representing the rate that our savings is projected to grow each year. The resulting compounding factor is 16.6268. Divide this factor into the final goal of $8,400 to get an annual savings target of $505. If the family starts by saving $505 per year when their son is born, under these conditions of inflation and savings growth, they would accumulate a nest egg thirteen years later large enough to give him a bar mitzvah that would cost $5,000 in current dollars.

Enlisting Help

You might not even foot the entire bill of an expense. Take, for example, a college savings plan. Friends and family members often ask what to give a child at birthdays and other holidays, so why not invite them to participate in your child's education by contributing each year to a college savings fund? Let's see how this might work.

Your assumptions are:

- Your child starts receiving college fund gifts on her second birthday.
- Her college savings account earns 4 percent per year.
- She receives $100 from each of her five relatives, totaling $500 on each birthday.

How much will the account contain when she turns eighteen? Using the Future Value of Annuity Factors—Chart C from Appendix B, we drop down the left column to seventeen (the total number of years between her second and eighteenth birthdays) and track over to the 4 percent earnings rate to find a compounding factor of 23.6975. This compounding factor, multiplied by her annual gifts of $500, equals $11,849. While many of her childhood birthday presents might be forgotten by this age, what college freshman wouldn't appreciate almost $12,000 as a Happy Eighteenth Birthday present!

Blessing and Curse

The compounding power of interest is highly potent, but when building a wealth plan it's important to understand both its powers and its curses. Here's an example of the darker side of compounding.

Let's say you and your family love to travel. Each year you go on one or two business trips and the family goes along with you to make a vacation of it. Combining business with pleasure is a good idea because you can deduct many of your expenses against your business income, saving tax dollars, although family members must pay their own way, which experience has shown to be about $3,000 per vacation.

How much do two $3,000 vacations a year, charged to a credit card, really cost? Here are the facts:

- Balance charged to the credit card = $6,000
- Credit card annual interest = 12 percent
- Total number of payments = approximately twenty-four

Like many Americans, you might be on a credit card roller coaster. You load up your cards, and then pay more than the required minimum payment to pay off the balances every two to three years. If you maintain an average balance of $6,000 on this card before paying it off you will pay an extra 25 percent or $1,526 for your vacations. This amount might even completely negate the tax savings you enjoyed by taking the family along!

How did we determine this cost? In the Future Value Factors—Chart A from Appendix B, drop down the left column to two years, then track across to 12 percent to arrive at the future value factor of 1.2544. Multiply this by the average credit card balance of $6,000 to arrive at $7,526. This amount is $1,526, or 25 percent higher than the original cost of the vacation.

By planning ahead and investing for vacations in advance, you could have enjoyed a 25 percent growth in your money by not paying the extra interest cost—an enviable return indeed!

CHAPTER 8

Your Investment Portfolio

A good investment plan is one that puts your money to work for you. A poor plan—or no plan—could force you to work increasingly harder for enough income to meet rising monthly expenses. Without adequate income, and with only an uncertain social security system as a fallback, you could find that, rather than retiring comfortably, you have to continue to work in order to support yourself later in life.

The Right Investment Plan

A good investment plan puts you on a methodical, achievable track toward your goals. It focuses on long-term "buy and hold" investment strategies that encourage you to research and purchase your investments with little regard to short-term returns, get-rich-quick schemes, or market-timing—trying to "outguess the market" by buying into investments when they're near a short-term low and sell out near a short-term high, a highly risky gamble. Wall Street is littered with the victims of market-timing, making it one of the most dangerous investment strategies.

FACTS

There are several different classes of brokers and brokerage firms. Full-service firms provide investment advice as part of the commission charged on securities transactions. Discount brokerages generally don't provide personalized advice. Be aware of the level of advice you are receiving.

In addition to lucrative long-term returns, a sound, wealth-making investment plan will consider the effect of income tax and trading expenses on your portfolio by planning for the most appropriate tax savings and paying as few commissions and other fees related to investment services as possible. Every dollar in a broker's commission check, or money manager's annual fee, can be traced to an investor's wallet, and money paid to brokers and managers carries an opportunity cost—lost potential investment return. Savvy investors are careful how they spend their money, whether it's for daily household expenses, investment transactions, or investment advice. Be aware of your costs, spend deliberately, and expect value for your money.

Asset Allocation: Determining Your Optimum Mix

Asset allocation is the financial equivalent of a piece of sage advice: Don't put all your eggs in one basket. In investing terms, that means you should invest in a variety of investment types in order to manage the risk in your portfolio. Each investor determines his or her customized asset allocation target based on two factors: time to invest, or "investment horizon," and risk tolerance, the amount of price fluctuation he or she can comfortably tolerate in their account.

Asset allocation is an important element in a sound investment strategy for the simple reason that no investor can predict which type of investment, stocks, bonds, or cash, is going to fare best over a short period of time. It may be that in the next year the stock market will outperform the bond market. Or, perhaps, both stock and bond markets will flounder and cash will be the most beneficial investment. By choosing a mix of these three basic types of investments—stocks, bonds, and cash and sticking with it, successful investors can create an investment plan that doesn't keep them awake and worried at night, while still helping them reach their financial goals.

Investment firms spend a great deal of time, energy, and money trying to help their investors properly allocate their assets. The research done by these firms can be a very helpful starting point in creating your own investment mix. We have listed a few helpful resources in Appendix A.

FACTS

Volatility is the amount of change in value your investment experiences over a specific period of time. Volatility is measured by various statistics, the most common of which is called standard deviation. In practice, volatility is a subjective measure. An investment that changes value 10 percent either way in a month might not bother you, but it might torture another investor.

Your asset allocation plan should begin with the three basic investment types: stocks, bonds, and cash. Each of these investment types—or "classes," as they are also called—grows at a different rate and with a different level of volatility. It is this growth rate and potential volatility that is the basis for the asset allocation. Let's look at these characteristics a little more closely.

Volatility Over the Years

Historically, each asset class has grown at a different rate, with stocks growing the most, followed by bonds and cash, in that order. Since stocks have the greatest amount of growth potential, it may seem logical to commit all your invested money to them and ignore the concept of asset allocation altogether. But most investors can't tolerate the often-dizzying fluctuations of a pure stock portfolio. They tire of the up-and-down cycles, and often focus inordinately on the downs. They start to look at the stocks as more short-term investments and feel that investments need to be sold off when they go down and bought when they go up. Some investors begin losing sleep over what their next investment account statement is going to say, and many, with their insides turning to water, choose to sell in a panic rather than investing in solid companies for years or even decades.

Historical investment performance really only tells you what *has* happened, not what the future holds. We use past performance because it's the only yardstick we have, no matter how imperfect, but you're not bound to it. Adjust your expected investment returns to match what you think the future holds.

Mixing dissimilar assets—bonds and cash, for example—into a stock portfolio creates a balance between risk and reward and creates a portfolio that you will be able to stick to long enough to reach your wealth goals. While bonds and cash don't return the relatively rapid growth of stocks over a long period of time, they suffer less volatility and risk. Having some of your assets in these lower-risk asset classes reduces the overall risk of your portfolio to a point where you can sleep peacefully and remain committed to your investment plan.

Choosing the Mix—Risk Tolerance and Time Horizon

The number of bonds and amount of cash to add to your stock portfolio (or, if you are starting with a portfolio of mostly bonds and cash, the number of stocks to add to your bond-and-cash portfolio) depends on your time horizon and your risk tolerance. This is purely a personal preference—there is no right or wrong asset allocation, though certain allocations could be more efficient than others.

To help you get started here are some guidelines:

The Aggressive Allocation

A growth portfolio asset allocation of 70 percent stocks, 25 percent bonds, and 5 percent cash might be suitable for you if you have a long-term—meaning longer than ten years—investment horizon, are informed about your investments, and feel comfortable with a large amount of risk and value fluctuation in your portfolio. If you scored 20 or below in our Risk Tolerance quiz in the previous chapter you might choose an allocation similar to this one, but you must be prepared to stay the course for more than ten years. This is not to say that you would not change some of your investments as conditions warranted (we'll talk about this in Chapter 9) but that you must be capable of maintaining your commitment to your asset allocation for at least that long.

The Balanced Allocation

If you're an aggressive investor with a shorter time frame (five to ten years) or have a more conservative investing temperament (scoring 21 to 29 on the Risk Tolerance quiz) and want to limit the volatility of your portfolio, you might choose a balanced portfolio asset allocation of 50 percent stocks, 40 percent bonds, and 10 percent cash. The projected growth of this portfolio is less than the growth of the more aggressive growth portfolio but it will not experience as dramatic a roller-coaster ride as the 70 percent stock allocation. If you are a moderate investor you might choose this allocation for your longer-term investments of ten years or more.

The Income/Conservative Portfolio

If you are an investor looking to generate income now, prefer to reduce fluctuations in your portfolio, or are within five years or so of reaching your investment goal, you might choose an income/conservative portfolio asset allocation of 15 percent stocks, 60 percent bonds, and 25 percent cash. This portfolio might work for you if you scored 30 or higher on the Risk Tolerance quiz. This mix enables the cash and bonds in this portfolio to generate income while the stock allocation continues to grow to help keep pace with inflation. This portfolio might also be a good starting point if you are a new investor and want to become accustomed to fluctuations in your stock investments while still keeping most of your portfolio in less risky investments.

ESSENTIALS

If you are honest with yourself, and barring any unusually bad investments, your risk tolerance should not change much over time, meaning your asset allocation should not change. Generally five years or so before retirement, start reducing stock and increasing bonds and cash to preserve the principal you have worked so hard to accumulate.

These asset allocation suggestions are not the only possible choices. You should consider them as starting points in developing your own investment mix. Talk to your investment advisor and other investors about their asset allocation strategies. Make adjustments to these suggestions by adding stock to increase risk and potential return or by adding bonds or cash to reduce the risk, and of course potential return, as you feel comfortable.

Different Allocation for Different "Money Baskets"

You may choose to create a different asset allocation for each of your investment portfolios based on the time frame of the investment goal they are meant to achieve. Your money can usually be divided into three or four "money baskets" based on your financial goals and the time frame until you expect to achieve them:

- **The short-term basket.** The emergency fund basket should be part of everyone's financial plan. This basket should contain enough money to cover three to six months' household expenses and is usually invested in safe, short-term investments like passbook savings accounts and money market funds. Having an adequate stash of cash is imperative if you hope to get rich because it will help you over the inevitable hurdles without piling up credit card debt or selling off wealth-building investments. If you live in a two-income household, one person's salary should count toward part of the emergency fund, reducing your needed set-aside.

- **The mid-term basket.** Your family situation and financial goals will dictate what goes into your middle basket. This is the place to accumulate for your goals that will not happen within the next five or six years, but will happen before retirement, such as purchasing a home, saving for a wedding, or starting a business. The money in the accounts earmarked for the middle basket can be invested more aggressively than the money in the short-term basket because more time can be allowed for the value to recover in the case of an investment downturn, but they shouldn't be invested as aggressively as the long-term basket unless they have a time horizon of at least ten years. A moderate to aggressive investor might choose the balanced portfolio for the money in their middle basket; a more conservative investor might choose something closer to the income/conservative portfolio.

- **The long-term basket.** Earmarked for your retirement basket are the accounts that you are using to accumulate assets for your retirement or other long-term goals. This money is invested for a longer term than the money in the middle basket so it can be invested according to an asset allocation with more risk, such as the growth/aggressive portfolio.

Smaller Breakouts of the Basic Three Classes

The basic asset classes of stocks, bonds, and cash can be further divided into smaller categories or types:

- **Stocks.** By company size: large cap (for the companies with the largest market capitalization), mid cap, and small cap; by company location: non–U.S. companies based in developed countries, and non–U.S. companies based in developing or "emerging" countries; by stock "style," or investing strategy: growth stocks or value stocks

- **Bonds.** By type: high-yield, treasury, corporate, and municipal; by maturity term: long-term, intermediate-term, and short-term
- **Cash.** Savings, money market, certificates of deposit

We'll talk about each one of these finer delineations of asset classes in the next chapter and how you might use them as part of your asset-allocation strategy.

FACTS

Market capitalization, or market cap, represents the total value of a publicly traded company's stock. For example, if a company has 30 million shares of stock outstanding—meaning that there are 30 million shares that are owned by shareholders as a group—and the stock is trading at $20 per share, the company's market cap is the product of the two numbers, or $600 million.

Dollar-Cost Averaging

Dollar-cost averaging is one of the most methodical and reliable investment techniques a wealth builder can use. Not only does it eliminate the uncertainties of market timing, it can reduce portfolio risk whenever you're making deposits or reallocating your investments more aggressively. These equal deposits made into a volatile investment that changes share price frequently are helpful because the regular payment becomes a habit—ensuring that you will invest regardless of the market environment—thus taking advantage of down markets.

Frequent Deposits

Regular deposits into an aggressive investment will slowly build the position—reducing the temptation to try to time the market by gambling on finding a price low point before buying. This wait-and-see approach is a dangerous strategy because it's impossible to be sure where the stock's price bottom is actually located.

Here's an example:

DOLLAR-COST AVERAGING

MONTH	INVESTMENT AMOUNT	SHARE PRICE OF SHARES PURCHASED	NUMBER OF SHARES OWNED	TOTAL NUMBER AT CURRENT PRICE	ACCOUNT VALUE
January	$1,000	53	18.87	18.87	$1,000
February	$1,000	55	18.18	37.05	$2,038
March	$1,000	59	16.95	54.00	$3,186
April	$1,000	62	16.13	70.13	$4,348
May	$1,000	47	21.28	91.40	$4,296
June	$1,000	43	23.26	114.66	$4,930
July	$1,000	40	25.00	139.66	$5,586
August	$1,000	39	25.64	165.30	$6,447
September	$1,000	40	25.00	190.30	$7,612
October	$1,000	41	24.39	214.69	$8,802
November	$1,000	52	19.23	233.92	$12,164
December	$1,000	54	18.52	252.44	$13,632

Total invested	$12,000
Total shares purchased	252.44
Average share price over 12 months	$48.75
Average price paid per share	$47.54
Average savings per share	$1.21
Percentage savings over average price	2.49%

In this example, you invested $1,000 per month into an investment that changed in value from $53 in January to a high of $62 in April and a low of $39 in August. In spite of these value fluctuations, the $1,000 investment was made at the same time each month. When the price was high—like it was in April when only 16.1 shares were purchased—fewer of the expensive shares were purchased. When the price was cheaper—like in August when 25.6 shares were purchased—more shares were purchased. At the end of the year the average price per shares was $48.75, but through dollar-cost averaging this investor only paid $47.54, a 2.49 percent savings that added to the performance of their portfolio!

Annual Deposits

An alternative to investing monthly would be to invest the entire balance on the first day of the new year. The result at year's end would be virtually the same as in dollar-cost averaging, right? In fact, in this scenario, the single-deposit outcome would be noticeably worse. Here's how the single-deposit scenario would play out:

		SINGLE DEPOSIT			
MONTH	INVESTMENT AMOUNT	SHARE PRICE OF SHARES PURCHASED	NUMBER OF SHARES OWNED	TOTAL NUMBER AT CURRENT PRICE	ACCOUNT VALUE
January	$12,000	53	226.42	226.42	$12,000
February	$0	55	0.00	226.42	$12,453
March	$0	59	0.00	226.42	$13,358
April	$0	62	0.00	226.42	$14,038
May	$0	47	0.00	226.42	$10,642
June	$0	43	0.00	226.42	$9,736
July	$0	40	0.00	226.42	$9,057
August	$0	39	0.00	226.42	$8,830
September	$0	40	0.00	226.42	$9,057
October	$0	41	0.00	226.42	$9,283
November	$0	52	0.00	226.42	$11,774
December	$0	54	0.00	226.42	$12,226

Total invested	$12,000
Total shares purchased	226.42
Average share price over 12 months	$48.75
Average price paid per share	$53.00
Average savings per share	-$4.25
Percentage savings over average price	-8.72%

In this scenario all the shares were purchased at the January price of $53, $4.25 per share more than the average price for the year and $5.46 per share more than in the dollar-cost averaging example. Not following a dollar-cost averaging strategy cost this investor $1,405.40, which is the difference in value between the dollar-cost averaging portfolio in December and the single investment portfolio in December. This underperformance amounts to 11.7 percent of the original investment!

Dollar-cost averaging won't always work out this well, and you must consider transaction costs that might be incurred for some investments each time a new deposit is made. In fact, in this case, if transaction costs had totaled more than the saving of $1,405.40, then dollar-cost averaging would not have been more favorable.

Dollar-cost averaging must still be coupled with wise selection of investment vehicles. Whether buying stocks, mutual funds, exchange-traded funds, or any other option, the advice of a trusted investment advisor should always be part of any investment decision, even when taking advantage of the virtues of dollar-cost averaging.

What's more, if the single-deposit investor had timed the market perfectly— far easier said than done—and made their investment in August when the share price was at its low for the year, the result would have outperformed dollar-cost averaging by $4,398. But timing the market perfectly is about as likely as winning a lottery, and dollar-cost averaging is an excellent alternative to the uncertainty of trying to buy a security at its short-term low price.

Analyzing Your Investment Portfolio: Making It Fit Your Allocation

Now let's take a look at your current investment portfolio and see if it matches your chosen asset allocation. List the value of your stock, bond, and cash holdings in a chart like this one:

YOUR INVESTMENT PORTFOLIO

Date: _____

ASSET TYPE	DESCRIPTION	VALUE	PERCENTAGE OF TOTAL PORTFOLIO VALUE
Stock			
Total stock:			
Bond			
Total bond:			
Cash			
Total cash:			
Total portfolio value:			

If you own individual stocks or individual bonds, it will be easy simply to list each in their respective categories. If you own pooled accounts like mutual funds (which we'll talk about in more detail about in Chapter 11), which may contain a little of each asset class, you will need to refer to a third party reference source like Morningstar or Value Line, or contact the individual fund company itself to find out what part of your mutual fund is invested in which asset class.

Once you have each of your assets categorized for the portfolio you are analyzing, add up the totals in each asset class and list it at the bottom of each category. Finally, calculate the allocation of each class by dividing the total of each asset class into the total portfolio value to arrive at your current asset allocation.

When you have finished this step, you should have something that looks like the following hypothetical portfolio. (Remember, these are hypothetical investments we are listing—they are not investment suggestions. Also, note the importance of valuing all your portfolio assets as of the same date.)

The following sample portfolio has 27.5 percent stocks, 47.2 percent bonds, and 25.2 percent cash. Since the balanced mutual fund owns all three asset classes, you will find it in all three categories. This portfolio would be considered a conservative balanced portfolio because it has a significant amount of bonds and cash, a total of 72.5 percent, and only 27.5 percent stocks. This portfolio would be an appropriate mix for you if you wanted to limit your investment risk while still creating some opportunity for growth, and if you need the extra liquidity offered by 25.2 percent cash.

If you don't need the liquidity, and you are a somewhat aggressive investor, you might consider using some of the cash to increase your stock allocation. Even if you are a relatively conservative investor and don't need the liquidity of 25.2 percent cash, you might opt to use your cash to buy more bonds. Remember to use dollar-cost averaging if you are planning to increase your holding of a volatile investment.

SAMPLE INVESTMENT PORTFOLIO

Date: *May 28, 2002*

ASSET TYPE	DESCRIPTION	VALUE	PERCENTAGE OF TOTAL PORTFOLIO VALUE
Stock	*Home Town, Inc.*	*$5,400*	
	Big City, LLC	*$3,489*	
	MacroCorp	*$1,286*	
	JCN Corp	*$3,278*	
	Balanced mutual fund	*$3,498*	
	Large-cap mutual fund	*$2,525*	
Total stock:		$19,476	27.5%
Bond	*10-year treasury bond*	*$20,000*	
	3-year municipal bond	*$5,000*	
	Balanced mutual fund	*$3,425*	
	Large-cap mutual fund	*$4,958*	
Total bond:		$33,383	47.2%
Cash	*Balanced mutual fund*	*$5,840*	
	Money market account	*$12,000*	
Total cash:	$17,840		25.2%
Total portfolio value:	$70,699		

Staying on Course:
Wealth Journals and Investor Profiles

It can be very difficult to stay the course with a carefully planned asset allocation at a time when your investments are losing value. It's important to spend plenty of time prior to making any investments to assess your risk tolerance and investment time horizon, then establish a proper asset allocation you can stick with, even when the market is against you. This process starts with your wealth journal.

Staying in touch with your feelings about money is an important part of building wealth. Your wealth journal is a helpful tool for gaining greater insight into your life priorities. It gives you a completely private area for expressing your feelings, thoughts, and aspirations. Your journal need not be fancy; a little quiet time, paper or notebook, and a pen are all you need to get started. Writing regularly in your journal will give you an outlet to vent your frustrations or concerns with the market. And, over time, it will give you perspective as you look over past entries at previous down markets and realize that these ups and downs are part of investing.

Don't look at a single investment and let it influence your thinking about your wealth plan. Instead, look at the big picture—your portfolio, your financial goals, and the economy. Most important: Sleep on any decisions to shift your investments before you take action.

Another helpful tool to summarize your investment objective, target asset allocation, and other information relating to your investment plan—and which can be shared with others—is an investor profile. This is a summary of your financial parameters and goals. On it you should list your asset allocation and other important summary information about your wealth plan. Your investor profile should be reviewed each time you review your investments or wealth plan. When it seems like your plan isn't working and you're tempted to make a dramatic change such as selling some of your investments, revisit your investor profile and contemplate your motivations for creating your wealth plan in the first place. You might also decide to continue your wealth journal and record the gains and losses in your portfolio and how the changes made you feel. After a time, you may begin to visualize your progress toward your wealth goals and become more accustomed to the ups and downs of investing.

Your investor profile, along with your net worth and cash flow statements, make up the legend for your map to wealth. Make it a habit to keep it updated regularly, and refer to it when reviewing your wealth and investment plan. Keep these documents in front of you as we continue to develop your course to wealth.

Try the following investor profile to get you started:

INVESTOR PROFILE

Date: _____

PRIMARY GOALS (List your specific primary goals, financial and otherwise.)

TIME HORIZON (When do you want to achieve each of your goals? For each goal, assign a year by which you intend to reach it, making it easier to see how your various goals work together and which ones are planned to happen around the same time. For example, how many years will pass between the time you finish paying for your children's college education and the year you would like to retire? The time between key financial goals is important to assessing how reasonable your overall goals are.)

RISK TOLERANCE (Are you a risk-adverse, conservative investor or are you a moderate or aggressive investor who doesn't mind volatility in your portfolio? Be as complete as possible here, especially if your partner has a different level of risk tolerance, in which case both of you should reflect on the risk tolerance of your shared portfolio.)

_____

_____

_____

_____

RETURN ASSUMPTION (This is the assumed growth rate of your portfolio. You should make it a conservative assumption, one that you will use to make financial planning projections. It is not necessarily the rate that your portfolio will earn each year.)

_____

_____

_____

_____

ALLOCATION TARGET (Fill in the allocation target you arrived at earlier in this chapter. If you have chosen different allocations for your each of different portfolios, you can list each separately here as well.)

_____

_____

_____

_____

MAXIMUM MARGINAL TAX RATE (If you're not sure what rate to enter, don't fill in this entry now. You will learn more about taxes in Chapter 16 and be better able to determine this rate.)

Tax Bracket %: _____

AVERAGE TAX RATE (This gives you an idea of how much of your wage earnings and investment earnings goes to Uncle Sam. To find this important percentage, add the total amount of tax you paid last year (federal, state, and local taxes if they apply to you) and divide it into your pre-tax income.)

Average Tax Rate %: _____

EMERGENCY FUND (How large an emergency fund did you decide you needed after our discussion earlier in this chapter? Enter that number here.)

Emergency Fund: $ _____

STABILITY OF INCOME (How stable is your income? Are you dependent on a job from which you are worried you might be laid off? Are you self-employed and find that your income fluctuates from month to month? Have you been working for the same company for some time and feel good about your job stability? It's important to think about the stability of your family's income and make a note of it in your investor profile so you can refer to it when you begin building a savings budget or considering your emergency fund. If you decide that your job may not be all that stable, you might want to increase your emergency fund.)

_____

_____

_____

_____

OTHER LIQUIDITY ISSUES (Are there any other big expenses coming up that are not part of your financial plan? Do you need to plan for a new roof, a new car, or some other occasional expense? It's helpful to have these budget busters listed here so that you can plan ahead for them.)

_____

_____

_____

_____

OTHER LEGAL ISSUES (As much as we would hope that this is not the case, are there any pending legal issues in your life? Are you planning a divorce? Are you helping to manage a family member's estate? Are you a party to a lawsuit? Like the liquidity issues above, it's helpful to list any legal issues here to help plan for them.)

_____

_____

_____

_____

CHAPTER 9
The Logistics of Investing

O nce you've purchased investments to implement your asset alloca- tion it's important to regularly review your portfolio's performance and its fit with your risk tolerance. You might need to make changes for a variety of rea- sons, including investments that don't live up to their expectations or a change of focus in your portfolio.

Diversification

In the last chapter, you built an asset allocation target that included the three basic investment types: stocks, bonds, and cash. A prudent investor works to manage risk whenever they can. One way to do this is by being careful not to put all your financial eggs in a single basket, a concept known as "diversification."

You don't have to make investing your hobby, but you should monitor your wealth plan. Watch television business shows, read popular investing magazines, visit reputable Internet sites, or take a class on managing money. Not all information is good, or even accurate, but experience will help you decide what's important to you.

For diversification purposes, we can divide each of the three basic asset classes into smaller segments called subclasses. An effective asset allocation including these subclasses can help reduce the overall risk of a portfolio while suffering only a small reduction in expected return.

Consider the possible subclasses under each basic asset category.

Stocks

Stock subclasses include domestic (shares of stock in companies that are based in, or do most of their business in, the United States); international (stock issued by companies that are based in a variety of countries and do business internationally, both inside and outside the United States); and foreign (stocks of companies that primarily do business in countries other than the United States).

Company Size

Company size subclasses include large cap (companies with market caps greater than $5 billion); mid cap (companies with market caps of between $1 and $5 billion); and small cap (companies with market caps less than $1 billion). Some analysts even add a category for mega-cap, companies with over $10 billion in market; and micro-cap, for very small companies.

Investment Style

Investment style subclasses include growth stocks (investors believe these stocks are likely to grow in value faster than the market as a whole) and value stocks (investors feel these stocks are good companies, but for some reason shares are being bought and sold below a price that the investor feels is the true value of the company).

Industry Sector

Industry sectors include financial, technology, healthcare, energy, retail, consumer durables (like furniture, appliances, and consumer electronics), and consumer staples (like household cleaning products, food, and tobacco). You may do a good job spreading your investment across large, medium, and small companies that do business inside and outside the United States, but if they are all in a couple of the same industry sectors you will not be as well diversified as you expect.

Preferred Stock

Preferred stocks don't technically constitute an asset class, but are still potentially part of a strong diversification strategy because of their expected dividend income stream. Preferred stock generally pays a dividend that is greater than the everyday common stock of a company. While the preferred stock may not enjoy some company ownership rights that the common stock does, this income stream could make preferred stock less risky than the common stock of the same company. This is because the investor has two potential avenues of profit: the regular dividend payment and the price increase of the stock.

Bonds

Bond subclasses include government agency (issued by a government agency like Fannie Mae, Ginnie Mae, or Freddie Mac); treasury (issued by the United States Treasury): municipal (issued by a city or a town); corporate (issued by a company); and foreign (issued by foreign governments or corporations).

Convertible bonds (or convertibles) resemble preferred stock in that they are not necessarily an asset subclass, but the option their owner has to change them into company stock makes them neither fully stock nor bond. They may be more or less risky than regular bonds; in the worst case, convertible bondholders may be in line for payment behind straight bondholders in case of a bankruptcy. Suffice it to say that potential investors in convertible bonds should get professional advice.

High-yield bonds are issued by an entity that has a greater than average chance of defaulting on the loan (not paying back principal or making interest payments.) The rates paid by these bonds are higher because of this additional risk.

The two most popular types of U.S. savings bonds are called EE bonds and Inflation bonds (I bonds). These safe investments can be very useful in an asset allocation because of the tax-deferred nature of their interest payments.

Cash

Cash subclasses include savings (money deposited at a bank or credit union that is typically covered by federal FDIC insurance, which protects up to $100,000 against bank default); money market (money deposited in a money market account that often earns an interest rate higher than a savings account but does not have FDIC insurance); and certificates of deposit or CDs (accounts available through a variety of financial institutions that offer a fixed rate of interest over a set period of time).

Buying and Owning Securities

Before the advent of computers, investors received paper stock and bond certificates as proof of ownership in the companies they invested in. Many people still prefer to hold their investments in certificate form, but there are two other, perhaps less cumbersome, ways to hold them.

To understand the various forms securities can be held in, it's helpful to understand a bit about how they are traded. Publicly traded stocks and bonds are usually bought and sold with the help of a broker, a transfer agent, or a principal. An investor may contact a broker or agent and request that a specific transaction, such as the purchase or sale of a specific stock or bond, be made in the name of the investor. It's then the broker's job to get the best price possible for the investor at the exchange where the stock or bond is sold.

FACTS

In these computer-dominated times, very few stock transactions are settled through the "open outcry" system that we see portrayed on television and in movies, in which a group of yelling, arm-waving traders surround a market maker's post on the exchange floor shouting out buy and sell orders. Most orders are matched electronically and are filled in seconds.

Bonds are typically bought directly from the broker's inventory. The broker has purchased these bonds at a "wholesale" price with the plan to mark them up for sale to its customers at "retail" prices. In this position, brokers are said to be acting as a principal, as opposed to when they are acting as an agent who sells bonds for a commission.

If an investor is buying stock, he or she must deliver the cash to the broker within a specific amount of time after the broker executes the stock purchase to "settle," or complete the trade. If an investor is selling, he or she has a deadline to settle the trade by delivering the certificates for the stocks or bonds to the broker who placed the sell order on their behalf.

If a stock or bond is held in certificate form, the settlement, also called "clearing," can be delayed. In fact, because the broker could be required to clear the trade with the exchange before he acquires your certificate, most brokerages will not sell a stock without already holding it under "street name" in an electronic account that resembles an escrow account. This means that you must first deposit the stock in an account with the broker before they will sell it for you. But, if you'd like to hold your securities in certificate form despite the complications involved, here are a few precautions you should keep in mind.

Safeguarding Certificates

Paper certificates are easily misplaced and are cumbersome to reissue if lost or destroyed. Some bond certificates do not indicate the owner's name on them and can be redeemed by anyone who possesses them!

Keep a photocopy of the certificate or a record of the "cusip" number (located on the front upper right corner of most certificates), company name, and number of owned shares or the face value of the bond in a separate location to smooth the reissue process. Keep the certificates themselves in a secure place such as a safe-deposit box. If you misplace your certificates, contact the company's shareholder services department or your broker to start the reissuing process.

Redeeming Certificates

Selling paper certificate shares quickly may be a problem. You'll need to deliver the certificates to a brokerage firm or to the issuing company for redemption. This extra time is an important consideration if you want or need to liquidate your position quickly.

Keeping Accurate Records

It's important to keep your address updated with your portfolio company's transfer agent so you'll receive correspondence and any dividend or interest checks promptly. If the company wishes to be bought, or merges with another company, as a shareholder you'll be given a chance to vote your approval or disapproval. If the company does merge or is bought, you will be mailed information explaining the disposition of your stock shares—whether you will be offered new shares in the new company or cash in exchange for your old shares.

Accurate record keeping will also help to avoid tax errors when you sell your stock. Keep a record of your initial investment plus any dividends you've received because they are taxable in the year they are paid. These payments, added to your initial cost, equal your "cost basis" and may be subtracted from any sale proceeds when calculating your capital gain.

Splitting Your Stock

If the company whose shares you own decides to change the number of shares they have outstanding by either doubling the number of outstanding shares, called a "stock split," or reducing the number of shares, a "reverse split," you will be given the opportunity to order a new certificate indicating the new number of shares.

FACTS

America's foremost wealth-builder, Warren Buffet, doesn't believe in splitting stock. Buffet, the head of Berkshire Hathaway, has never permitted its stock to split, meaning it has traded well above $10,000. The downside, of course, is that only wealthy investors can afford to buy more than a handful of the company's shares!

Companies split or reverse split their stock for a variety of reasons, but one of the most common is to manipulate the price of their shares. If the price of a share becomes too high, investors may not want to trade in shares for fear that too much money is tied up in each share. This could mean the volume of trades per day could go down and the price of the stock might drop. Each company has an opinion about the range in which they feel their stock should trade, and if the stock gets much above that range they may decide to make a change.

A share price that sinks too low can also harm a stock. That's because the New York Stock Exchange and the Nasdaq stock market enforce rules that prevent poor-quality companies from selling stock to investors. If a stock falls below certain benchmarks for too long, or if other conditions aren't met, the trading organizations can "delist" the stock, meaning bar them from trading except on the more speculative Over-the-Counter Bulletin Board. In order to sustain a sagging stock price, and to dodge the "delisting" bullet, some struggling companies will stage a reverse split where, in the case of a one-for-three reverse split, for example, three 50-cent shares are converted into one share worth $1.50.

Holding Your Investments Electronically

Holding your stock or bonds in electronic form, known by the industry term "street name," will help avoid the problems of lost certificates and delayed transactions. To hold your securities electronically, simply open a brokerage account enclosing either cash or bond and stock certificates with your application. Be sure to ask about expenses and transaction limitations or requirements before opening an account, as the amount of account activity and the level of service the firm provides may affect your transaction expenses. Full-service firms usually provide a personal stockbroker to help you with your account, but may offer a telephone or Internet system at lower per-transaction commissions.

Services you purchase by holding your investments in street name at a brokerage firm include the following:

- **Convenient record keeping.** The brokerage firm will make record keeping easier by providing monthly account statements. These statements will include the account balance (usually compared to the previous month), a list of transactions made during the month, and sometimes the cost basis of your investments.
- **Insurance backup.** Most firms carry "SIPC" insurance from the Securities Investor Protection Corp., and you should ask about the amount of coverage when you open your account. Basic SIPC insurance covers investors' securities up to $500,000 per account, and cash up to $100,000 per account, against losses due to brokerage-firm bankruptcy.
- **One account, fewer hassles.** A brokerage account will allow you to hold a variety of investments in the same account. So you may have a number of stocks, some bonds, and some mutual funds all in your individual brokerage account, and you can choose how you'd like to "register" the account ownership. You may even decide to open one account for all your retirement assets, another for your non-retirement

investments, and still another for the investments you hold jointly with another person. If you maintain these accounts with a single brokerage firm, the accounts might be combined into a single monthly statement called "householding."

- **Making the trade.** The brokerage firm will buy or sell securities at your direction and will clear all transactions through your account. This means you'll need to keep adequate cash in the account for any purchase you order; when the firm sells stock for you, it will deposit the proceeds, minus commission and transaction costs, into a money market account for you. Interest payments from your bonds can be deposited directly to your money market account or paid directly to you, depending on your instructions.
- **Checkbook ease.** Most firms make your cash readily available by providing some form of checking account.

Investor Services Programs

Another way to hold stock is to participate in an investor services program. Not all companies provide this service, but some have registered with the Securities Exchange Commission to offer shares directly to the public without using a broker. This is an inexpensive way to hold shares electronically, because the transactions don't involve paying brokerage commissions. These programs typically involve transaction fees, however, so ask about expenses when you talk to the company.

Dividend Reinvestment Plans are great gifts to give your children or grandchildren. With a small initial investment in a high-quality stock, your youngster can begin to learn about stocks and investing, and maybe even take a few steps toward wealth!

To enroll in a plan, contact the company whose shares you'd like to purchase. In turn, the company will put you in touch with its transfer agent or the trustee that administers its shareholder programs. EquiServe LP is the largest of these plan administrators. Contact them at ✍*www.equiserve.com*

or by mail at EquiServe, Shareholder Services, P.O. Box 43010, Providence, RI 02940-3010, to learn if they administer a plan for your prospective portfolio company. You will usually receive monthly statements from your plan, and may make a transfer to a brokerage account at any time.

There are two types of investor services programs: direct investment plans and dividend reinvestment plans. Through a direct investment plan you may purchase shares of company stock for a nominal transaction fee. A dividend reinvestment plan, sometimes called a "DRIP," will purchase new stock with dividends paid on the shares you already own.

A Closer Look at Stocks

Now that we've introduced a variety of methods of managing your ownership of stocks and bonds, it's time to define them in more detail. Simply put, a stock is a share of ownership in a company, a percentage dictated by the total number of shares "outstanding"—that have been sold to the public. Companies issue shares—or sell ownership interests—in themselves in order to fund growth or pay for some major corporate initiative.

Diversifying Your Stock Risk

When building the stock allocation of your portfolio it is important to purchase the stock of a variety of companies. These companies should differ in size, industry sector, and country of origin. Larger companies will tend to be in the later growth stages of their business. They typically experience more predictable growth and often pay dividends (payments that represent a return of a portion of the company's profit to shareholders), which add to your investment growth.

Mid-size or smaller companies are usually in the start-up and fast growth phase of their business. They don't typically pay dividends because earnings are usually reinvested back into the company to help it grow. These companies' stock may outperform their larger peers but are not without risk. What might sound like a wonderful new idea could turn out to be a money-losing bust overnight, as Internet-based companies have proven in the late 1990s and early 2000s.

Diversifying the industry sectors that you invest in is also important because not all parts of the economy do well at the same time. For example, energy companies might be thriving while technology companies are struggling, or retail companies might be growing while the health-care industry struggles. Since it is difficult for anyone to project which industries might do well at any particular time, it's important to own a little of each.

ALERT

Small companies don't have the track record of larger companies, so make sure to fully research a small company before investing in it. An average investor with a moderate risk tolerance would probably choose to limit their small-stock exposure to no more than 10 percent of the stocks in their portfolio.

It's also important to diversify across geographical regions because different economies will be growing at different times. By investing a large part of your portfolio in U.S. securities and perhaps 10–15 percent in overseas investments in developed economies (for a moderate-risk investor), you will decrease the risk of your overall portfolio.

Stock Indexes: Built-in Diversification

The broad stock market can be divided into smaller markets based on the type of stock involved. These markets are tracked or measured by the market's "stock index," a representative list of typical stocks for that market. For example, the broad domestic stock market is often measured by the Standard & Poor's 500 stock index. This index is a list of 500 stocks that securities research firm Standard & Poor's feels are representative of the overall large-company stock market.

The value of these 500 stocks is tracked throughout each trading day and reported to represent the overall direction of the stock market. Other indexes are used to represent other markets: The Nasdaq 100 index represents the large stocks (most with a technology orientation) that trade on the Nasdaq electronic stock market. The S&P 400 mid-cap index tracks medium-size companies and the Russell 2000 index tracks the performance of small companies.

By identifying which indexes best mirror your portfolio, you can make some assumptions about what future performance you might expect.

Here are some commonly used stock indexes and their twenty-year annual performance histories:

- Standard & Poor's 500 Index (S&P 500) average annual return of about 14 percent
- Dow Jones Industrial Average's annual return of just under 14 percent
- Russell 2000 Index average annual return of about 14 percent
- Wilshire 5000 Index average annual return of about 13 percent
- Lehman Brothers Aggregate Bond Index average return of about 10 percent

The past twenty years have not necessarily been representative of the performance you can expect in the stock and bond markets. The older stock indexes tell this story. Over its entire history (1928 to present) the Dow Jones Industrial Average has returned closer to 5 percent average per year. The S&P 500 has averaged about 7 percent per year since 1924. What will stocks and bonds return in future years? No one can say for sure. But, a certain wealth plan is to assume relatively low returns and save extra for your nest egg, just in case.

A Closer Look at Bonds

Rather than sell ownership in their company by issuing shares of stock, some companies choose borrow money from investors by issuing bonds. An investor purchases the bond from the company for a set dollar amount in cash, which the company can then use to expand its plant, gear up for a new product, or fund any number of corporate programs. The company then promises to pay back the loan, plus interest, at some future date.

Bonds formalize a loan the investor has made to the issuer. The investor can choose to keep the bond until it matures and the loan is paid back, or he can sell the bond to another investor before it matures. Bonds may change hands this way many times before they finally mature and, depending on the financial stability of the bond issuer, they can be a less risky investment than stocks. A variety of issuers use bonds: Companies, the federal and state governments, foreign governments, municipalities, and government agencies are the most common. We'll refer to the bond issuer as a company, but it could also be one of these other entities.

ESSENTIALS

Bonds may not seem as exciting as stocks, but their values are a very important part of a wealth builder's portfolio. In fact, bonds can form the rock upon which the rest of a portfolio stands. High-quality bonds can earn interest year after year, while the stocks you own may vacillate wildly in value.

Bonds are good wealth-building tools because they react differently to economic factors than stocks do. This means that, in general, bond prices go up while stock prices are going down, and vice versa. This difference is an important factor when attempting to diversify. If the part of your portfolio invested in stocks is losing value, you hope the part you invested in bonds isn't.

Also, because bonds are a loan, not part ownership like stocks, the investor will usually receive interest payments and the payback of the loan at some predetermined point. Again, this is different from stocks, which make no such promise. And bondholders are essentially in the front of the line, ahead of shareholders, for money if the company goes bankrupt. Should a company suffer through a bankruptcy, stock shareholders are unlikely to get their money back, but bonds holders—as creditors of the company—may receive some payback.

The credit rating of the bond issuer is an important factor in deter-mining the risk of the bond. If the company has a poor track record or weak financial standing, the investor may not receive the interest payments and loan payback on the bond. Companies with low credit ratings usually offer higher interest rates to their bond investors as compensation for the added risk. If you are looking at a bond that carries a higher interest rate than its peers, check the issuer's credit rating.

There are six basic terms that are important in understanding the mechanics of bonds:

- **Face value.** This is the amount a bondholder loans to the issuer by buying the bond. The term stems from the fact that the amount of the "loan" is printed on the front, or face, of each bond certificate.
- **Principal.** Principal and face value can mean the same thing when it comes to bonds. The principal is the amount of money the bond represents—i.e. a new $10,000 bond is purchased for $10,000, has $10,000 printed on its face, and the bond principal is $10,000.
- **Interest rate.** The rate of interest the bond pays is fixed at the time of issue and is a factor of the bond issuer's credit rating and the term of the bond. If the term is very long, say several years, the interest rate, or coupon rate, will be higher than a bond with a shorter term. If the credit rating of the issuer is poor, the interest rate will be higher than a bond from an issuer with a higher rating.
- **Coupon payments.** Coupon payment refers to the interest payment paid by the bond. Bonds held in certificate form have small squares of paper attached to the bottom of the certificate representing the interest payments due at particular dates, functionally similar to a loan payment booklet. The bondholder can clip these squares of paper, which are called "coupons," from the bond and submit them to the issuer for payment. Paper coupons are growing less common, in part because it's more convenient to hold your bonds in a brokerage account and receive interest payments electronically. Even then, the payments are still called "coupon payments."
- **Maturity.** At the maturity date, or the expiration of the bond's term, the bond issuer is required to repay the face value amount of the bond to the bond owner.
- **Yield.** Yield represents the total percentage return to the investor from the bond. It is a combination of the coupon payments, plus any profit generated because the investor bought the bond for less than face value. It could also represent a loss that resulted from buying the bond for more than face value.

CHAPTER 10

Finding Investment Information

Researching your investments might not be something you want to do alone. Without sound financial advice, many individual investors are sorely tempted by investments that later turn sour. A responsible investment advisor can help you grow your wealth by reviewing your investment choices and research, and ensure that your choices are in keeping with your wealth plan.

The Good, the Bad, and the Costly

Just as a healthy economy has generated a sweeping interest in the stock and bond markets, and investing in general, the popularity of the Internet has enabled a blossoming in the quantity and variety of information that is conveniently available to investors. There are Web sites, newsletters, magazines, books, seminars, radio shows, TV shows, entire cable stations, sales professionals, and investment analysts all offering information about the economy and investing.

Who do you believe? How do you separate the sound advice from the foolish, the trash from the treasure? There are three important questions to ask about financial information and the people who offer it: What is their personal interest, how much does their advice cost, and what is their track record?

FACTS

The important thing to remember when building and maintaining your investment portfolio is that your wealth plan is your responsibility. Ask for professional help when you need it. Read about and research your investments and the investments your advisors recommend. Keep current on investing trends. Your portfolio represents *your* wealth—it should be *your* priority.

Evaluating the Source

It's no surprise that the people who disseminate financial advice and commentary often have a vested interest in the matter. These people often have a great deal of experience in their field and can become valuable resources. But be aware of who you are working with, ask questions, and consider their advice in light of their personal interest. As long as you're making your own decisions from a position of informed awareness, you can glean helpful investment advice from almost anywhere—because you'll know what information is credible and what is doubtful.

Responsible commentators disclose their interest, but in many cases it's up to each member of their audience to discern where the interest of a commentator and an individual investor might clash. When listening to or reading financial advice or commentary, ask yourself, what is this source's special interest? Is the Web site, magazine, TV show, or radio program oversimplifying an issue for the sake of clarity, while sacrificing the comprehensive details that investors must pore over when making informed decisions? Have they looked at all the angles? Are they giving equal emphasis to all the factors involved?

It's also important to consider the track record of any investment promoter. Has this source consistently provided sound advice? Does the author of the article, book, or TV program work in the field they are discussing? Have they been working in the field long enough to establish a track record, or are they a newcomer with a flair for marketing and getting their name in the press? Of course, you can be less picky when you're reading for general advice and ideas than when you're hiring an investment adviser, but you still need to be cautious. Don't waste your time or your money on advice from a source you're not sure you can trust.

Attention Grabbers

As media conglomerates spread their influence further and further abroad and into more and more areas of daily life, an even more troubling conflict of interest could arise: Is a media outlet owned by the very company they are commenting on? Some media outlets are very careful to disclose their potential conflicts of interest, but mere disclosure doesn't guarantee impartiality. When in doubt, turn to more than one—preferably several—independent sources of information.

What's important to realize about investment advice in the media is that it is designed to hold your attention, not necessarily to be comprehensive—or even overly responsible. After all, would you buy a magazine whose cover story read "Steady, long-term investing is surest road to wealth"? Probably not. The magazine that screams "Seven stocks that will turbocharge your portfolio!" might get your attention, but articles like that probably won't offer much information that will help you with your lifelong wealth plan. In the final analysis, the surest way to wealth—a carefully mapped-out, long-term plan combined with a frugal lifestyle—is probably the least compatible message for print or electronic media whose mission is to grab attention.

Ignore the daily swing in sentiment between frantic optimism and hopeless pessimism that can characterize some media, particularly cable networks such as CNBC and CNNfn. That's not to say these networks aren't entertaining, even informative and educational. But take the market's good days with a grain of salt, and shrug off its bad days. As a sober, informed wealth builder, you're in it for the long haul.

Pay particularly close attention to the publications or programs with a more grounded perspective that offer insight into investment strategies that might complement your own. Do they discuss asset allocation or the government's economic predictions? Do they feature interviews with noted economists, business owners, or CEOs? These grounded, pragmatic stories are more often the ones that will teach you something valuable and help you refine your investing habits. Getting rich is a process and a lifestyle—not an overnight phenomenon.

Hidden Costs

Watch out for sales pitches in sheep's clothing! Some commentary is authored by professionals whose business is based on sales commissions, and their advice is potentially slanted in favor of the higher-commissioned products. Of course, you must pay for sound financial advice, but be aware of what you're paying for. If you receive a bill from your advisor, it's easy to see the cost of advice. With commissions, whose cost is often hidden, it's not always as obvious. Ask your advisor about their compensation. Purchase investment advice deliberately.

Like other salespeople, investment sellers naturally press harder to promote products that carry higher, more lucrative commissions, or are part of an incentive program. It may not be obvious to investors which products these are. Ask your advisor if this is the case with any of his recommendations.

Does the author of a financial commentary or the expert cited in a business feature article own the investment they are touting in the media? If you invest in such a vehicle, are you enriching them rather than yourself?

With so much independent, third-party investment advice available, why not stick with the ways that don't come loaded with a sales pitch?

Workshops, Seminars, and Classes

Workshops and seminars are often a pleasant and inexpensive way to gather general investment information and learn about financial strategies. But there are some warning signs that a seminar is meant more as a sales pitch than an evening of informative discussion. For example, it's a dead giveaway that a sales pitch is in store if a free meal is offered!

Presentations with broad subject matter such as "Making the most of today's investment environment" or "Fixed-investment strategies for retired people" will probably prove more fruitful than workshops about a specific product, technique, or system. For example, a seminar titled "Putting life insurance to work for your retirement" is sure to be a sales pitch.

Investment newsletters can be a fun way to learn about new investment ideas and opportunities, but even these seemingly harmless scribes can spell trouble for a uninformed investor. Like other media outlets, the newsletter must be attention-getting to justify its subscription fees. It's up to you to take the research further and choose your own investments.

Try never to enroll in a costly "beat Wall Street" program or commit to any purchases solely on the information you hear at a workshop. Take home any information you're interested in and consider whether it meets with your financial goals before making a commitment. Talk to your other advisors about the ideas you're considering. The old wisdom is best: Sleep on it!

Classes and workshops offered by colleges, continuing-education programs, and nonprofit groups are often a good bet for finding helpful investment advice and are often offered at low cost. The presenter may be a local professional, and possibly even tied to a local company whose profits stem from commission sales. But host colleges or organizations generally screen their speakers and insist they adhere to a "no sales pitch" policy in the classroom.

If you're lucky, a teacher of this kind of seminar might be someone you feel comfortable with, and you might opt to consult him or her outside the classroom as a financial advisor. What better way to screen an advisor than to see them in action first? We'll talk more about how to hire a wealth advisor and what to expect from them in Chapter 17.

FACTS

Magazines, newsletters, TV and radio shows, Web sites, and most workshops and seminars are good resources for low-cost financial and investment advice. But this advice is general in nature. You'll learn about basic strategies and trends but you won't get advice about your individual situation. You have to do your homework beyond these general sources and get personal help when you need it.

Investment Oracles

You can find a variety of sources for more detailed, specific information on your investments. Some are third-party researchers who sell their analysis; others are investment houses themselves that offer information about their own products or the investments they suggest. Let's look at a few.

Morningstar and Value Line Reports

Morningstar and Value Line are two independent research firms that provide information about mutual funds and stocks. These firms track specific fund and stock information and use it to compile standardized charts and reports. The formats are clear and simple, and enable you to compare apples to apples. That's not always possible when you view reports published by the mutual fund companies or the stock-issuing companies; those reports can be framed any number of ways and can sometimes leave out telltale information. Third-party researchers don't have this conflict. And they're getting a lot easier to access, especially with Morningstar and Value Line information available on the Internet by subscription and at most libraries. (See Appendix A for more information.)

Bond Credit Ratings

You're probably familiar with bond ratings from some of the financial headlines that screamed about the financial disasters of "junk bonds." The junk-bond debacle stemmed from people like "Junk Bond King" Michael Milken, who sold high-risk bonds, called junk bonds, to investors who weren't told of the very high likelihood that the bonds they were buying might default. And many of those bonds eventually *did* default, saddling investors with worthless investments. When federal investigators looked into the sale, they found that investors were fleeced by high-pressure bond salesmen who didn't properly explain the very high risks. Some junk-bond salesmen went to prison because of the scandal, and it ruined many wealth-seeking families.

Think of bond ratings as report cards for your investment portfolio, with the most reliable bonds earning top marks, called "triple-A" ratings, and the very least-reliable earning an S&P rating of BB+ or below, or junk-bond ratings.

ESSENTIALS

Like bond ratings, personal credit ratings are important for more than borrowing power. If you have a poor (or no) credit rating, you may pay higher credit card interest, higher rates for mortgages and consumer loans, even higher insurance premiums! Companies with poor bond ratings pay higher rates on their loans, including the bonds they issue.

Bond ratings are a lot like credit ratings. In both cases, a credit-rating agency is judging the individual or entity's ability to repay a debt. In the case of a person's credit rating, a credit-scoring agency is reviewing a person's history of paying their bills. Other lenders like a bank or a mortgage company can use that history to anticipate the likelihood that he or she will pay a new debt, for example a new bank loan or a new mortgage.

Bonds are given credit ratings by many of the same agencies that rate insurance companies. The best-known bond-rating agencies are Moody's Investor Services, Standard & Poor's, and A.M. Best. The bond ratings they publish are available online (see Appendix A for more information) and at well-stocked libraries. Your broker may also provide you with these reports as a customer service, and if he or she doesn't volunteer the information, be certain to ask.

Accountants, Lawyers, and Other Professionals

You might be surprised about how many nontraditional sources can offer sound investment advice. For example, your attorney and tax advisor may be able to offer you advice about investments. That's because, as professionals of all types participate in the evolution of the financial services industry toward a broader menu of services, more and more attorneys and tax experts are creating multifaceted practices. And if they don't offer financial expertise directly, most have created a network of financial experts from which they can offer excellent referrals.

FACTS

An increasing number of lawyers and accountants are offering investment advice. Interview them about how this works into the rest of their practice, and be certain they can wear both hats and still provide sound, thorough, and unbiased advice. Ask them how many clients they provide with investment advice and how long investment advice has been part of their practice.

Professional Managers and Other Managed Accounts

The investment community recognized many years ago that, if small investors were going to grow into bigger investors, the financial services industry had to offer some help. That's because not all investors had the wherewithal to purchase a diversified portfolio of stocks and bonds, and even those that did, often didn't know how.

One solution the investment community arrived at was the pooled, managed accounts through which the individual could enjoy diversification and professional money management. Over the years, this market has grown to include many types of products and services. We'll talk about the most common pooled accounts: mutual funds, exchange-traded funds, professional money managers, variable annuities and life insurance, and folios, in the next chapter. Before we get into the individual pooled accounts themselves, let's look at the two different styles of investing that pooled accounts employ: active and passive.

Active

Actively managed accounts are overseen by institutional investment experts who research companies and investments in detail, then actively buy and sell stocks and bonds, sometimes making many trades each day involving many thousands of shares. The gains from buying when stocks are inexpensive and selling when they've increased in value are enough to outweigh the added tax and transaction costs incurred from fast-paced trading, or so the theory goes. Actively managed accounts rely heavily on the stock- and bond-picking ability of the fund manager or management team. When researching these actively managed funds, investigate the manager's track record compared to the average performance of other managers of similar funds. How long has the manager been overseeing the fund? Is the fund managed mostly by a single person, whose departure from the fund could send it into disarray, or by a team of managers in which a single defection wouldn't make much difference in its investment behavior? This information is available from the company the manager works for or, better yet, from third-party, independent sources like Morningstar and Value Line.

Passive

There's another side to the active management philosophy: the passive management style. Managers running passive accounts employ a long-term buy-and-hold strategy, often called an index strategy, in which they purchase a broad array of securities that mirror the general makeup of a broad market index such as the Dow Jones Industrial Average or any one of a number of industry indices.

The idea behind this less active approach is to provide the investor with an account that mirrors a particular market or asset allocation, but at the same time cut down on the costs of trading and the tax consequences. Uncle Sam takes a bite out of the profits that pooled funds earn when they sell a stock for more money than they paid for it because the fund is considered a "flow-through" entity; it doesn't pay its own taxes. The shareholders of any flow-through entity share the tax on capital gains and other income generated in the fund based on the number of shares they own. Tax on these so-called "capital gains" count against the profits earned by selling the stock because the investor has to reach into their pocket or sell shares of the fund to pay them. Capital gains tax can be one of the biggest drains on mutual fund returns. That's why some investors love passive funds, because the lower tax exposure means less tax headache.

QUESTIONS?

What is the purpose of a market index?
Indexes were created as a way to easily track the performance of particular parts of the market. Investors use indexes as a yardstick against which to measure their own portfolio performance.

There's another reason passively managed funds are favorites with some investors: Passively managed funds are typically "no-brainers" when trying to pick funds to match an asset allocation. This means that computer programs are able to tell a manager how many stocks to buy and sell in order to continue mirroring a specific index. With that kind of simple, quantitative direction, there's no need for a fund company to employ a high-priced investing "all star" as its fund manager. Investors in an index fund have only to examine the fund itself and its ability to match the index. They don't have to worry about a manager who leaves, loses a stock- or bond-picking touch, or changes investment philosophy.

Not having a portfolio manager all but guarantees that the passive fund will remain within its "style," or investment philosophy. That means that, for investors with moderate or conservative risk tolerance, they can be more certain that a low- to moderate-risk fund won't gradually morph into a moderate- to high-risk one, as can happen when active-fund managers surrender to the temptation of investing in the latest stock fad.

Investing with Style

A fund's "style" describes the philosophy used to pick the investments in a portfolio. This portfolio can be your own portfolio or any pooled account. Style is most often divided into two segments: value and growth.

Value managers look to buy stocks that they feel are selling at a discount to their true value. The investor disagrees with the market, thinking that the rest of the market doesn't see what he sees in the value of the stock. In his opinion, he's buying the stock cheap. Disciplined, pure value investors will sell the stock when the price reaches their estimate of its true value.

Growth managers generally assign a lesser value to price in their analysis. Growth investors look for companies that are part of quickly growing industry sectors or regions and that they believe are poised to grow beyond their current stock price. Growth investors don't completely disregard price, but they do use different criteria when choosing investments than value investors. For diversification purposes, it's important to have both types of investment philosophies in your portfolio.

There's no reason not to mix both actively and passively managed accounts in your portfolio. Both bring their own advantages and disadvantages, and the two can combine for a well-diversified portfolio.

For investors concerned with "style drift," the tendency among mutual fund managers to move away from a targeted style, passively managed funds may be just the ticket. For example, if an investor needs an allocation that includes large stocks, they can invest in the S&P 500 index. If the investor wants to invest in small stocks they might choose to target the Russell 2000 index. The investor probably won't have to make a change to this selection until they need to balance their portfolio, take profits, or change their target asset allocation.

Active or Passive Accounts: Which Is Better?

A huge controversy has swirled inside the industry over which type of account, active or passive, is the best choice for investors. As with anything, the more informed you are, the wiser your choices will be. It might even be smart to hedge your options and consider a mix of management theories. For example, you might consider using the actively managed choices in your accounts that are tax-deferred—retirement accounts like IRAs and 401(k)s, for example—and thus less sensitive to the tax expense of an actively managed account. Or you may prefer a portfolio completely composed of passively managed accounts, with their more tax-sensitive investment strategy, in your accounts that are not sheltered from tax. You might even decide that the cost of an actively managed account is worthwhile in an investing sector where an astute fund manager might be able to create enough value reflected in better performance to justify his cost, including research-intensive international or small-stock funds, for example. Whatever the case, it's important to understand the difference between styles, and to be deliberate about which type of account you choose.

CHAPTER 11
Managed Investments

I nvestment companies have, for a very long time, been discovering new ways to help investors diversify and choose their investments—for a fee, of course. Investment trusts, the ancestors of mutual funds, were used by British and Scottish investors to diversify their investments as early as 1860. These trusts came to the New World with European immigration, and, in the United States, were used primarily by institutional investors who were involved in market speculation.

Mutual Funds

A mutual fund is actually a company whose service to its customers is providing pooled investment accounts. Rather than building widgets or providing insurance coverage, the business of a mutual fund is to invest the money of its subscribers in a particular way. When you deposit your money in a mutual fund you buy a share of the mutual fund, not a share of the investments it owns. Your investment value will mirror the value of the whole pooled account less overhead expenses: called net asset value, or NAV. If you choose to sell your mutual fund shares, the fund will pay you for each share based on its current value, and when you choose to buy a larger share of the fund, it will generally accept new deposits on a daily basis. Shares are not traded the way stocks and bonds are. Instead, at the end of the trading day the values of the fund's holdings are tabulated and the fund processes purchases and withdrawals from individual investors and reconciles their accounts.

Prospectus: The Lowdown on Your Fund

An individual manager or team of managers professionally manages the mutual fund following the guidelines outlined in the fund's descriptive literature, called a prospectus. The prospectus also provides information regarding the fund's expenses, investments, purchase and sale procedures, and its risk profile.

Carrying the Load

Mutual funds charge fees to support themselves in a couple of ways: management fees and sales fees. The sales fee, also called the load, is a sales commission that the company charges when you buy or sell your shares in the fund. Funds collect their commissions by adjusting the price at which you buy or sell your shares, adding or subtracting a percentage of each share's NAV. For example, in the case of up-front commissions you pay when you buy shares—called front-end loads—the shares are priced at NAV plus the commission percentage. Once the shares arrive in your account, you'll see them on your account statement at NAV—a price lower than what you paid for them. The broker or mutual fund salesman collects the difference.

Commissions that are paid when you sell your shares—called back-end loads or withdrawal fees—work similarly. When you sell shares, your proceeds are something less than NAV; the difference, again, pays the manager's commission. Ask the broker what the effect of this charge will be before you sell. Since it's based on the full value of what you sell, you might be surprised how much it can add up to.

Lifting the Load

The best time to grill your broker on how much of your wealth you'll sacrifice to front-end or back-end loads is before you buy into the fund. That's because there are a wide selection of funds that don't charge these fees and prefer to distribute their shares directly to the public without the assistance of a sales force. These funds are called no-load funds. They are bought and sold at NAV without adjustment.

That no-load fund you bought may at some time abruptly add new sales charges, which may or may not affect current investors. Review all the material your fund company mails for this and other important information. Mutual fund companies are required by law to disclose all fees in their prospectus.

Sales Fees

Mutual funds, load-carrying and no-load alike, sometimes also charge sales fees called 12b-1 fees, after the tax law paragraph that defines them. These fees help cover distribution costs of the fund and may be used to pay ongoing commissions to salespeople and other marketing and advertising costs. Small no-load mutual funds that don't yet have enough assets so that their annual management fees can support their sales efforts will also charge a 12b-1 fee to help support the distribution costs of the fund until it grows.

Paying the Fund Manager

Mutual fund management fees are paid by the fund to support its manager or management team. The fees are paid by the fund, not the individual investor, but ultimately affect the growth of the investor's shares. Management fees should reflect the difficulty and expertise of picking the investments in the fund and the manager's knack for picking good investments. Funds requiring more expertise—say, a foreign health-care fund or a small-cap value fund—may pay their manager 1.5 percent per year or more. Funds with more generic investment objectives—say, large-cap blend funds or large-cap growth funds that seek to mirror the S&P 500—will typically pay their manager closer to 1 percent. Be aware of the fees your mutual fund is paying for management—the information is in the prospectus—and be sure not to overpay.

FACTS

Prospectuses are published by the investment provider, and outline the potential benefits and risk of a particular investment. Some may be difficult to understand, but with practice you will learn to navigate through these important documents. Never invest without reading the accompanying prospectus!

Making Mutual Funds Work for Your Wealth

Let's look at some wealth-building tips for investing in mutual funds.

Check the Track Record

Look for funds with at least a five-year track record of strong performance. Be sure that the current manager or management team is responsible for this record, and that most of the good performance has not been the work of someone else. In an actively managed fund, you're paying for the manager's expertise.

Lighten the Load

Think twice about using commission-bearing "loaded" funds in retirement accounts. You're only allowed to deposit a limited amount of money each year into these accounts, and there's generally no good reason to spend part of your limited deposit to pay a salesperson's commission. You're ahead of the game if you invest in no-load funds, and spend the commission savings on investment advice—purchased separately—that can help you wring the most wealth out of every dollar.

Diversify

Use mutual funds to diversify your investment styles. Some funds invest with a value philosophy and others for growth. There are funds that invest in large companies, some in mid-size ones, and still others in small ones. And the diversification options go on and on. Use the variety to create diversity within your portfolio.

It's hard to overstate the importance of putting your eggs in different baskets. But beware of overdiversification, meaning a portfolio with too many individual investments. Such a pool of holdings can become unwieldy, and the trading costs and tax complications of managing so many assets can rob wealth.

Guard Against Overlap

Watch for overlap among your mutual funds. For example, you might own one fund that invests in large companies and another that invests in retail stocks. With these two factors guiding their holdings, both funds could be heavily weighted with Wal-Mart stock, for example. Mutual fund managers don't like to publicize their holdings because savvy individual investors could "mirror" their positions by buying the same selection of stocks themselves without paying commission and 12b-1 fees. But funds are required by regulation to publish their holdings twice a year, so check these lists to be sure that you are truly diversified and not simply in a variety of mutual funds that are all buying stock in the same few companies.

Watch for Drift

Review your mutual fund portfolio regularly and watch for style drift, which occurs when the fund you originally bought for one asset allocation purpose—say "large-cap value"—strays from its original investment purpose. Your large-cap value fund could morph into a large-cap growth fund if it kept its stocks after they grew past their target prices rather than taking profits and rebalancing into new value stocks. Unchecked, you could end up with all your large-cap holdings in growth style, for example. This phenomenon can also happen with small- or mid-cap mutual funds whose holdings grow into larger companies, meaning your small- or mid-cap growth fund could find itself holding mid- or large-cap growth stocks. That style drift doesn't necessarily mean your returns suffer, but regardless of return, your wealth plan works best when you keep your allocation properly diversified.

Be Deliberate

Don't chase performance—stick with your asset allocation. By that, we mean, just because growth stocks, or value stocks or Japan stocks, say, might be performing particularly well, you need to stay disciplined enough to reject the temptation to sell investments that might be temporarily underperforming in order to funnel cash into the "flavor of the moment." If your fund is not doing as well as others you've seen in the news lately, rather than succumb to the urge to invest in the latest stock-market fashion, remember two things. First, the funds in the news are probably already past their peak—they've already enjoyed their fastest run-up and are attracting attention—so they may now be overpriced. Second, go back to your investor profile and review your reasons for buying a particular mutual fund in the first place. Remember, your wealth plan is based on patience and long-term investment.

Don't Toy with Your Investments

Just because you're able to shift your investments as often as you like from one fund to another in the same family of funds without a sales charge doesn't mean that you should. Resist chasing the market, and make significant changes only after consulting your advisor, and only for a sound reason. Discipline is the hallmark of a successful investor.

Track the Pedigree

If you decide to purchase a mutual fund with a sales load, be sure that the fund family offers a variety of strong funds in different sectors and with different styles. Most families of funds waive additional sales loads when assets are moved to another fund in the family. If the fund family offers diverse selections, should the need arise to adjust your asset allocation target and change investment focus, you'll have other fund selections to move to without paying another sales charge. Check the prospectus on this to be sure this is the case with the family you choose.

Trim the Charges

Pay attention to which sales charge you are paying. Loaded mutual funds come in three different styles, labeled A, B, and C. "A" shares charge an up-front sales charge, and maybe a 12b-1 fee. "B" shares impose a sales charge if you sell the shares within a certain period of time, and usually charge a higher 12b-1 fee than "A" shares (the fund pays its salespeople up front, then often a trail of annual commissions for these sales, so they must charge a higher 12b-1 fee to cover this higher up-front cost). "C" shares often don't carry a front- or back-end load, but they typically have a higher annual 12b-1 fee. Because 12b-1 fee charges are based on a fixed percentage of the invested assets, the fees grow as your investments grow. And as you investigate the best mutual-fund investments, keep an eye on a fund's performance *after* accounting for its sales load.

SSENTIALS

Funds-of-funds, or several mutual funds that are grouped together in a managed account, can be helpful "one-stop-shopping " for some portfolios. These FOFs, as they're sometimes known, offer asset allocation in addition to money management. Their asset allocations are targeted for specific years or for risk tolerance or a combination of both.

Watch the Calendar

Be alert for year-end capital-gain distributions. Mutual funds are known by tax experts as "flow-through" tax entities, which means they pass their tax obligations directly to their shareholders. If the fund sells a security at a profit, the capital gain is passed along to shareholders, regardless of whether the shareholders have actually gotten richer. This pass-through usually takes place between September and December of the year, so be cautious about buying into a mutual fund that is about to make its distribution. After all, the growth that contributed to the distribution has already been enjoyed by the investors that bought into the fund earlier, making the fund effectively more expensive for investors buying in for the first time just before a taxable distribution takes place. Buying shares of a fund right before a distribution translates into taxes for new investors who didn't reap the benefit.

Keep Careful Records

If you don't keep track of your investments, you could ultimately pay more in taxes than necessary when you sell your mutual fund shares. Mutual funds typically pay dividends, interest, and capital gains that many investors opt to reinvest in their fund. These reinvested amounts are reported on a tax form called a 1099. Investors pay taxes on these distributions at year's end, but often forget to count these transactions as additional deposits to their investments. This oversight causes them to underestimate their cost and overestimate their profit. Tax is due on the profit and, if they think their profit is too large, they'll pay too much tax. Talk to your financial or tax advisor if you're unsure about figuring this important tax.

Don't Overpay the Traders

Consider trading costs when choosing a fund. There are two types of trading charges to watch for: commissions charged by the fund and transaction charges applied by the brokerage firm holding the account. If you're holding your account directly at the fund company, you won't pay the latter charge. Some funds can be purchased directly from the fund family itself without a sales charge, but others are only available through a commissioned broker. If you opt for the convenience of a brokerage account, your broker may charge a transaction fee over and above the commission he collects from the mutual fund. But, with the huge selection of available funds on the market there isn't much reason to pay this double charge. Ask the broker for a list of the funds in their no-transaction fee fund supermarket, sometimes called NTF funds, which are funds available without this additional fee. These funds may or may not also charge a commission themselves, but at least you are avoiding the extra fee at the brokerage level. Many NTF funds are also no-load funds. A fund with no sales load and no transaction fee can be especially attractive because they can be bought at effectively no cost at all!

The Incredible Index Fund

When it comes to investing inexpensively, the most frugal method of investing in the stock and bond markets could be the index fund. Index mutual funds are passively managed. An index fund's manager or management team purchases only the stocks or bonds contained in a particular market index. For example, in an index like the Nasdaq 100, a particular company might make up 4 percent of its stock holdings. An index fund trying to mirror the Nasdaq 100, then, would be sure to invest 4 percent of its assets in that stock. It would then buy stock in the other ninety-nine companies that make up the Nasdaq 100 index, again in the exact proportion as the index.

FACTS

Index funds will help reduce the time you spend managing your portfolio. Index funds are impervious to managers' whims or departure, and don't react every time a company listed in the index changes strategy. In the final analysis, index funds can be enormous timesavers.

If an index is very large, like the Wilshire 5000, where an index would have to buy stock in 5000 companies in order to exactly track it, an index fund might take a shortcut by purchasing a representative selection. But the idea is the same: Build a stock portfolio that exactly, or at least very closely, matches the performance of a market index. The managers don't try to beat the market by actively buying and selling the securities in their portfolio. They simply gather the index investments and get out of the way!

Index funds are useful in a personal portfolio because their passive management approach keeps trading expenses and taxes lower and limits style drift better than their actively managed cousins. The funds are more tax efficient because their buy-and-hold style limits trading activity, reducing capital gains distributions and keeping trading costs low. Style drift is limited because of the strict market index parameters the fund is mandated to follow. If the only stocks the management can buy are the ones in the index, it goes without saying that they can't change style by buying something else. Essentially, the managers are not making active buy and sell decisions, so they aren't in a position to succumb to market influences.

Exchange-Traded Funds

The American Stock Exchange created exchange-traded funds, or ETFs, to tap into a portion of the index-fund market. In essence, the American Stock Exchange created ETFs as baskets of the same securities tracked in a specific index, but not susceptible to the cash inflows and outflows of a mutual fund because they do not offer their shares directly to the public.

ESSENTIALS

Exchange-traded funds, like stocks, charge a commission for each purchase. If you're planning a dollar-cost averaging strategy in which you're investing a certain dollar amount per month, a mutual fund that carries no transaction fee or commission might be a better choice.

Because the selection of securities in these funds scarcely changes at all over time, and because the shares are traded among institutional investors rather than between a fund company and an investor, they incur almost none of the trading costs and tax obligations of index mutual funds. And as the icing on the cake, they pay none of the princely manager salaries that actively managed funds must pay. Because ETFs have lower expenses, and they don't hold a portion of their assets in relatively unproductive cash, as most mutual funds must, they are able to more closely mirror their target index than a mutual fund.

However, ETFs aren't without their detractions. That's because ETF shares are traded through the market among investors themselves. Being able to sell your ETF when you need to is not a certainty. ETF liquidity depends on the willingness of another investor to buy your shares. This isn't a concern with mutual-fund shares, because the fund company is required to buy back your shares any time you choose to sell them.

And while ETFs are traded throughout the trading day like stocks, enabling investors to take advantage of intraday price changes that are not available to investors in mutual funds—whose daily prices are only calculated at the end of each trading day—each ETF trade costs a commission, which may not be the case with a mutual fund.

Variable Annuities and Life Insurance

The insurance industry has also tried to get in on the money-management game by finding ways to serve individual investors looking for professional money management and diversification. Their answer to this market is the variable annuity and variable life insurance contract.

Variable Annuities: The Investor Takes the Risk

Variable annuities are different and more risky than the familiar fixed annuities. With a fixed annuity, a life insurance company promises that an investment will pay a specific rate of interest or grow at a particular rate, meaning that a few years later, the account can produce an income stream. But in the increasingly popular variable annuity, the investment risk is transferred to the investor. That means the investor must choose from a variety of investment accounts, which are managed like mutual funds by the insurance company, and the investor bears the risk of the future growth. Investors can change the accounts held in the annuity without paying any tax penalty because annuities are tax-deferred investments. In other words, you don't pay taxes on the annuity until you begin pulling income out of it.

ALERT

Pay close attention to the footnotes in the expense portion of the variable annuity prospectus. Sometimes managers will refund management expenses to fluff up sub-account performance. This refund is not guaranteed each year, and could deflate your investment performance, if skipped.

By tax law, annuities levy an annual life insurance charge that is one of the things that enables them to remain tax-deferred. This charge becomes a drag on the annuity accounts performance so that, all things being equal, an investment in a stock mutual fund will perform better than a variable annuity stock account. And if each account grew at the same rate, the mutual fund would incur less tax at sale because its gains are taxed as capital gains rather than the higher personal income–tax rates that apply to annuity withdrawals. And since annuities are tax deferred, they're an especially bad match for retirement accounts, which are already tax deferred without bearing the burden of extra insurance cost.

Variable Life Insurance

Variable life insurance policies work much the same as annuities in that the insurance company transfers the investment risk of the cash portion of the policy to the individual investor. The investor may be able to reduce the amount of their premium payment for the life insurance depending on the performance of the stocks and bonds they hold in their variable life sub-account, or they can continue to pay the same premiums and leave the cash account alone to grow. The investor can change the selection sub-account anytime without taking a tax hit that might occur with a mutual fund, ETF, or other investment outside of a retirement account.

And if any part of the cash value is needed, it can be borrowed against the remaining cash balance. The cash value may or may not increase the death benefit of the life insurance plan, depending on the features of your individual policy. If you need life insurance, this may be a good fit. But, as always when investing, scrutinize the fine print; if your accounts don't grow as expected, you could be forced to pay a higher premium to support the policy. So if the market is in a downswing, this might not be the time that you want to have to make this extra dollar commitment.

ESSENTIALS   If your insurance policy lapses before you repay a loan against your cash value, part of the loan can become taxable. Be especially careful when taking loans on your policy to avoid this wealth-robbing scenario.

Be sure you examine your need for insurance before making this commitment, and calculate the potential advantages of buying a less expensive term insurance policy and investing the premium savings. (See Chapter 6 for more on term insurance.) You may find that this strategy gives you greater flexibility and lower cost. If you're not sure how to make this comparison, ask your financial, tax, or legal advisor for help. They will either have the expertise you need or will be able to refer you to someone who does.

Folios

Folios are relatively new accounts that are a hybrid of mutual funds and ETFs. In fact, they are currently exempt from the investment rules that regulate other pooled accounts. Firms that offer folios create "prefabricated" investment portfolios that investors can buy "off the rack" rather than construct new portfolios from scratch. The investor can then customize the folio by buying new stocks or selling old ones. Most firms permit folio investors to buy or sell stocks as often or as seldom as they like, though generally not more than twice in a trading day. Since the investor has some choice of when to trade, they have better control over the tax implications of their investments and can control tax as well as transaction costs. Folio providers often offer cut-rate trades or annual-fee trading, which can also reduce trading cost.

Folios are generally a bit easier to manage than ETFs because they can be purchased in dollar lots like mutual funds rather than by shares like stocks and ETFs. That means an investor can dictate the exact sum of money they wish to invest, even if that amount doesn't divide evenly into a specific number of shares; like mutual funds, folios don't mind trading in fractions of a share.

Folios are a new beast in the financial services menagerie. There are still a number of unanswered questions about how they fit into investment portfolios. But for savvy investors who are willing to do their homework and uncover the virtues and vices of a particular folio, they may offer a good way to diversify their investment.

What Should Investment Advice Cost?

Good investment advice can be worth many times its cost; bad advice, no matter how cheap, can cost you many times the amount you save compared to more costly, and more sage, counsel. It's critical in building wealth that you understand the interests of the person or firm offering the advice, including the potentially hidden conflicts of interests. Don't be afraid to pay for a good, independent opinion of your investment plan, but always bear this in mind: You and you alone have the final say about your portfolio, and the responsibility for getting rich falls solely on your shoulders. Stay informed about all costs that are linked to your investments. Ask questions, read widely, and do your homework, and you will enjoy every step on the road to riches.

CHAPTER 12

Mapping a Sound Retirement Plan

Retirement planning is a very important part of your wealth plan. For most of us, a retirement that offers us the chance to do what we want, when we want to do it, is an important goal. Others love their life's work and want to continue doing it as long as possible, but prudently plan for financial security in case poor health or other circumstances intervene.

The Retirement Planning Worksheet

How much income do you need to make your post-career years comfortable and rewarding? What should be your nest egg goal to ensure future financial security? How much money must you save each month to reach that goal? This worksheet will help you find out. By using the time value of money principles you learned in Chapter 7, you'll be able to put specific numbers on your financial condition and future goals.

Take a minute to review the work you did in Chapter 2. What are your retirement goals? Do you plan to stop working completely upon retirement, or will you work at least part-time? Perhaps you hope to change jobs and do something you truly love, for less money. Are you planning to travel? Start your own business? With your retirement goals in mind, let's begin to craft your retirement plan.

This retirement worksheet serves as only a stepping-off point for your wealth plan. Your initial results are likely to be somewhat startling, although with careful review and adjustment you should ultimately arrive at a plan you can live—and grow rich—with.

Step 1: Describe Your Retirement Goals

Before you get to the charts and numbers, briefly describe your retirement goals:

_____

_____

_____

_____

_____

_____

Now, go back and rewrite your retirement expectations as specific and measurable goals. Review Chapter 2 to learn how to define your goals in a specific and measurable way, and then write them here:

_____

_____

_____

_____

Now that you've done that, this worksheet will help you with the second and third parts of your goal: making it realistic and making it achievable.

Step 2: Make Guesstimates

Much of wealth planning comes down to making four educated guesses about the future:

- **How long will you live in retirement?** It's critical that you're realistic in your planning and create enough financial security to remain in independent retirement for the rest of your life. Be sure to plan for a long life. If you retire in your early sixties you should plan to live thirty years or more in retirement. This worksheet assumes you will run out of money on the day you die—so plan for a few extra years to avoid cutting it too close.
- **How much will inflation average each year?** Inflation is the silent killer of retirement nest eggs. In the 1990s inflation started around 5.4 percent and fell to 2.3 percent in 2001. In order to err on the conservative side, assume inflation will remain at least equal to the current inflation rate plus 1 percent. If that number seems too low to you—or if you are planning a retirement that is a long way off— you might add 1.5 percent or even 2 percent.
- **What will your average annual investment return be?** For this part of the plan you'll need to make an assumption about the future growth of your investments that is not overly optimistic. Review what your

portfolio returned last year. Did you earn 5 percent? 25 percent? Did your portfolio shrink? Plan on earning less on your portfolio after retirement than you did while you were working to allow for rebalancing toward more income-generating investments that don't return as much. Subtract at least 2 percent from the portfolio growth assumption you used for your preretirement investments to better reflect this reality of slower growth after retirement.

- **How much income will you need each year in retirement?** It's a conservative approach to at least plan for the same income you spend now. Obviously, there will be expenses you bear while you're working or while your kids are young that will disappear when you retire, but these expenses may be replaced with new ones, such as travel and medical costs. Your investments will replace your paycheck. Some financial planners suggest that you plan for retirement income of 80 percent of your working income at the time you retire, which could be years in the future. We suggest you start with your current budget and make adjustments from there. Revisit this worksheet frequently and make adjustments to it as you approach your goal.

SSENTIALS

It's generally good retirement planning to cut out as many "fixed costs" as possible before retirement. With that in mind, you may want to plan to pay off your mortgage before you collect your gold watch, meaning that any extra mortgage principal you pay now toward your mortgage can be counted as retirement savings.

Fill in your assumptions here and circle each number to make them easier to return to as you progress through the worksheet:

1. How long will you live in retirement? _____ years
2. How much do you think inflation will average each year? _____ percent
3. What will your average annual investment return be before and after retirement? _____ percent before; _____ percent after
4. How much income will you need each year in retirement? $ _____ in today's dollars

Finally, state your retirement target: In how many years from now do you want to retire or change your lifestyle? _____ years

Step 3: Determine Your Sources of Income

Let's research how much of your retirement income will flow from each of your income sources: savings, part-time work, social security benefits, and pensions. Some income sources will be provided in future dollars (social security and possibly pension information) while others like part-time work and your actual income desired will be better expressed in current dollar terms. Be sure to keep these two types of numbers separate. We will show you how to properly account for them in a minute. Remember, the numbers generated here are only estimates. Accurate retirement planning considers many factors that are not dealt with in this worksheet. One of these factors is the effect of taxes on your retirement plan funds when they are withdrawn from your account. We'll talk more about these effects in Chapter 15, but please review the results on this worksheet with your financial or tax advisor as well.

What monthly income will you need in retirement? This is the same number you listed in the last question of step 2 above, then divided by twelve. $ _____ per month

How much monthly income will you earn during retirement from a job (part-time employment, new business, dream job, etc.)? If your retirement vision doesn't include working, leave this line blank. $_____ per month

How much retirement income will come from other sources that are not under your direct control, such as social security or an employer pension? Social security: $_____ per month; employer pension: $_____ per month; other: $_____ per month

(Your social security statement should arrive in the mail three months before your birthday every year. If you don't have a current statement, you may request one for free by going to the Social Security Administration web site ✍ *www.ssa.gov,* or by calling ✆ (800) 772-1213.)

Total your income sources that are expressed in today's dollars here: $_____ per month. For clarity, we'll call this income "A." Total your income sources that are expressed in future dollars here (be sure that all income sources are as of the same year): $_____ per month. This income amount will be referred to as income "B."

Subtract income A amount from your retirement income goal to get the first part of the income that you need to receive from your savings: $_____. Multiply it by twelve to get the annual amount: $_____. Circle both these numbers so you can come back to them easily as you complete the rest of the worksheet.

FACTS

Many retirees enjoy working part-time during retirement. They enjoy the contact with friends, the chance to learn new skills, and they find the extra income helps pay for some luxuries. Planning for a period of part-time work after your full-time career is over may help you retire earlier.

Step 4: Estimate Your Nest Egg

Now let's estimate the total retirement investment required to generate enough income to fuel your lifestyle. We'll call this amount your "nest egg target." Obviously, your nest egg is a very important part of your retirement plan because it is the one element that you have the most control over. The government controls social security, your employer controls your pension, but you control your savings, the source of your wealth power. After all, you're the one who decides how much to set aside for your nest egg. You decide where and how to invest it and, therefore, how large it will grow. This step will help you calculate how big your nest egg needs to be—at a minimum—to supplement social security and other income when you can retire.

Up to this point in the retirement planning worksheet we've been using today's dollars to describe your income. Now let's calculate the effect of inflation on your income from now to the time you retire. This will move your income estimate forward from today's dollars to the dollars that you will be spending at retirement. It will answer the question "What income will you need at retirement to support the lifestyle you have today?"

Refer to Future Value Factors Chart A from Appendix B to see the "factor" or multiplier by which any quantity will grow over time. This quantity could be almost anything: your income, your investments, or your retirement income goal, as in this example. Chart A lists years along the left-hand column and percentages along the top. In this example, the left column represents the number of years your retirement income goal will have to grow before you reach retirement; the percentages represent the average inflation rate per year. To use Chart A for this example, find in the left column the number of years between now and the time you plan to retire, then track across to the column for your assumed rate of inflation. Circle the number at the intersection of these two columns. Multiply your income A by this factor to calculate the new inflation-adjusted income. Factor _____ multiplied by target income in today's dollars $_____ equals income in future dollars $_____. Now, subtract your income B (income sources already adjusted for inflation) from this adjusted income amount. This new number is your income needed from investments, adjusted for inflation. Circle this new income target so it's easy to return to later.

For example, if you planned to retire in ten years, and you projected average inflation in those years of 4 percent, the equation would look like this: Growth factor **1.4802 × $60,000 = $88,812.** This means that, in ten years, with 4 percent average inflation, the lifestyle you support with $60,000 per year income will then cost $88,812 per year.

Inflation Adjusted Income in Retirement

Inflation, of course, will continue after you retire and will become even more critical once you're no longer working and receiving cost-of-living increases in your salary. The easiest way to calculate the right allowance for inflation's bite on your wealth during retirement is to assume that part of your nest egg's investment return will go toward providing you inflation-increased income and part of it will go toward growth for use in the future. The whole investment return cannot be used exclusively for income. For example, if your investments equal $1,000,000 and they are generating 5 percent growth of $50,000 per year, only part of that growth—say, closer to $38,500 if inflation is 4 percent—can be used as income. The remaining earnings must be reinvested so that the portfolio can continue to keep your income at pace with inflation.

Here's how this calculation works. Let's assume that you're planning for a 5 percent return on your investments and a 4 percent inflation rate. You won't be able to use that whole 5 percent return on your investments for income because part of that growth will have to be reinvested to counteract future inflation. By reducing your growth assumption to account for inflation, you will find the new investment-growth assumption will allow you enough of a nest egg from which you can draw an ever-larger income. The result of this calculation is the real rate of return on your investments. It's effectively the rate of return reduced to account for inflation, but there is also a compounding characteristic involved. The mathematical calculations to determine this compounding amount are quite detailed. For simplicity's sake, let's use a real growth rate that is simply the total growth rate, less inflation.

What the result means is that, if the investment return rate is 5 percent and inflation is 4 percent, then you should only assume a 1 percent return on your investments to provide income.

Use the following chart to summarize your assumptions and what you have calculated so far. If you've been circling your answers they should be easy to pull out of the earlier text:

NEST EGG ASSUMPTIONS

Target retirement year =	
Time in retirement =	years
Inflation =	percent
Average investment return =	percent
Annual income need =	in today's dollars
Income from part-time work or business =	in today's dollars
Income from social security =	in future dollars
Income from pension =	in future dollars
Income needed from savings (total income wanted in future dollars less social security and pension) =	in future dollars
Rate of return on your investments before retirement =	percent
Real rate of return on your investments after retirement (adjusted for inflation) =	percent

Predicting inflation is like trying to catch a falling knife, but planning to offset its effects is more feasible. Look for investments that grow with inflation, such as stocks, inflation bonds, and real estate, and be prepared to adjust your spending in the years that inflation is high.

Step 5: Figure the Nest Egg Target

This next section of this worksheet will help you estimate your target nest egg to provide the income from savings you'll need in retirement. First, turn to Present Value of Annuity Factors Chart B from Appendix B for the factor you need for this calculation. Find the number of years you'll be in retirement in the left-hand column, then track across to the column that represents your real rate of return. (Remember, this is not the full return you expect from your investments, but the return adjusted for the effects of inflation that we just calculated. Be sure to use the lower growth rate of your investments after retirement, not the higher preretirement rate.)

Circle the factor at the intersection of the year row and the percentage column and write it here: Factor from Chart B: _____.

Now simply multiply your desired annual income from investments by this factor to find your target nest egg: Desired annual income $_____ × Factor B _____ = Target nest egg: _____.

Let's take it step-by-step in an example:

- Years in retirement = 30
- Income from savings = $60,000 in today's dollars
- Income from savings = $202,000 in future dollars (31 years remaining until retirement, average 4 percent inflation)
- Real rate of return on investments = 1 percent (5 percent return, 4 percent inflation)
- Growth factor from Chart B (30 years, 1 percent real rate of return) = 25.8077
- Income from savings × 25.8077 = nest egg target
- $202,000 × 25.8077 = $5,213,000 = your nest egg target!

More than $5 million might seem like a huge number, but remember that it's expressed in future dollars. This is the actual amount of money you will need in your nest egg if you plan to retire in thirty-one years. In today's dollars, assuming 4 percent inflation, this would equal about $1,500,000—not quite the unreachable sum that $5 million seems to be.

Step 6: Determine How Much to Save Annually

This next part of the worksheet will help you determine how much to save on an average annual basis to meet your retirement goal. Since this number is an average, your actual savings will likely start below this target and move up over time to be above this target. For example, if the average savings needs to be $1,000 per month and you start at $750 per month and increase the amount over time so that by the end of ten years you were saving $1,250 your average should work out to $1,000 per month. This could work something like what is illustrated in this chart:

AVERAGE ANNUAL SAVINGS

YEAR	AMOUNT SAVED PER MONTH	YEAR	AMOUNT SAVED PER MONTH
1	$750	6	$1,028
2	$806	7	$1,083
3	$861	8	$1,139
4	$917	9	$1,194
5	$972	10	$1,250
Average			$1,000

The compounding power of money earning interest over time is a very potent force. If you plan to start with a savings budget that is below your average annual target, you must increase this savings as quickly as you can. If you wait too long to increase your savings, you may achieve your target average but the larger sums invested later will have far less buying power than if they'd been invested earlier, before value-robbing inflation took its toll.

Partway There

If you've already begun investing, you're partway to your goal and you won't have to save for your entire nest egg. Before you begin planning your savings budget, calculate how much your current retirement assets might grow by the time you retire. Here's how to calculate how much saving you have remaining when you factor in the investments you've already made:

First, look up the growth factor by which you're assuming your investments will grow from Future Value Factors Chart A in Appendix B. To find the factor, drop down the left column to the number of years remaining until retirement, then track across to the expected percentage return on your investments. Factor A _____

Now, multiply the amount of your current retirement savings by the growth factor you arrived at in the previous step to find the potential future value of your savings. Current savings $_____ × Factor A _____ = Potential future nest egg from current investments $_____

Your calculation might look similar to this:

- Growth factor from Future Value Factors Chart A (31 years until retirement, 7 percent investment return) = 8.1451
- Current investments of $30,000 x 8.1451 = $244,000, value in future dollars

That means your current investments of $30,000 are projected to grow to $244,000 in 31 years assuming 7 percent per year growth.

Now you try it:

Enter the value of your current retirement investments here:

$_____

Write the growth factor from Future Value Factors Chart A here:

_____

Multiply your current investments by the growth factor from Future Value Factors Chart A.

$_____ × _____ = $_____

This is the amount you have already saved toward your retirement.

Avoid the temptation to sell all stocks and move to bonds when you retire. This rapid change could prove a tax disaster. And your portfolio still needs to keep pace with inflation, something that stocks are better at accomplishing than bonds.

Step 7: Calculate the Amount You Have Left to Save

Now let's calculate how much more you need to save to reach your goal and how much per year, on average, you need to budget toward this savings. First, subtract the amount your current savings will grow to from your total nest egg target. This will give you the additional amount that you'll need to save. Nest egg target $_____ minus Estimate of future value of current saving $_____ = remaining amount to save $_____. Circle this figure because you will need it later.

When we do subtract this sample amount of current retirement savings from our sample target nest egg, we find that $3,716,000 remains to be saved, in future dollars: $3,960,000 – $244,000 = $3,716,000.

Now, divide this remaining amount by the factor from Future Value of Annuity Factors Chart C (see Appendix B) to discover the average annual savings to fill this nest egg gap. Chart C is read like all the rest of the charts. The left-hand column is the number of years until retirement. The top row is the expected growth rate per year from now until then. In our example we find: Remaining nest egg to save **$3,716,000** / Factor C **102.0730** = $36,405 target average savings per year.

This means that our retirement investor with thirty-one more years before retirement, and $30,000 already saved, needs to save an average of $36,405 per year for the next thirty-one years to reach a nest egg goal of $3,960,000. It might be possible to begin saving that much right away or some adjustments may be necessary first. What's most important is that saving begin right away. In Chapter 12 we'll look at some ways to accomplish this.

Now, you try it. Using your own retirement savings situation, calculate the average amount you need to save until retirement in order to reach this target nest egg.

Divide the amount remaining to be saved by the factor from Future Value of Annuity Factors Chart C. Factor C is found by dropping down the left column to the number of years until retirement, then tracking across to the expected percentage rate of return. (You're an old pro at these calculations by now!) Enter your figures here: Remaining nest egg to be saved $_____ /factor from Future Value of Annuity Factors Chart C _____ = required average annual savings $_____. Circle this number twice because it is the final result of this worksheet!

Some Things to Keep in Mind

Like anything that looks far into the future, predictions are far from guarantees. Here are some things to keep in mind about retirement planning and the figures you take away from this exercise.

• This worksheet only estimates what you should be saving towards your retirement or lifestyle-change goal, and will need to be reviewed and changed as you move towards that goal.

FACTS

Once you've made the rough calculations in this worksheet, you should consult with your wealth advisor for a custom-tailored retirement plan. After all, the worksheet is based on fixed assumptions and compounded growth. Your advisor should be able to project variable growth, inflation, and the number of years you're likely to be in retirement using what's known as a Monte Carlo simulation.

• The assumptions you select are critical to the accuracy of your results. If you overestimate your investment returns or underestimate inflation you may find—hopefully before you're uncomfortably close to retirement!—that you've saved too little, and, at the current savings rate, you're going to fall short of your needed nest egg when you retire.
• If the savings goal appears completely beyond your reach right now, don't despair. If you are more than fifteen years from retirement, you can start at a lower savings rate as long as you manage to ratchet up the savings rate over the next couple of years.

- If you are less than fifteen years from retirement and the retirement savings goal is out of your reach, consider adjusting your goal to make it more achievable. You can delay your retirement date and continue saving while you work a few more years or you can reduce the income you need from investments by either adjusting your budget or by working part-time during retirement.

A Wake-Up Call?

If the retirement worksheet in this chapter sets off a startling wake-up call, you're not alone. Many Americans have failed to adequately plan for retirement, thinking—probably mistakenly—that the social security system will offer a relatively lucrative retirement income. The fact of the matter is, social security is far from a sure bet, and the younger you are, the less certain it is that this safety net will offer a soft landing when you retire. The system is likely to undergo so many changes in coming years that it could be unrecognizable in decades to come, and its financial security is a matter of heated debate. The future uncertainty of this public assistance system mandates that you take your future security into your own hands. You pay many bills during the month, but the most important is for your retirement security—pay yourself first!

Ask yourself some sobering questions about the true value of your spending during your working years, when every dollar of lavish spending is a dollar that is not being saved and invested for retirement. The opportunity cost of the money that could be invested, but instead is vanishing in the form of luxuries or undeliberate expenses, can be staggering when looked at in terms of how much that money could add to your retirement nest egg in years to come if it were invested now. Is the second $2,000 vacation each year worth losing $82,000 of your retirement nest egg? Is the extra $400 per month lease on a luxury car worth more than $208,000 added to your retirement pool? Is the $70 per week you spend dining out worth over $158,000 of your retirement fund? Your answer to these questions might be "yes," but make sure your answer is an informed one, and that you are deliberate about spending money only on those things you truly value. Happy saving!

CHAPTER 13

Common Retirement Investment Plans

C hapter 12 started you on course by calculating your nest egg and savings goals. Now, we'll discuss where to invest those savings for the most potent return in line with your risk tolerance. In this chapter, we'll discuss common retirement investment vehicles such as Individual Retirement Accounts, 401(k)s, and Roth IRAs. You'll learn what distinguishes one type of account from another, and when you should select one over the others.

Why Is Retirement Saving So Important?

Social security is coming under increasing pressure from demographic trends that rely on a shrinking number of contributors to pay an exploding pool of recipients.

Remember, social security is a pay-as-you-go system rather than a pension-style program with an account for each participant. That means that the very money that comes out of your paycheck this month has been funneled directly into the hands of that elderly couple standing in front of you at the bank teller's window to cash their social security check. A pension system, by contrast, would invest your dollars now so they could be paid out years from now, having grown over the intervening years thanks to the leverage of its time value (see Chapter 7).

Social security's pay-as-you-go characteristic is what spurs some critics to label it a government-run Ponzi scheme, which is any investment that relies on the continued deposits by new subscribers to pay returns promised to earlier subscribers. Social security depends on this same premise. Later investors—or in the case of social security, today's workers—support the returns, or social security income, of earlier investors. At some point, the number of new investors diminishes. Under a true Ponzi scheme this happens because people lose faith in the pyramid and refuse to deposit money. Under social security, the pool of workers can diminish, leaving fewer depositors supporting an ever-growing pool of retirees.

Some officials have already conceded that the program is doomed by undeniable demographics—which show three workers will soon be paying the benefits for each retiree, compared to more than forty workers sharing the support of each retiree during the early decades of the Roosevelt-era program. By the program's own admission, by 2016 it will pay out more than it takes in. It seems clear that without significant changes, the social security trust funds will be exhausted by 2038.

So were does that leave you? Very possibly, responsible for your own retirement security without a dime of help from a government that might mean well but may not be able to pay benefits to all its citizens. Fortunately, the government has provided some of the tools you'll need to go it alone, thanks to certain tax-advantaged retirement plans.

Growing Wealthy by Delaying the Tax Man

Retirement investing has two parts: the investment itself and the "tax wrapper" or the account that cloaks the investment in a tax-advantaged haven. In earlier chapters, you learned about stocks, bonds, and pooled accounts. But these important wealth builders tell only half the story. The accounts that hold these investments tell the other half, because the federal government encourages retirement saving by offering tax breaks to long-term holdings if they are kept separate from other investments in accounts targeted only for retirement income. The separate packages to hold these investments are broadly called retirement accounts, and they're identified by a variety of acronyms and numbers.

Understanding this alphabet soup of investing and the maze of tax issues that surround them is critical to a strong retirement plan. Otherwise, valuable nest egg dollars could be lost to unnecessary taxes. Some rules affecting these plans change often and will likely continue to change as baby boomers retire in growing numbers.

Tax laws affecting retirement savings and retirement accounts change more frequently than you might imagine. The political clout of the aging baby-boomers will likely only encourage more change. Stay in close contact with your tax advisor to be sure you take advantage of all the wealth opportunities these laws have to offer.

There are several different types of plans that we'll look at here: employer-sponsored retirement plans called 401(k)s and 403(b)s; individual retirement accounts (IRAs); rollover individual retirement accounts (Rollover IRAs); retirement plans for self-employed workers and small companies called SEPs and SIMPLEs; Roth IRAs and Roth 401(k)s; and a plan for self-employed people called a KEOGH.

Taxes Make the Difference

Taxes are what differentiate retirement accounts from ordinary investment accounts. You may see retirement accounts referred to as tax-deferred accounts and regular investment accounts labeled as taxable accounts. In fact, the only thing that distinguishes the two types of accounts from each other is their tax status.

Both accounts can hold the same types of investments. Both can be moved from one investment manager to another. Both can be moved from one type of investment to another—i.e., from stocks to bonds or from mutual funds to exchange traded funds (ETFs). But both accounts are not taxed the same. In Chapter 16, you'll learn more about managing the taxes in your entire investment plan, taxable and retirement plans alike. But first, this chapter will pay special attention to retirement accounts and their tax benefits.

Retirement accounts, with a few exceptions, all share the same five tax characteristics:

- **Deferral.** Money within the account is protected from taxes unless it's withdrawn. The tax that's regularly due on realized capital gains (the profits on the sale of a successful investment), interest, and dividends are delayed until the money is withdrawn from the retirement account. Delaying taxes typically is a good wealth-building strategy because the money that would have been paid to Uncle Sam can remain invested. This deferral is one of the most powerful retirement account characteristics.
- **Withdrawal window.** Money withdrawn before age fifty-nine and a half incurs an extra 10 percent penalty. There are a few exceptions, as you'll see shortly. You must begin making withdrawals (again with some exceptions) when you are seventy and a half.
- **Earned-income requirement.** You must have earned income, or be the spouse of a worker, to make a deposit to a retirement plan. The "non-worker" retirement plan is called a spousal IRA. Your deposit is often deductible against income, so it's limited by the amount of earned income or the special deposit limit of the plan, whichever is less. We'll review each of these deposit limits later in the chapter.
- **Taxing withdrawals.** Withdrawals from retirement plans are taxed as regular income. This is an important consideration, because income-tax rates are higher than capital gains tax rates. We'll look at this more closely in Chapter 16.

- **Ownership.** Retirement plans can only belong to one person at a time—generally the worker—with one exception, the spousal IRA. The owner can name a beneficiary to receive the assets in their account when they die. This transfer takes place outside of a legal process called probate. Regular investment accounts can be owned by more than one person, or can be owned by a parent or other adult for the benefit of a child. If you name your spouse as beneficiary and die before withdrawing your money, your spouse can transfer the balance to an account in his or her name without paying tax.

FACTS

Probate is a legal process through which the court distributes your assets after your death. This is a public proceeding that many people seek to streamline through the use of trusts, among other things. But probate could also be a valuable part of the estate-closing process. Talk to your attorney about how to handle this controversial part of wealth transfer.

Employer-Sponsored Plans

Employer-sponsored retirement plans can be categorized into two basic types: defined contribution and defined benefit. Defined-contribution plans regulate the amount that you can contribute, or deposit, in a plan. Defined-benefit plans, often called pensions, specify the benefit, or income, provided by the plan at retirement.

When you retire, the balance in your defined-contribution plan is the sum of your deposits over the years plus the appreciation of your investments. They are what they are—big or small. Such plans place the burden for saving and investing on the employee.

On the other hand, in a defined-benefit plan the employer makes a commitment to pay a specific pension benefit—usually related to the employee's salary and years with the company. The employer, not the employee, is responsible for depositing enough to fulfill this promise. The employer is also responsible for choosing the investments in the account, and usually does so without input from the employee.

Because of the expense and risk associated with defined-benefit plans, many private employers have closed them in favor of offering less expensive, less risky defined-contribution plans. (Defined-contribution plans are less risky for employers because they shift the responsibility for saving and investing to the employee. That helps shield an employer from the risk of being sued by disgruntled workers, or having to deposit extra funds to support a promised benefit, in case the pension invest-ments perform poorly.)

FACTS

Plan ahead to pay off loans on retirement plans before you leave your employer or lose your job. The balance of unpaid loans is taxable if the remaining portion of the plan is rolled over or otherwise distributed.

If you work for the federal, state, or local government you may be covered by a pension. Many younger, private-sector employees prefer defined-contribution plans because they're portable, meaning they can be moved from one employer to another as the employee changes jobs. And, unlike pensions, which have little value until the employee reaches retirement, the defined contribution plan is worth more during the early years in the employee's career. The demographic and economic changes that have made the workforce more mobile are rapidly sending the security of a gold watch and a thirty-year pension the way of the dinosaur! (We'll tell you more about how to maximize your defined-contribution plan in Chapter 15.)

Defined-Contribution Plans: 401(k)s and 403(b)s

401(k)s and 403(b)s are the most powerful wealth builders in an employee's toolbox. They are offered by larger employers and get their names from the sections of the tax law that created them. 401(k)s are available to all corporate employees, while 403(b) plans are available only to employees of schools, nonprofit organizations, and other similar institutions.

The large deposit allowances that the law permits for 401(k) and 403(b) retirement plans, and the feature that allows companies to match a portion of their employees' contribution to the plans, make them a critical part of your wealth plan that cannot be ignored if you hope to get rich. In addition to the five characteristics listed above, these plans share these features:

- **Tax savings.** Deposits are allowed up to a specific percent of your salary—say 15 percent, or a maximum of $11,000 per year before tax— which means your taxable income is reduced by that amount, which translates into tax savings. This defers the tax on that income until it's withdrawn (hopefully at retirement, and not before). The current maximum dollar limits will gradually adjust upwards over time so that inflation doesn't eat up too much of the retirement savings benefit.
- **Borrowing allowed.** Workers are permitted to borrow against their account if they want to buy their first home, pay education expenses, medical bills, or in case of some emergencies.
- **Catch-up deposits.** Workers over age fifty are allowed to make additional "catch-up" deposits beyond the normal contribution limit.
- **Employer match.** Employers are provided the opportunity to match contributions to the employee's account as an incentive to participate in the plan or as a general business incentive sometimes called a profit-sharing contribution. Employers can choose to deposit this usually annual contribution to employee's plans regardless of whether the company posts a profit that year.
- **Fifteen percent and beyond.** Offer employees an option to make additional after-tax contributions to their plans if they want to go beyond the 15 percent and $11,000 limit.

Employer Option

In 401(k) and 403(b) plans, the employer selects the investment firm that will manage the employee's accounts and handle the logistics of deposits and withdrawals. Employees choose their investments from a pool of choices picked by the employer, and can generally change those choices on a regular basis. Some plans allow daily changes in investment choices, although a smart wealth builder knows better than to succumb to the temptation to time the market.

Some employers are now offering an individual brokerage account option to employees who want to choose their own investments rather than settle for the choices offered by the company. This brokerage account is part of the employee's 401(k) or 403(b), but the employee himself chooses the investment. Examine the expenses on this option to be sure they don't outweigh the benefit of choosing other investments; the ones picked by your employer may be just fine.

ALERT

Complete your ex-employer's retirement plan distribution paperwork with special care. Whether you wish to transfer your funds to your new employer's account, roll them over into a personal IRA, or withdraw them altogether, you could suffer unintended results—and unintended tax consequences—if the paperwork is completed incorrectly.

401(k) and 403(b) plans offer employees the most tax-deductible bang-for-the-buck. As a part of your plan to get rich, it's very important that you participate in your employer's plan. If your employer doesn't offer one, or doesn't match at least some of your contributions, encourage it to do so right away. If your employer offers a plan, it's important to understand that the wealth-building power of these defined contribution plans is so potent that, at the very least, you should be investing the amount your employer matches. Think of it this way: This match is free money, but if you don't contribute, there's no way for you to collect it.

When you leave your employer you can take your account with you, but the dollars must remain in some type of retirement plan or you will owe income taxes and a penalty payment on the amount you withdraw. You may either transfer your account to your new employer's plan or you may roll it over to a personal account called a rollover IRA. We'll look at the logistics of this in a minute.

Individual Retirement Accounts and Rollover IRAs

Individual retirement accounts, known as IRAs, are available to anyone with earned income, and their spouse. Depending on your income you may be able to deduct your deposit, but even if not, that doesn't mean these are not good accounts.

Each spouse of a worker can also open his or her own individual retirement account in addition to and separate from the worker's account. They each can deposit an amount equal to the greater of their combined earned income or $ 3,000 each (starting in tax year 2002). So if the wife works and makes more than $6,000, both husband and wife can deposit the full $3,000 into their own plans. Remember the earnings in these accounts grow tax-deferred, meaning they aren't taxed until you withdraw them when you retire. That's what makes these accounts such favorites with wealth builders.

ESSENTIALS

Good wealth planners make it a point to contribute to their IRA each year, whether they earn a tax deduction for it or not. And they begin early. With the power of compound interest, depositing $2,000 per year for even the first few years of your working life can result in a significant addition to your future nest egg.

If you don't have a retirement plan through your employer, you are also eligible to deduct the amount of money you contribute to your IRA each year. If your employer provides a plan, your deduction will be phased out based on your income. The income limitations on this change yearly, but for tax year 2002 single folks will start losing their deduction at $34,000 per year income. Married couples filing jointly will start to lose theirs at $54,000. This loss of the deduction shouldn't stop you from saving, though. The account will still grow tax-deferred regardless of whether it was initially deductible. For retirement tax management purposes it's important to keep separate accounts for your tax-deductible and non-deductible contributions. You certainly don't want to pay a double tax on your withdrawals.

Guarding Against Overtaxation

Let's look at how this works. Deductible contributions to an IRA have not yet been taxed. This is because you were allowed to deduct them on your tax return. Non-deductible contributions have already been taxed.

This is because you paid them from your after-tax income and weren't allowed to deduct them on your return. When you withdraw these non-deductible contributions from your IRA you don't owe income tax because the tax has already been paid.

Be diligent with your record keeping, unless you don't mind Uncle Sam scooping up more than his fair share of your money. If you mix the types of deposits in these two types of retirement accounts, you might not be able to remember which contributions you paid tax on and which you didn't. You run the risk of overpaying your taxes when you make withdrawals from your retirement accounts. And nothing erodes wealth faster than paying too much tax!

Portable Plan

As we mentioned, if you leave your employer you have the option to take your 401(k) or 403(b) plan assets with you. You can redeposit them in your new employer's plan or into one of your own, called a Rollover IRA. Since this money is from an employer's plan it is called qualified money to set it apart from the money you might deposit in your own plan, which is called unqualified money or an unqualified plan. In fact, "Rollover IRA" is often printed right on your account statement to help differentiate these special accounts from regular IRAs. Since the Rollover IRA is under your control, you can choose your own investments. If your new employer offers a qualified plan whose investments you prefer, you can transfer the Rollover IRA dollars back into that employer's qualified plan, or you can continue with the Rollover IRA.

ESSENTIALS

If you're married, your spouse will be asked to acknowledge your request to transfer assets out of your employer's retirement plan. This acknowledgment often needs to be notarized to be valid. As a spouse, be sure you're aware of where these assets are going.

But be careful! You can only transfer money back into a qualified plan if all the money in the Rollover IRA is qualified. If you "taint" the Rollover IRA with "unqualified" money that you deposited yourself, outside of your employer's plan, you won't be able to redeposit it into a qualified plan. Past tax laws have made it smart to keep as much money as possible in qualified plans. Check with your advisor to see if this is the case with your plan.

Self-Employed Retirement Plans and Plans for Small Employers

The government offers special plans to assist small employers and self-employed people with their retirement savings. These plans are "turbocharged" IRA accounts that don't have the expensive administrative fees of 401(k) plans and still allow workers to invest more than the small IRA limit. These plans are called Simplified Employee Pension plans, or SEPs, and Savings Incentive Match Plan for Employees of Small Employers, or SIMPLEs. If you're self-employed—or have self-employment income from a second job or business—you can contribute to a SEP or a SIMPLE in addition to your 401(k) or 403(b) contribution. The SEP or SIMPLE contribution limit is based on your self-employment income.

What Is a SEP?

SEP plans allow the employer to deposit up to 15 percent of the employee's salary or $24,000, whichever is lower, into the employee's IRA account each year. The employee may choose the investments in the SEP and the place where the SEP is established—bank, mutual fund companies, and brokerage firms are the most common choices.

QUESTIONS?

Who is a sole proprietor, and what retirement options does he or she have?
A business owner becomes a sole proprietor if he or she makes no election to be a corporation or a partnership. A sole proprietor may or may not have employees, and has many choices of retirement plans available to them beyond the individual IRA account.

When you leave a job, your SEP goes with you. If you earn self-employment income, you can continue contributing to the SEP—or if you go to a new employer who has a plan, your SEP can accept contributions from that employer. The SEP is the employee's IRA—other than making the deposits, the employer doesn't have any say about what the employee does with the account. If you are a sole proprietor who runs a business without any other employees, you might choose a SEP as your retirement plan because it has a higher contribution limit than a regular IRA and a SIMPLE. Since a sole proprietor is the employer and the employee, he or she is making the deposit from the profits of the business. The contributions to a SEP are tax deductible.

What Is a SIMPLE?

Think of SIMPLE plans as 401(k) plans for small companies. They allow employees to make contributions that are matched by the employer rather than requiring the employer to make the full contribution. The employee can contribute up to $6,500. Since the employer has a flexible match, they must be sure all employees, not just the owner or highly paid employees, are treated equally. They can do this under two different formulas. One formula requires them to make deposits equal to 2 percent of each employee's pay (those participating in the SIMPLE as well as those who are not) into their accounts, or they can match with 3 percent of employees' salaries into participating employees' accounts. Since not all employees participate—although they should—many employers follow the matching formula instead of the guaranteed 2 percent deposit. If your employer does this, be sure to participate. Hey, it's free money!

Roth IRAs and Roth 401(k)s

Roth IRAs—and their counterparts, Roth 401(k)s—are the best retirement planning deal Uncle Sam has offered in a long time. Named after the senator who proposed them, they are like the regular IRA, but with two differences: non-deductible deposits and tax-free withdrawals.

Like regular IRAs, the maximum you can deposit into a Roth IRA in 2002 is $3,000. If you're over fifty, you can deposit an additional catch-up amount of $500 for a total of $3,500 (minus any amounts deposited to your regular IRA) into a Roth account. The deposits are not deductible, but when you withdraw the earnings at retirement, they're not taxed, as long as your Roth has been open for at least five years. What a wealth-creating deal!

Unlike regular retirement accounts, whose earnings are taxed as income when you withdraw them, withdrawals from Roth accounts are tax-free. Not only are you deferring taxes, you are actually avoiding them. Uncle Sam doesn't allow that very often!

Predictably, because these accounts are such good deals, they have some restrictions. Most importantly, if you are married and filing a joint tax return and your adjusted gross income (AGI, which is basically your income after a few conditions are met) is more than $160,000, you are not eligible to make a deposit. This ineligibility starts to phase in at $150,000, so, for example, if your AGI is $155,000 you may only deposit one-half the annual limit into a Roth IRA. If you're single, this phase-out starts at $95,000 AGI and you become completely ineligible at $110,000 AGI. These limits may change, so be sure to check current rates.

FACTS

Unlike regular IRAs, there's no rule forcing you to withdraw money from a Roth, so the growth on the investments in your account can be continued tax-free for some time. With proper estate planning, Roth IRAs can passed to beneficiaries.

Otherwise, the investments for Roth IRAs are the same as other IRA accounts and, like rollover IRAs, they must be kept separate from your other accounts in order to preserve the tax-free nature of the earnings. Roth 401(k)s are essentially identical to Roth IRAs, but are managed like 401(k) accounts and are offered through employers.

Roth IRA Conversions

If you already have a regular IRA or a Rollover IRA account, and would like to take advantage of the tax-free growth in a Roth, you can transfer your money to a new Roth IRA in any tax year that you make less than $100,000. This rollover money shouldn't be combined with your other Roth account that you've been regularly contributing to. This could be a good opportunity to save taxes on the future growth of the account but the up-front tax hit may not be worth it. The money you use to pay the taxes could have been invested, so it's important to calculate the future value of this tax money before deciding to convert.

Keogh Plans

If you're self-employed and you'd like to deposit more than a SEP or SIMPLE will allow, you can open a Keogh plan. Keogh plans use the same investments as other retirement plans but have much higher maximum contribution limits. This type of plan is more expensive to administer because the contribution amount varies based on your business success and must be calculated each year. And you may have to file a separate tax return called a 5500 for the plan. But the increased tax savings on the extra deposit may be worth it. Ask your financial advisor for details on whether this plan is right for you.

CHAPTER 14

Staying on Track with Your Wealth Plan

W ealth planning is not a project that can be done once, and then forgotten. As your life changes, you must review and adjust your plan, or risk veering off track. A wealth plan is never cast in stone. Your finances are always moving and changing. New opportunities come and go. Tracking and perfecting your wealth plan isn't rocket science, but it does take some smarts and a little effort.

The Forgotten Key to Wealth

Investors often neglect the crucial final step of reviewing and adjusting their investments, as it becomes inconvenient to keep up with the plan. Sometimes, this neglect stems from an investor's fear that he might fail to manage his portfolio toward wealth, or a perception that his finances will grow beyond his ability to manage them. Sometimes it's plain and simple complacency that keeps would-be wealth builders from the important work of tracking and refining their investment plan.

Rich people are meticulous about reviewing their plan and making adjustments. And these adjustments are typically relatively simple and straightforward. Often, a review of your wealth plan is nothing more than just that, a review, with no adjustments needed. In fact, if you're reviewing your progress on a fairly regular basis—say monthly or quarterly—you may find that the adjustments you make are so small they take virtually no time or effort.

FACTS

Typically, when folks receive a raise, a bonus, or some other windfall, they automatically adjust their spending upwards without realizing it. A regular budget review will spotlight these spending changes and enable you to make adjustments before ill-advised spending patterns become habits.

In a wealth plan, time does indeed equal money. If you have a lot of time before your retirement, you can afford to save slowly. If you have less time, you'll have to save more aggressively. But without a regular review you'll miss the chance to make small corrections to your plan. By the time you realize you're off course, the needed corrections might be very large and you might not be able to afford to make them! Different parts of your plan should be reviewed at different times, as we'll discuss in the following sections.

Budgets and Cash Flow

Budgets and cash flow should be reviewed monthly or bimonthly. If you're diligent in monitoring how much money comes in and goes out of your wallet each month, you'll be able to keep a tidy check register and accurate bank records, not to mention easing the sometimes-daunting task of tracking down missing transactions. What's more, you'll be more likely to discover bank or credit card errors before they get out of hand. And you'll be able to adjust your own spending before you and your family squander too much cash in "non-deliberate" spending.

Investment Accounts

Investment accounts should be examined each month to reconcile transactions, but the investments themselves generally don't need to be reviewed more frequently than once a quarter. Since most mutual funds only report their holdings semiannually, it's difficult to make adjustments more frequently than that. But portfolios should be reviewed for balance and to make sure they're hitting your target asset allocation, especially if you're making regular contributions. You may not necessarily decide to sell a position in favor of another, but you might adjust where you are making your regular deposits.

FACTS

In its simplest form, a stock option is the right to buy or sell a stock at a certain price. "Buy" stock options are "in the money" when the market price is higher than the option price, meaning if you were to exercise your option, you could quickly sell the stock and make a profit. If the option price is higher than the market price, the option is "underwater."

Short-Term Goals

Short-term goals, cash position, and expected large cash outlays should be assessed at least three times every year. You may find that you're saving for one large payment—for example, a new roof on your home or a down payment on a new car—but that your plans are derailed by an emergency replacement of a household appliance, for instance, or unexpected medical bills. By deliberately reviewing and discussing with family members any potential upcoming large expenses, you can better manage your emergency fund and cash position and head off much of the "it's-always-something" syndrome that can be so damaging to a long-term savings plan. If you feel like you can't get ahead because these major expenses seem to continually surprise you, you may be hesitant to save for the long term, and that could cause you to fail to achieve your long-term goals.

Tax Planning

Tax planning should be reviewed at least once during the tax year—well before the year is over. It doesn't do any good to wait until after New Year's Day to visit your tax preparer and discuss your tax plan. (We'll talk more about tax planning in Chapter 16.) If you wait past January 1, it could be too late to make tax-saving transactions that must be made during the tax year. If your tax circumstances are particularly complex—for example, if you receive employee stock options or are self-employed—you may already visit your tax accountant more frequently through the year. Your accountant will prepare a tax projection for you at mid-year to project what your tax situation may be at year's end. With this projection they can make suggestions that will help you adjust your plan.

Estate Planning

Estate planning should be reviewed every two to three years, and whenever anything significant happens to alter your life situation, such as a birth or death in your family or a change in your marital status. Without this kind of review, your plan may no longer reflect your wishes, and it may not take into account changes in the tax and estate laws. If estate laws change, as they may do for the next few years, you may find it helpful to give your lawyer a call for a review of how the changes could help you or hurt you.

An estate planning review needn't involve an expensive meeting with your lawyer. On your own, you can pull out your estate documents and check that the beneficiaries, executors, trustees, powers of attorney, and health care proxies you've named are still the ones you would prefer. (We'll talk about more about these roles in Chapter 18.) Also check that you've listed second choices for all of these vital roles in case your first choice is unavailable or unable to serve. If you have questions you can contact your estate lawyer and they'll be able to determine whether the question warrants a formal office consultation.

Insurance

Insurance plans should be reviewed annually. A quick call to your agent for a review will generally not cost any money unless you need more coverage. A review of your homeowner's, umbrella, and automobile coverage may reveal that the limits need to be increased because of inflation or because of a change you've made to your home or property. Your disability insurance might need to be adjusted to fit a new job with higher pay or higher monthly expenses. Life insurance might need to be expanded to provide coverage for new children or a spouse who has stopped working, or reduced after a child leaves home or you retire.

With a regular review, you'll be sure that nothing gets missed and no needed coverage is overlooked. Remember, when it comes to insurance, you must stay a step ahead of the unexpected: Once you've had a loss, you can't turn back the clock and buy coverage. For example, once your health has deteriorated, you can't then buy life, disability, or long-term care insurance as easily or as cheaply as when you were in the pink. A regular insurance review will protect the wealth you are working so hard to build, and ultimately save you money.

Look at the Big Picture

While you should be reviewing each part of your plan at various intervals as we just discussed, don't get so caught up in the details that you don't occasionally take a broader perspective and review the purpose of your wealth plan in the first place. Even after you've started on your course to wealth, continue to add to your wealth journal. Write about how you feel about your plan, your lifestyle, and the progress you are making. Write about the obstacles you've run up against and how you conquered them. When you're feeling uncertain about a financial decision, or are up against a challenge that seems insurmountable, thumb through your wealth journal and revisit your goals and your achievements thus far. You may find you come away reinvigorated, with new strength and commitment to your plan.

Changes and adjustments to your wealth plan will continue even after you have retired. To maintain your wealth and to continue to build financial security, you must review your goals and make adjustments. You may find after years of retirement that you don't enjoy the same things you did when you were working. You may decide to indulge a new hobby, open a business, or get a new job. All of these things will affect your plan. You may even find yourself rebuilding your plan completely once you retire.

Managing Your Wealth During Retirement

Saving and investing for retirement can be a lot of fun. Even the ups and downs of the stock and bond markets and the cycles in your portfolio can hold fascination when you are many years from retirement. But the tables are turned, and the volatility loses its charm, when you have to rely on your investments for income.

Managing your wealth and making investment and asset allocation decisions in the years approaching retirement is an important part of your wealth plan. Good decision-making at this time is critical to avoid big losses in your portfolio as you approach retirement, though not as critical as when you're already retired. When you're working, you have the choice of delaying retirement to recover from a bad investment decision. It may not be your favorite option, but in a pinch, you really could work just one more year. But once you've been out of the workforce for a few years, it's not so easy to get back in it, and it could take much longer to generate enough income to make up for a wealth-planning mistake.

Managing your portfolio in retirement is a bit trickier than when you're working because the stakes are higher. Let's look at some of the most common mistakes.

Optimistic Expectations

The best situation for a content retirement is to be so rich, to have such a large nest egg, that you don't have to take any risk whatsoever to meet your income goals. If everyone had such a nest egg, one that they only had to invest in perfectly safe savings accounts and government bonds, every investment advisor would be put out of business! Unfortunately, not everyone has such wealth, so people need to make assumptions about the growth rate of their investments and take risks even in retirement.

What's the best substitute for an impossibly massive nest egg? Strive for the lowest, most conservative rate-of-return assumption you reasonably can, and save the biggest possible nest egg. The lower the rate-of-return assumption you use in forecasting your investment returns, the lower will be the risk that you'll be unable to maintain your lifestyle. Betting that sky-high return rates of 10 percent or 12 percent on a portfolio will continue through a thirty-year retirement—even if it's been earning that kind of return for the past few years—is irrational and very risky. If you start spending money early in your retirement on the assumption your investments can sustain that kind of outrageously optimistic growth, you may erode your nest egg to such a point that even high-risk investments won't help you recover from an economic downturn.

ALERT

Don't necessarily wish for high interest rates on your bonds. After all, a 13 percent bond in a 10 percent inflation period is no better than a 4 percent bond in a 1 percent inflation period. Look for your bond portfolio to stay marginally ahead of inflation and disregard the bare numbers.

Remember that the "risk-free" rate of return, the one that you should be able to count on, year in and year out and without a lot of risky investments, is about 4 to 5 percent. If inflation is 4 percent, this translates into a real return rate of only 0.96 percent. This means that your portfolio's growth will just barely stay ahead of inflation, so taking some risk is necessary even in retirement. But don't make assumptions that require you to take too much. If you're planning for average inflation of 4 percent, your investment return assumption should be no more than 3 percent than that or 7 percent.

Clearly, investment return rates fluctuate with inflation. As inflation increases, the return rates on bonds and cash should increase as well. By mixing inflation-hedged bonds—like government inflation bonds, treasuries, and agencies—with a small proportion of stocks, you should be able to achieve an asset allocation that controls volatility while outpacing inflation. Compare your portfolio's growth rate to the rate of inflation to see how well you're doing. Plan to stay ahead of inflation by at least 2 to 3 percent. When you review your investment returns, look not only at the overall return but also at how well you are staying ahead of inflation. For example, your return might be 14 percent but if inflation is also 14 percent—admittedly, not a very likely scenario!—you're not making any progress. Even a comparatively low return like 5 percent can be good in a year in which inflation is 2 percent.

FACTS

The U.S. Treasury Department borrows money from the public by selling treasury bonds, notes, and bills. They differ mostly in their maturity: Treasury bonds mature in ten years or more; treasury notes in one to ten years; and treasury bills, or "T-bills," in either three months, six months, or one year.

Experienced retirement advisors are practiced in making assumptions about retirement income, investments, and inflation. It's often worthwhile to get an outside opinion or two when making decisions about something as critical as your lifelong financial security.

Underestimating Lifespan

Don't underestimate the number of years you'll live in retirement. You may spend as much time spending money in retirement as you spent earning it and saving it—maybe more! Even rich people must sometimes look for ways to stretch the retirement dollars they worked hard to accumulate.

Retirements are now lasting longer as people retire earlier and live longer. You may retire at age fifty-five and still have a forty-year investment time horizon as your health enables you to live well into your nineties. You may decide to work part-time to reduce your early dependence on your nest egg. In this case you'll have to plan your asset allocation strategy accordingly, but with less risk than you took while you were working at your career.

Plan your expenses with long life in mind. Allow yourself more flexibility by not entering retirement with a lot of debt, such as a big mortgage, a home equity loan, credit card balances, and the like. Get these things cleared up before you retire so you can enjoy yourself and not feel captive to inflexible expenses.

Could You Outlive Your Wealth?

Reviewing and managing your assets and portfolio risk in retirement could take on lifesaving proportions should you run the risk of outliving your wealth. Pay close attention to the health of your nest egg as you progress through retirement. You might even want to develop a new hobby in your golden years: inflation watching.

SSENTIALS

To avoid overspending and outliving your retirement nest egg, plan each year how much you can afford to spend (you may want to check with your financial advisor), then set up your retirement account to send one-twelfth of this annual income directly to your checking account each month. Spend only this amount and keep your nest egg safe.

The federal government regularly reports inflation as the "consumer price index," or CPI. This number is used by regulators to adjust social security payments and the interest rate on "inflation bonds" called I-bonds. Many companies and state governments use the CPI to adjust pension payments and wages. But the CPI does not tell the whole story. It is a broad measurement that encompasses a large number of products in the economy, but it may not represent anything close to the actual buying habits of you and your family. Your family's medical expenses, rent, condominium fees, real estate taxes and other housing expenses, gasoline, car repairs, groceries, travel expenses, and other regular payments may actually increase each year by a factor greater than that reported by the government's

CPI number. If you're comparing your portfolio's growth to the CPI, you may be underestimating the influence on your financial security of your personal inflation rate and long life.

The solution is to take a close look at your family's spending and track the gradual increase in the cost of those daily necessities. Do this every couple of months, or whatever suits your habits. Determine your own cost of living index, then judge your portfolio's performance and growth against it and change your asset allocation or spending habits accordingly with an eye towards longevity.

Inadequate Insurance Coverage

Once you're retired, just as when you were still working, you can choose whether to retain a risk or transfer it to an insurance company. When you're relying on maintaining your income and nest egg in retirement, risk management becomes even more important. A little foresight can make the difference between a comfortable, carefree retirement and a money-troubled one.

QUESTIONS?

How do I make insurance decisions when I'm surrounded by salespeople?
Trained advisors can help you for a fee, meaning they're not shackled to sales quotas and commissions. Look for the designation "Licensed Insurance Counselor" or "Licensed Insurance Advisor," depending on the state you live in.

Medical expenses can be a large drain on your retirement wealth. Of course you'll be healthier—and spend less on medical care—if you take care of yourself before you retire, as well as after, by eating right and getting regular exercise. To help protect against the health hazards you can't prevent, be sure you have strong insurance coverage. Federal Medicare part A coverage is provided to everyone beginning at age sixty-five. Purchase a supplemental part B policy and consider a "medi-gap" policy to pay deductibles and some expenses that Medicare doesn't.

To protect against long-term health care expenses, earmark some of your retirement nest egg, or purchase a long-term care insurance policy. If you're not rich enough to set aside $300,000 to $400,000 for medical care, consider purchasing a policy that would essentially do the same thing for you. For a simple premium, you can purchase coverage that would protect some of your nest egg against these potentially catastrophic medical expenses.

Make sure your life insurance is paid up, or decide whether there's any need to carry it at all. If you have accumulated enough of a nest egg to support you and your partner in retirement, you may not need to continue paying life insurance premiums. Check Chapter 6 for a more in-depth discussion about the use of life insurance. You may decide to keep a policy to create an inheritance for a child who is not receiving a family business, for instance, or to protect a disabled child if you die. By planning ahead, these policies can be funded while you're working so they don't become a burden when you retire.

Changing Investment Types: Are Bonds Really Best?

As we've mentioned, the best retirement scenario is to have such a large nest egg and frugal lifestyle that you can retire by taking no greater risk with your investments than you would with a passbook savings account. Most of us are not that fortunate, even though we should strive to be. Obviously, the less risk you must take in order to generate sufficient income from your retirement portfolio, the safer you'll feel.

Most retirement nest eggs still must not only stay one jump ahead of inflation once their owners retire, but they'll also have to actually continue growing. This kind of growth can really only be found in stocks—but how large a stock allocation is appropriate, and when should you make adjustments?

Over the long term, stocks have returned far more than bonds, albeit with a higher degree of volatility. From January 1, 1975, to December 31, 1999, stocks in the S&P 500 stock index returned, on average, 14.67 percent per year, while bonds in the Lehman Brother's Aggregate Bond Index, during the same period, returned 10.32 percent. But, stocks were a lot more volatile. Over this period, their best year was 1995, when they returned 34.11 percent; but in 1981, their worst year, stocks lost 9.73 percent.

Bonds may not have averaged as high a return. In their best year, 1982, they returned 32.62 percent. But they haven't lost as much either. In 1994, their worst year, they only lost 2.92 percent.

ESSENTIALS

Asset correlation applies to how alike the performances of two assets are. If two stocks are positively correlated, they move up and down together. If they're negatively correlated, they move in opposite directions to each other, one gaining while the other loses value. In the real world, nothing's perfect, but strive for negative correlation in your portfolio.

To manage the risk of both a market downturn (in which your stock holdings could lose value) and the chance of rising inflation (against which your bond holdings could lose value), you must mix the two types of assets. But, though there will be less volatility, owning all bonds after retirement is no better an idea than owning all stock before it. By strategically mixing the two asset classes in your portfolio, under a theory called "negative correlation," you can reduce the overall risk of your portfolio without significantly reducing return. The mathematical calculations to determine negative correlation are too complex to go into here, but simply put, they underscore the importance of selecting a range of investments in which some should rise in value when others are in decline.

Your investment advisor will be able to calculate these correlations and advise you how much stock and how many bonds—and what type of each—to hold in your portfolio. This calculation and advice is one of those things that are best left to the professionals. We'll talk in Chapter 17 about how to find an advisor to help you. In the end, you'll be surprised what a wealth-building difference the dependable payments of bonds can make to reduce the gyrations of your portfolio.

Long-Term Investing in a Changing Economy

The time you spent developing your financial goals and creating your wealth plan was very important. This careful preparation will help you stay on course through the storms and distractions between now and the day you reach your goal. Too often, investors are drawn off course by promises of easy money, or chased away from a successful plan by warnings of failure.

The hard work of creating a budget and savings plan and researching investments can be utterly nullified if an investor has a wandering eye. Don't be drawn off course by magazine articles or television business programs that promise the "the five best stock picks of the season" or "the fifty best mutual funds of the fourth quarter." The short-term outlook of these kinds of suggestions is a sure warning sign: Wealth-robbing advice ahead!

Investors who continually shop for bargains in clothes and gifts seem to lose their bargain-hunting instincts when buying stocks. Don't fall into the "best of last year" trap. After all, a store advertising "All merchandise marked up 40 percent over last year" won't attract many buyers, so don't fall for costly stock markups just to "wear" the latest fashions.

True, the stocks might be top performers and the mutual funds may have produced superb results, but reacting to lurid headlines and breathless declarations is no way to build a sturdy, long-term portfolio. Choosing investments is a methodical process, but an investor with adequate experience can find it a challenging and rewarding pursuit.

The satisfaction of building a sound, though perhaps unspectacular, portfolio is driven home as you watch "active traders"—those who generally chase hot stocks with an eye toward timing the market's swings—suffer through stomach-churning rises and tailspins in the value of their fashion-driven portfolio. Stick to your plan, be frugal, and enjoy your slow, inevitable progress toward your goal.

CHAPTER 15

Finish Line: At Last, You're There!

I t's time to put the finishing touches on your wealth plan by discussing how to measure and manage your success once you've achieved it and how to make that important decision to finally retire. You'll also discover ways to contribute to the social causes that are important to you through charitable giving, and how to manage your money after you're gone for your children's benefit.

Measuring and Managing Success: Knowing When to Retire

Deciding when and how to retire can be one of the most momentous decisions you'll ever make. For many of us, our careers, as satisfying as they may be, are a means to an end. Our ultimate goal is to be able to put work behind us so that we can spend years pursuing those interests that we developed as we matured.

Now, you're making decisions to cut yourself off from a way of life and an income stream that you enjoyed for decades. There's one crucial piece of advice that you should heed at the outset: Take it slowly.

Planning Your New Lifestyle

All too often workers retire to a weekend lifestyle that leaves them bored and wanting for challenge. While you're working, develop the hobbies and outside interests that will make your retirement as fulfilling as your job. Seven days a week of nothing but golf may sound good now, but it could get tiresome pretty fast when it's the only thing in your date book. Remember, you could be retired for thirty years or more! Plan to make the most of it.

FACTS

There's no rule that says people have to stop working. You may find that the transition lifestyle of part-time work or consulting and part-time retirement fits you just right.

Part-time work is a great way to transition into retirement. Not only does it provide an income—which could be enough to let you shift down and ease into retirement earlier—but it also helps keep a sense of schedule and routine during the important transition years. Few habits are easy to quit cold turkey, and many workers find that their jobs and careers fall into this category, too. Reducing hours at their current job, consulting to their old company, or even moving into a completely different—although lower-stress and less schedule-intensive—job has helped many a retiree downshift from the rat race into retirement.

Planning the Finances

Planning that final day at work can be financially stressful, too. In fact, this is the problem many workers anticipate but few know quite how to handle. You've made the budget calculations and are sure that your retirement nest egg will support you. Still, the first few months—or years, for some folks—can be a difficult transition as the paychecks stop and investments start supporting the budget. Here are a few tips to help this first part of retirement run more smoothly:

Making the change to your new retirement lifestyle may not be easy. Many people identify themselves with their job or their business. Giving this up can be difficult. Talk to your advisor or a retired friend for a referral to a counselor experienced with this type of life transition for help over the tough spots.

- **Pay the big bills.** Get big-ticket items like college education and home renovations out of the way while you are still working. Do any necessary maintenance on your home, such as replacing old appliances, fixing an aging roof, and painting the house. The major advantage in reducing the huge bills that you have left to pay is psychological, but after all, so is much of the bliss and comfort that comes from retirement.
- **Erase debt.** Plan to pay down your mortgage and reduce debt as much as possible while you're working. Not having high fixed expenses in retirement makes your monthly budget more flexible and easier to manage on a fixed income.
- **Care for your car.** Buy a new car or complete major repairs on your current one while you're working. Avoid the frustrating budget-buster payments of an older car, or one that needs repair, by taking care of this small but important task before your paycheck stops.
- **Move in.** Buy your new retirement home a couple of years before you retire. Yes, you may be maintaining two homes in those last few years before retirement, but you may discover that you don't care for the new home or its location, or that there are major repairs needed on

it. If you're still employed, you'll have the option to add a couple of years to your career to pay for the repairs, or to sell the house and find a new location that more closely fits your expectations. Give yourself the last few years of your working career to make new friends in your new retirement home, if you intend to move, and grow accustomed to your planned retirement environment.

Maximizing Your Pension for Wealth

A pension plan promises to provide the worker an income for life. These plans offer the ultimate employee benefit—retirement income—and are often based on a formula that benefits the loyal employee. The longer the employee worked for the company, or the government agency, the better the pension. For example, a pension encouraging longevity might pay 30 percent of salary for every ten years worked for the company. In this case, a twenty-five-year veteran would receive 75 percent of their salary as a pension in retirement!

ESSENTIALS

Your pension plan may have a default payment option to care for your spouse if you die before retirement. Check with the plan administrator or human resources at the company that provides the plan to find out what that default is, and whether you can change it to another option that better fits your spouse's needs.

Pension plans are becoming rare because they are expensive for employers to maintain. The expenses lie in the administration and funding of the benefit. It would take a great deal of money to ensure a lifetime income to a retired workforce at a level equal to 75 percent of their working salaries. What's more, these retirees are no longer adding to the bottom line of the company and are now only a liability. The money to support the plan must be invested, and the company must retain the risk of those investments. Many companies in recent years have stopped offering these defined-benefit plans in favor of defined-contribution plans like 401(k)s and 403(b)s (which we discussed in Chapter 13).

Defined-contribution plans are favored by today's more mobile workforce where few employees stay with a company long enough to draw a large pension. Current employees of a company changing their plan are bought out through a plan "rollover" into something called a "cash-balance plan." In this transition the employee essentially receives an account worth what the employer has set aside for his pension benefit to date. If the employee is young, this account will be small because most of the money for a pension plan is deposited in the last few years before retirement. If the employee is older, their cash-balance plan may be larger than that of a younger employee's, but it will still be a smaller benefit than the pension plan would have provided.

To support the income streams for all past employees, employers who provide pensions set aside a certain amount of assets each year into a separate account. This account is managed by a trustee who invests it to support the anticipated payments. The trustee uses the law of large numbers to calculate how many retirees will be due a benefit each year, how much the total benefits are likely to be, how many retirees will die and how many will begin retirement. These calculations are based on the same actuarial statistics that insurance agencies employ. For the employee planning to retire, an analysis similar to a life insurance analysis must be completed. Pension plans contain a life insurance component, which is readily seen in the different payment options that are offered.

Choosing a Pension Option

The most common options are usually:

- **Full pension for life.** The full pension is paid for the life of the pensioner, meaning the retired employee who is now receiving the pension. In our example that follows we'll call this option A.
- **Reduced payment.** A reduced payment is made to the pensioner, say two-thirds of the full benefit, then one-third of the benefit to the

pensioner's widow or widower if the pensioner dies. In our example that follows we'll call this option B.

- **Half payment.** A half-pension payment is made to the pensioner, which continues to be paid to the widow or widower. In our example that follows we'll call this option C.

Let's look at an example to see how the insurance part of this analysis works, and how you can use it to wring the most wealth out of your pension. Say the full benefit the pension will pay the retiree is $3,000 per month. Under option A this benefit would be paid to the retiree for their entire life, but no benefit would be paid to the spouse when the retiree died. Under option B the retiree would receive a reduced benefit of $2,000 per month and the spouse would be left a one-third benefit of $1,000 per month. Option C splits the benefit in half, paying the retiree $1,500 per month and the spouse $1,500 per month at the retiree's death.

Many pensioners and their spouses pick their company's equivalent of our option B or option C—the spousal benefit. Companies encourage pensioners to do this because they loathe having an angry widow or widower banging on the company's door to collect pension money after the pensioner dies leaving them no benefit. Widows, like orphans, are not easy adversaries in a lawsuit. Company interest aside, is the reduced benefit the right choice for the retiree and their family? It depends on the retiree's circumstances—can the surviving spouse live comfortably on the remaining nest egg that they have accumulated?—and on the insurance premiums involved.

Under option A, the retiree is not purchasing any insurance because they are receiving the full pension benefit. Under the pension options that don't pay a full benefit—options B and C—the insurance premium effectively is paid out of the reduced benefit the retiree collects. This insurance benefit provides the income to the spouse if the retiree dies first. Under option A, the retiree pays for no insurance. They receive the full benefit, $3,000 per month in our example, and when they die there is no benefit left for their beneficiary—their spouse. Under option B in our example, the retiree pays $1,000 per month insurance premium to ensure the $1,000 per month benefit for their spouse. In option C, the retiree pays $1,500 per month to cover this benefit.

Choosing a pension option is an important and irrevocable decision. The gravity of this decision makes a second opinion from a trusted advisor very valuable. Talk to your financial, tax, or legal advisor for help in making this important decision.

What happens if the spouse dies first? The pensioner is often stuck at the lower pension amount—essentially paying a premium to protect the financial well being of someone who has passed away! If you're eligible to receive a pension, ask yourself: Is the insurance premium worth the benefit to the spouse? Could equal coverage be bought through other means? What is the risk of the spouse dying first? Here are some tips to help you make this decision.

Cost of Private Insurance

How much would private insurance cost to cover the spouse's future income needs? Taking the full pension benefit and paying part to an insurance policy to provide a death benefit to the spouse may be cheaper than taking the reduced pension benefit. Also, by purchasing insurance separately, the policy can be canceled, and the full pension benefit retained by the retiree, if the spouse passes away before the pensioner. Also, if the retirement nest egg is large enough to support the spouse in lieu of the pension benefit, no insurance coverage, private or pension-sponsored, may be needed.

Age

Who is older or less healthy, the retiree or the spouse? If there is a large difference in age, or if one person has significant health problems, some retirees and their spouses will opt to "bet" on who might pass away first. For example, if the retiree is significantly older than the spouse, they might think it a good bet that the retiree will die first and opt for one of the spousal benefit options (option B or C). On the other hand, if the spouse is older, the full benefit (option A in our example) might be the smart choice. The same could be the case if one person had significant health problems that might reduce their life expectancy. There are few cases in which this type of chance could be clear-cut. Be sure when choosing a benefit based on your belief of the future that you back it up with financial security as well.

Uninsurability

If the retiree cannot purchase private insurance outside of the pension, the decision is all but made for you. If the spouse doesn't have adequate income or assets to support them if the pensioner passes away first, one of the spousal benefit options is probably the only good choice.

Don't get drawn into the expensive trap of stubbornly thinking: "It's my pension and I want it." You may not need to spend the extra money protect-ing your pension for your spouse. Look to your other assets to cover the spouse's income needs in the case of the pensioner dying before the spouse. If you have plenty of assets for their support, consider taking the higher pension benefit and keeping the nest egg invested as long as possible.

Philanthropy: Building a "Foundation"

There are many ways to benefit the world with the wealth you've accumulated. Some can be supported while you're alive—through volunteer work and annual contributions—and some after you're gone—through trusts, gifts, and foundations. The variety of estate plans that you can use to benefit the causes you believe in are as varied as the wealth builders who use them.

Benefit Your Charity

Life insurance plans that are no longer needed to support your family can be reassigned to a charity. You'll have to keep paying the premiums, of course—but this may be a great way to leave a legacy to your favorite cause. Life insurance can also be used to compensate your children for assets donated either from your estate or while you were alive by providing a benefit to replace what was donated to charity.

Pay Your Charity a Salary

If you don't need all your income, your estate-planning lawyer can develop a plan to provide your selected charity with an income while you are alive, with the principal from those investments going to your kids, grandchildren, or other heirs after you die.

Donate Creatively

Every little bit helps. Small and large charities and nonprofits alike are always grateful for every little bit their supporters can spare. Get in touch with your favorites and find out what's on their wish list. You may be surprised. The work wardrobe you no longer need or the fax machine or computer you won't use now may find a second home at a local charity. Nonprofits may even welcome the donation of a vehicle that you no longer need to commute to work in!

If you plan to donate your used computer equipment after you retire, make sure the memory drives are free of confidential information. Just deleting the files isn't good enough. Talk to your computer specialist about reformatting the drives so that the information on them is permanently removed.

Pour a Foundation

Foundations are a wonderful way to get involved in the community and to diversify your charitable contributions. Foundations are essentially pools of money that are pledged to support a specific type or group of causes. You can pledge to an existing foundation or you can develop your own with a charter to support the types of charities you love. Think big! Recruit your retiring friends to contribute and serve as directors, and together you could really change the world!

Leaving Money to Your Children

Deciding how and when (and if!) to leave your kids money is often fraught with difficulty. When you are in a first marriage with young kids, the decision may seem obvious—"We want to leave all our money to our children for their well-being and education," many people say. But how would your bequest differ if your kids were grown? What if they're adults with jobs and families of their own, and are not doing a good job of managing their own money? How confident are you that they'd responsibly manage a large inheritance? What if they're disabled? Or what if there are kids from previous marriages? What about grandkids?

FACTS

Tax authorities are scrutinizing the plans touted by many insurance companies to provide both a charitable donation as well as benefits to the survivors when you die. These complex plans involve insurance policies owned by either a trust or the charity and "gifts" of the annual premium payments. Pay close attention to these schemes and discuss your plans with an independent advisor before signing anything.

Folks in the wealth-accumulation phase of their lives often have little need for complex estate plans to control the distribution of their wealth if they pass away at an unexpectedly young age. In most cases, if they have kids, the money gets left in trust for the children, with the plan that much of it would be spent raising and educating them. Couples and individuals without kids often worry even less about the distribution of their wealth because there are no family members that depend on them. They leave their assets to charity, or divide it up equally between siblings and parents. Let's look now at some of the planning dilemmas that plague wealthy parents with children.

When You're Still Building Your Wealth

If you are building wealth but are not yet rich, you should have already put an insurance plan in place to help your family achieve your wealth goals if you're not around to do it for them. Wealth builders should have enough life insurance in place as a matter of course so that even though their bank accounts don't yet make them wealthy, their insurance policies do.

FACTS

Talk openly about your money wishes with the folks you select as your children's caregivers in the event of your death. They may be hesitant to spend the children's inheritance, using their own money to raise them to save your money for when they're older. Be clear if you want your money spent to help raise your kids.

That said, let's agree that either you have enough wealth accumulated that you'd need to be cautious and forward-thinking in distributing it, or that your life insurance is plentiful enough that a large estate would be left if you died prematurely. What do you do with it? When should you let your kids have the money?

When Kids Are Young

With young children, the first thing you need to determine is whether there will be a significant amount of cash left over after—if this is your goal—your kids are educated. A well-managed trust fund is most parents' wish, to help educate their kids and send them off into their adult life with a little cash in their pockets—just as the parents would have done had they lived longer. The simplest of trusts can be written to provide the kids with their needs, but what if the inheritance is large enough to last until adulthood? Or what if your kids are already adults and out on their own?

When Kids Are Grown

Little is more frustrating than being a committed wealth builder with adult children who are wealth wasters. Spending a lifetime accumulating wealth is very rewarding, but contemplating the possibility of all that hard work going for naught because your kids are spendthrifts can be very disheartening. This can be avoided, to a point, with a little bit of planning.

Don't tell your kids how much money you have. If you're focused on accumulating wealth, you probably haven't spent a lot of money helping your young children keep up with the Joneses. Don't start doing this when they are older, either. Encourage all the important family money discussions with your kids without telling them how many zeros there are in your net-worth statement. If they are not expecting a windfall, they will not be tempted to count on a big inheritance and you won't find yourself in the uncomfortable position of trying to support their spendthrift habits.

You may find that your kids are frugal wealth builders like yourself. If this is the case, they will probably be glad to know more about your finances to put their minds at rest about supporting you in your old age. A well-timed discussion may put everyone's mind at ease.

Most beneficiaries blow the first amount of inheritance they receive and regret it later. Talk to your attorney about creating a plan to distribute a small amount to your kids right away—say 20 percent or less. Then, have them wait five years or so before distributing more. Give your kids a chance to develop economic self-confidence of their own without the burden—yes, we said burden—of having too much money too soon. They'll probably do a better job of managing their own money, building careers, and raising their families on their own without the added pressure of managing a big inheritance too early.

If you're worried about your kids confronting an emergency without the support of your money to rescue them, ask your lawyer to put a provision in your estate plan that gives them access to a small amount in the event of a dire emergency—but be very careful about the parameters that merit an emergency withdrawal. If the provisions are too lenient, they may defeat the purpose of delaying the full distribution by giving the kids the money early anyway.

A Disabled Child

If your child is disabled and receiving disability benefits, special care must be taken to avoid disrupting their benefits by leaving large inheritance assets. Talk to an attorney experienced in this area to be sure your plan doesn't conflict with or reduce the benefits your child may be receiving, or may at some point be eligible for.

Children from a Prior Marriage

If you have, or your spouse has, kids from a previous marriage, you should carefully plan how to distribute your assets in the case one of you dies before the other. This may sound obvious, but many have been left in financial dire straits because money had been channeled prematurely to the deceased spouse's kids from another marriage. And many a spouse's kids have been disinherited by an estate that considers only the couple's own children. The estate planning involved doesn't need to be unnecessarily complex, but should be dealt with soon after you're remarried.

What About Grandkids?

Grandchildren are the welcome beneficiaries of many wealth builders. And with a little bit of planning, they too can benefit from their grandparents' frugal habits. Grandchildren can be benefited by trusts that pay their school tuitions or help in other ways toward their care and development. But, you may want to consider also helping them during life rather than after you die—you'll enjoy it more, and you'll have more control over the results. Be sure not to trample the parent's desires, though. Even the most spendthrift parent will resent meddling grandparents who attempt to exert control over the family through money. Your gifts to grandchildren should come with no strings attached.

To help preserve harmony, some expenses—like school tuition—can be paid directly to the institution without the limitations of gift taxes (more about gift taxes in Chapter 18). And be careful not to overspend. Remember, for the most part, your own financial well-being comes first. You made it on your own, and are a better person for the experience—they can, too.

CHAPTER 16

Your Fair Share: Managing Taxes

While most people are happy—or at least resigned—to pay their fair share of taxes, there is no reason to pay more. This chapter includes some planning hints that may help you save on tax expenses. As with all of our suggestions, it's important that you talk to your professional advisor about how these tips may apply to you.

Real Estate Owners

For the experienced investor, direct real estate ownership (as opposed to pooled real estate funds called real estate investment trusts, or "REITS") can be a great way to diversify your portfolio. Stocks, bonds, and cash are all key components of a diversified asset allocation, but real estate can add an extra twist with some potential management responsibilities and quite a bit of risk. Fortunately, though, even the less-than-savvy investor often can tap into the advantages of holding real estate in their portfolio—their home. Yes, we all need a roof over our head, and the tax-deferred appreciation, mortgage-interest tax deductions, and potential capital gains shelters really sweeten the deal.

Primary Residence: Tax-Deferred Growth

Your primary residence, simply, is the place where you live. If you have more than one house, like a vacation home or condo, your primary residence is the house in which you spend most of your time. Case law over the years has added a great deal of complexity to this definition as folks have tried to interpret the rule in more tax-advantageous ways. For our purposes, though, you should consider your primary residence to be the place that you call home.

Why is the primary residence definition important and how does it create tax-deferred growth? Like your investments in retirement accounts, you don't report your home's appreciation in value until you sell it. This tax-deferred growth can contribute to a great deal of wealth accumulation over a period of years or decades, if you are lucky enough to live in a desirable neighborhood, take good care of your home, and have neighbors who do the same. In addition to this tax-deferred growth, your primary residence is also eligible for a capital gains tax exclusion that other property isn't. This is why it's so important to maintain your home as a primary residence so that up to $500,000 in capital gains, for married taxpayers, and $250,000, for single taxpayers, can be sheltered from tax. This wonderful exemption is only available if you have lived in your home for at least two of the past five years, and you are only eligible to take an exemption once every two years. This seemingly simple rule can get a little tricky, so let's look at an example.

As a fresh college graduate you bought your first home. Let's say you paid $20,000 for your small home in 1970. Now, let's assume that you married, raised your kids, and it's now 2002 and your home has appreciated to $500,000 in value. This appreciation is due to additions and improvements that you made, and to the growth of the housing market in your area. Let's say that the improvements you made cost $100,000. These additions were essentially additional investments in the home, like making additional deposits to a bank or investment account, and they bring your total home cost to $120,000. What is the tax on your profit when you sell this home? What would the tax be if instead of being your primary residence the home were a rental property?

FACTS

Real estate investment trusts, or REITs (pronounced "reets"), are pooled accounts that own a variety of real estate investments and are managed by professional managers. They resemble mutual funds in many ways, except they invest in real estate properties rather than stocks and bonds. Rather than investing directly in an individual property, you may consider the diversification and professional management of a REIT.

Your profit in this example is $380,000 ($500,000 in current value minus $120,000 of invested cost). If you owed tax on that profit—as you would if you had sold it as a rental property—you could owe as much as $76,000! But, in part to encourage home ownership, the tax law says that you can shelter up to $500,000 profit from the sale of your primary residence. In this example, we'll assume that neither you nor your spouse has taken advantage of the exclusion in the past two years, and that you both have lived in the house for two of the last five years. Since the profit is less than $500,000, you owe no tax. If your capital gains tax rate is 20 percent (and these rates are changing, so don't bet on it) you have saved $76,000!

If you decide to sell your home and downsize to a smaller home, you could potentially sell for $500,000, pay cash for a smaller, less expensive home and still have money left over for retirement income. If you or your spouse had used the exemption for another home within the last two years, you could have taken half the exemption of $250,000. This would leave $130,000 subject to capital gains tax but, even at a 20 percent capital gains tax rate, the $26,000 due is still a great deal less than the $76,000 in capital gains taxes that other investments would be subject to.

If you are planning to sell your home—which can be a condominium, houseboat, house trailer, or stock held by a tenant-stockholder in a cooperative housing corporation—pay particular attention to this rule. You and your spouse are each allowed only one exclusion every two years, and if you do anything to exclude your residence from eligibility—like permanently moving to your summer home and renting out your residence—you could lose this wealth-saving exclusion.

Home Office Pitfalls

If you have a home business, you may be able to deduct office expenses, including depreciating the space in your home that you use for your business. But, if you plan to sell your house within the next few years, you should be very careful about making this choice, as the "business" part of the house loses its primary residence exclusion and becomes commercial property, at least for tax purposes. The business deductions and depreciation that you take may or may not make up for the loss of the capital-gains exclusion when you sell. Let's look at another example.

A home office could lose its definition—and therefore, its exemption—as a home office if it's also used for personal purposes. Keep the area free of personal items. If your home office consists of a desk in the family room, claim only the actual amount of space you use—not the whole room.

Let's say you paid $20,000 for your house in 1970, and made the $100,000 improvements we previously mentioned. After raising your kids, you decided to start a business from your home, and deducted expenses and depreciation on the upstairs bedrooms that you used as an office. Suppose the bedroom measured 144 square feet, roughly 5 percent of the total size of your home. Effectively, you have converted 5 percent of your house to commercial property. Commercial property does not enjoy the same capital gains tax exclusion as your home does, so when you sell your home, you will owe tax on the profit you made selling the bedroom as "commercial property." This sounds strange and bureaucratic, but it's worth paying attention to because it could cost you some of your wealth. If your total profit is $380,000, as in our previous example, and 3 percent, or $11,400, of that profit came from the sale of your commercial property bedroom-turned-business office, your capital gains tax could be as much as $2,280. Were your business deductions equal to or more than $2,280? It's important to plan well to be certain that exposing yourself to this extra tax is worth the deductions you were able to take in the business. Ask your business accountant to help you with the calculations if you aren't sure.

Mortgage-Interest Deduction

Another benefit of home ownership is that you can deduct much of the interest you pay on loans against your home. Interest on a mortgage up to $1 million and home-equity loan interest on a loan up to $100,000 can be deducted against income. Also, because your home is used to secure the loan as collateral, the lender will probably offer a lower interest rate than an unsecured loan. The extra tax savings, plus the lower interest rate savings, can save you big bucks over the course of the loan.

FACTS

Mortgages are the first loan on your home, meaning that the mortgage holder has first dibs on cash from the sale of your house if you default. An equity loan or second mortgage is "subordinate" to the mortgage, so the loan is often at a higher interest rate.

Think back to the house in our example that you bought for $20,000. By 2002, you've paid off the first mortgage, but you decide to remortgage to get enough cash to start a new business. Regardless of whether you choose a mortgage or a home equity loan (two different types of loans with different interest rates and other characteristics), the interest you pay on the loan will be lower than an unsecured loan, and may be deductible because the home is used as collateral.

The Tiered Tax System

Under our tiered tax system, everyone pays tax on their first amount of taxable income at a low rate of 10 or 15 percent (depending on which direction current tax law changes go). Once that first tier of 10 percent to 15 percent is surpassed, higher income amounts are taxed at marginally higher amounts: 28, 36, and 39.6 percent as of 2001. These tax brackets are scheduled to possibly change in the future, but the concept of the tiered structure will remain the same. And the incentive to try to keep as much income as possible in the lower brackets will continue for wealth builders and tax-aphobics alike.

Business Owners

Business owners may have a few unique opportunities to save tax by redistributing some of their income to their kids and their retirement plan. Children under the age of fourteen are subject to a "kiddie" tax on their unearned income over about $1,500. This means that income like interest and dividends over $1,500 will be taxed at their parents' highest marginal tax rate. So, if your twelve-year-old has an investment account for college that generated $4,000 in interest and dividends last year, the amount over $1,500—or $2,500—gets taxed at your rate instead of your child's. If that was all the income your child earned, his or her rate would be 15 percent. Your rate is probably much higher than that, as your income is probably higher. If your top rate were 36 percent, your child will pay a tax of $900 on his or her $2,500 instead of the $375 she would have owed if taxed at 15 percent. Once children turn fourteen, they are no longer subject to this extra tax.

The kiddie tax does not apply to earned income, so wealth-building business owners may consider hiring their children to help with the business as a way to build a sense of responsibility and to shift income.

Let's say that as part of your consulting practice, you've hired your twelve-year-old daughter to file, make copies, clean the office, and open and sort mail. You pay her $4,000 per year. You're able to deduct the expense of your daughter's services and related payroll costs and taxes as a business expense from your gross income. This lowers your net—taxable—income, saving you some tax obligation. If she invests $2,000 in an individual retirement plan, her remaining income of $2,000 will be sheltered from tax by the standard deduction, which in 2001 was $4,550. Therefore, she owes no tax and you've saved your business tax payments in the 36 percent bracket of over $1,440!

Paying your child a wage is an audit flag item for the IRS. Be absolutely sure that the duties you hire your child to do are within their abilities, that they actually perform those duties, and that the wage you pay is a fair (not inflated) wage.

Retirement Plans

As an employee, your employer may offer you a retirement plan that allows you to defer 15 percent or more of your income. You don't pay tax on this deferred income until you withdraw it from your retirement plan. This saves current income taxes and builds wealth to fund your retirement. If you're really lucky, your employer may also offer a pension or defined-benefit plan that provides a retirement "salary" or benefit in the form of a set income after a number of years of employment.

As a successful business owner focused on building wealth, you can create your own defined-benefit plan that could allow you to save quite a bit more than 15 percent of your income. This type of plan has greater annual costs than the basic 15 percent defined-contribution plan, but the added tax savings of deferring more income and the added nest egg growth are often hard to resist. The wealth-building potential of this strategy becomes even more powerful if you are the oldest or, better yet, the only employee at your company.

Let's say that your consulting practice has been going well the past few years, and you decide to invest more profit toward your retirement.

You're the sole employee, and you have the choice between a defined-contribution plan and a defined-benefit plan.

The defined-contribution plan can come in many different flavors—some of which, like a Simplified Employee Pension plan, or SEP, we discussed in Chapter 13—but all will limit your contribution to between 15 percent and 25 percent of your income. Since the defined-benefit plan calculates the deposit needed to fund a steady retirement income at a future date, the contribution is not limited. It's essentially "all you can eat" investing that lets you decide how best to reach your desired income. You will need an actuary to calculate this deposit based on established parameters, but the amount you will be able to invest each year could become a very large part of your business income.

Making Early Withdrawals from Retirement Plans

Many wealth builders are eager to enjoy their wealth, and they lament that much of that wealth is tied up in retirement-plan accounts—locked away, they think, until they reach age fifty-nine and a half, before which age distributions are taxed an additional 10 percent. With a little bit of planning, though, this age-based "lockbox" can be opened well before the magic retirement age.

Certified Public Accountants (CPAs) are invaluable resources for successful business owners and wealth builders alike. Tax laws change far too frequently to leave the specifics up to a layperson, no matter how smart you are, so be sure to discuss any tax-saving strategies with your CPA before implementing them. You'll be glad you did.

The 10 percent penalty on retirement plans is waived if, for at least five years, the account owner withdraws a regular amount based on their life expectancy. Therefore, you can start regular withdrawals at fifty-four and a half and continue through retirement, or make changes at fifty-nine and a half—five years later—as needed. If you would like to retire earlier—and your nest egg is large enough—you can begin the withdrawals sooner. Just be sure that they are based on your life expectancy.

Managing Taxes on Income

Part of building wealth is managing the amount of it you pay in taxes. One important aspect of this is to understand the different types of income and a little about how the tax system works. As an introduction to this, we'll discuss three types of income here: gross income, adjusted gross income, and taxable or net income.

- **Gross income** is the total of all that you bring in during the year, including wages and salary, unemployment compensation, tips and gratuities, interest and dividend income, alimony received, up to 85 percent of social security benefits received, rental income after expenses, business income after expenses—your total income.
- **Adjusted gross income** is the next step down from gross income. From gross income you deduct your IRA, SEP, or other self-employed retirement-plan contribution, some student-loan interest, alimony paid, self-employed medical expenses, moving expenses related to your job, medical savings account contributions, and one-half of your self-employment tax. Adjusted gross income, or AGI, is important because it affects certain deductions and phase-outs on other parts of your tax return.
- After deducting your itemized or standard deduction, your personal exemptions, and eligible credits, you arrive at your **taxable income**. Your tax due is calculated on this income amount.

Business owners are able to defer income by managing their billing and receivables, and they are able to transfer income—to a point—to other family members involved in the business. Folks who work as employees, though, are not afforded these options. Yet, there are still ways for them to manage wealth and taxes by deferring and transferring income.

Deferring Income

The most successful way for an employee—or an employee's spouse—to defer income is to take full advantage of an employer-provided retirement plan, as outlined in Chapter 13. These plans generally allow the employee to defer a significant amount of current wages by depositing them to the account rather than receiving them. This reduces the employee's take-home income and taxes, and builds wealth for the future. If your employer provides such a plan, there is little excuse for not taking full advantage of it. Some employers will even make matching contributions to your plan—free money!

With planning, the money in a Roth IRA can be deferred past your own lifetime and into your children and grandchildren's. Talk to your tax advisor about how you can set this up.

If your employer doesn't provide a plan—or if your income is below a certain limiting amount—you can deposit money in an individual retirement account, or IRA. The money deposited in such an account may be deductible—thus deferring tax on that income. The growth of the account is tax deferred, saving taxes along the way until you make withdrawals. And even when you do begin to pull money out of the account, only the amount withdrawn is counted as income for that year's tax purpose. To be sure that withdrawals will be made eventually, and the tax man will eventually get his share, the tax law requires that distributions begin by the April following the employee's turning age seventy and a half. These distributions must be made for each subsequent year by December 31, so don't delay making the first withdrawal. If you do, you will have a double distribution that year—one in April and one in December—poor planning that can cost you extra tax on the higher income.

Transferring Income

Even though, as an employee, you can't transfer part of your earned income to a child, you can transfer some unearned income, in the form of an investment account in your child's name. Under the Universal Transfers to Minors Act (UTMA) or the Universal Gift to Minors Act (UGMA), depending on what is recognized in your state, you can transfer up to $10,000 per year in investment principal to your child. If you are married, you can transfer up to $20,000: $10,000 from each spouse. If you choose to transfer investments that are producing income—say bonds or certificates of deposit—your children age fourteen and over will pay taxes on the interest at their probably lower tax rate. If your child is younger than fourteen, this strategy won't work as well, as income over about $1,500 will be taxed at your top rate. Still, you may still consider transfers in preparation for the year they turn fourteen.

Remember, the money transferred to your child becomes theirs, and must be used for their benefit. If the money is not spent for school, college, or other legitimate expenses, it becomes theirs to do with as they please when they reach adulthood—age eighteen for UGMA accounts, twenty-three for UTMA accounts.

Managing Taxes on Investments

Managing when you receive investment interest—and recognize it on your tax return as part of your gross income—is an important part of building wealth. Investments grow in two ways: capital gains and interest/dividend payments. Capital gains are generated when you are able to sell your investment for more than you bought it for. The realization of this value is deferred until the investment is sold. Interest and dividend payments are paid by various investments as compensation to shareholders (if paid by a company to its stockholders) or creditors (if paid by a company, government, or other entity to its bondholders).

Be sure to keep good records about how you used the money in your child's UTMA or UGMA account. In general, parents are responsible for sheltering and feeding their own children. Use the UTMA for extras like private school, college tuition, or special summer camp, not school clothes or regular living expenses.

A diversified portfolio is one that holds a variety of investments—generators of capital gains, dividends, and interest. If your goal is to generate growth in your investments during your working years and to defer use of your investment income and appreciation—and the associated tax payments—until retirement, you might choose accounts and investments that will allow you to defer realizing the interest and dividends generated by the investments.

Before we look at the accounts you could choose, let's review a little about the difference between taxes on interest and dividend income and taxes on capital gains that we touched on in Chapter 13. Interest and dividends from investments are taxed at regular income-tax rates. These rates are higher than capital-gains tax rates. When tax planning for an investment, consider that the interest or dividends from that investment will be taxed at your top marginal tax rate—your top bracket. These brackets are scheduled to adjust over the next few years, but at this writing they are 15, 28, 31, 36, and 39.6 percent.

Capital gains are taxed at either 10 percent (if your regular top income tax bracket is 15 percent) or 20 percent (for all other taxpayers.) If you are in the top income tax brackets, capital-gains rates can be quite a savings compared to the 28 to 39.6 percent rates you could be paying.

FACTS

If your investments have lost value, you can sell them and count the capital loss against other capital gains, and even some income. Extra caution should be used when rebalancing a portfolio using this strategy to avoid the "wash sale" rules. In a wash sale, if the same investment is repurchased within thirty days the capital loss could be disallowed.

Retirement accounts such as IRAs, SEPs, 401(k)s, and pension plans grow tax-deferred. The money in these accounts is not available until retirement age (fifty-nine and a half without penalty—or earlier with restrictions, as we saw earlier in the chapter) but the taxes generated by capital gains, interest, and dividends are not due until the money is withdrawn. This can be very beneficial if you're in a high tax bracket while working and plan to be in a lower bracket after retirement. However, assets withdrawn from retirement accounts are taxed at income-tax rates, not the lower capital-gains rates, so special care should be given to the investment choices in these account. This should not be the only consideration, though. Here are some facts to consider when choosing investments in a retirement account.

Income-Tax Treatment of Withdrawals

This consideration sometimes works against the time horizon consideration. (We never said wealth planning was a science—it's definitely an art.) If you have an investment that is risky or that you think will generate significant capital gains for you, you might think twice about holding it in a retirement account. If you think the investment will generate mostly capital gains, the tax-deferred nature of the retirement account is not needed, and when you finally sell the investment, the growth will be taxed at higher income-tax rates rather than capital-gains rates. If the investment is risky, and you are holding it in a regular, nonretirement account and decide to sell it at a loss if it doesn't pan out, you can deduct the capital loss (the opposite of capital gain) on your tax return. If you have decided to hold the investment in a retirement account, this deduction is not available.

The Quality of the Available Investment Choices

If your employer is providing the retirement plan, they may be offering only a limited choice of investment options. Often the quality of these investment options leaves something to be desired. Employees are then left to try to choose the investment option that has the highest quality among its peers, regardless of whether it is an income or capital-gains producer.

Deciding what to hold in a retirement account and what is best held outside a retirement account is a controversial issue in the investment world. The best wealth-building approach is to be informed about your decision, make it deliberately, and seek a balance between the different strategies.

Investment Selection

If you are trying to defer income for tax purposes, but stocks are either too risky for your portfolio or your portfolio already has a sufficient allocation of them, you may consider investing in bonds with preferential tax treatment. The most common of these are: treasury bonds, municipal bonds, and I-bonds.

Both treasury and municipal bonds provide interest payments that are either state-tax free (treasuries) or federal-tax free (municipals). If you buy municipals issued by your state of residence, they're also state-tax free. However, the interest rates that these bonds pay are adjusted to reflect their tax treatment. If you are in the lower marginal tax brackets, you may find that even though other bonds (corporate bonds) pay a taxable interest payment you are money ahead, after tax, of where you would be with the lower government-bond interest rate.

Inflation bonds, or I-bonds, are a type of government savings bond that provide an interest rate that adjusts for inflation. The bonds pay a base rate of interest plus a premium rate based on the prevailing inflation rate. Every six months, the government adjusts this inflation premium so that the growth of the bond keeps up with inflation. Taxes are not due on this income until the bonds are redeemed, so they can act as a great vehicle for deferring interest income without the concern of investment risk or the limitations of a retirement account. I-bonds will earn interest for thirty years and are redeemable at anytime—with three months of interest penalty for bonds that are redeemed before their fifth anniversary.

What the Future Holds

Every few years or so, there is a new sweeping change in tax law that sends wealth builders and business people to their CPAs, and CPAs into extra classes. All indications are that this will continue to be the case as baby boomers age and retire, and government spending on the war on terrorism continues. The best policy for wealth builders regarding tax law changes is to stay in close contact with your tax advisor or CPA, and to stay informed about potential new laws and rulings that may affect you or your plan. As you build wealth, you should find yourself talking to your tax advisor more and more during the year to assess your investment and tax plans, and to make adjustments to anticipated law changes.

CHAPTER 17

How to Find a Wealth Advisor

Although you are ultimately responsible for the success of your plan, a trusted financial advisor can help guide you on your path to wealth and be an important part of your success. However, even an experienced advisor can be a hindrance if your ideas conflict or your communication isn't open.

Finding an Advisor with Whom You're Comfortable

By now you know that creating and implementing a wealth plan is not something to take lightly. This plan is more important than your vacation plan, weekend plan, interior design plan, and even wedding plan. After all, this is your life plan! Even if you finally decide to do much of the work on your own, you'll still need to build a team of financial advisors to support you. Unless you plan to get into wealth planning full-time, there's no way you can stay sufficiently up-to-date on all the information that would help you take advantage of all the financial, legal, and tax opportunities offered to investors.

And even the most avid do-it-yourselfers understand that a reliable second opinion will do them good—or at least the smart and successful do-it-yourselfers do. Significant mistakes on your wealth plan could cost you a lot of money and a lot of time. You're probably going to need expert help.

The Importance of Trust

Financial advisors have widely varying levels of training and a host of different specialties. But training and experience should be only minimum requirements for the advisors you decide to consider. The single differentiating characteristic of the advisors you eventually select should be trust.

FACTS

Not all advisors work well with all people. Don't be intimidated by an advisor who is loved by all but whom you find difficult to understand or don't trust. This advisor may work with your friend or your parents but that doesn't mean he or she is right for you. Choose your own advisor.

No matter how altruistic your advisors are, their attention to your money will not always be as close as yours. They have businesses and other clients to worry about in addition to you. Never totally hand over your financial affairs to an advisor, no matter how much you trust them; an advisory relationship is a partnership, not a surrender of power. Your relationship with your advisors must be a two-way street if it's to be a success. Once you find advisors whom you trust and build trusting relationships with them, they will become a valuable part of your wealth-building team. One that, hopefully, you'll have for a very long time.

What Advisors Do You Need on Your Team?

As you build wealth, you will find that you need a team of advisors to cover all the special parts of your wealth plan. You'll need a financial planner to help create or review the plan, an investment advisor to help implement the investment portion of the plan, a lawyer to oversee the legal aspects of the plan, an accountant to help with the tax part of the plan, and an insurance advisor to help you work with the insurance needs of your plan.

This doesn't necessarily mean that you need to work with five different people. More than one of these specialties may be found within one person. Most commonly you may find that your financial planner or accountant also has expertise and can offer assistance with investments and/or insurance. In fact, the training to be a Certified Financial Planner includes courses in all aspects of a wealth plan: budgeting, insurance, investments, tax planning, retirement planning, and estate planning. For this reason, most wealth builders will start interviewing Certified Financial Planners first—as a general rule the financial planner can act as their point person—then the other team members can be added, as their expertise is needed.

A Cordial Atmosphere

Whomever you decide to welcome onto your team of advisors should not have a high-pressure sales approach. If you feel like each meeting with your advisor is going to be filled with the winner-and-loser posturing of a sales call, you may hesitate to meet with them as frequently as you should for the well-being of your wealth plan. Important parts of your wealth plan might then go unattended—a situation that can lead to financial disaster.

A meeting with your advisors may not be the jolliest time you ever spent, but it should be cordial, professional, educational, and productive. Your advisor should create a welcoming atmosphere. They should be well prepared for your meeting and unhurried. Be sure your advisor is giving your situation the time and attention it deserves, and that they're responsive to you. They should finish the meeting by confirming that you understand what was discussed and that all your questions were answered.

Here's a good rule to live by: Don't ever leave a meeting with an advisor with questions left unanswered in your mind. One way or another you are paying for the advisor's time, so be sure you feel involved in the discussion, not merely lectured to.

Big Firm or Little Firm

With the highly efficient technology available today and the large network of colleagues and business acquaintances that most successful advisors accumulate, the size of a financial planning firm is not necessarily a good indicator of the value of an advisor. You will find good advisors and bad in both large and small firms, for reasons as numerous as the advisors themselves. For example, an advisor in a large firm may be under pressure to cross-sell the firm's other services, leading to conflicts of interest and inappropriate recommendations. An advisor in a small firm may lack some of the in-house expertise found in a large firm, requiring you to consult other advisors.

Both of these situations have pluses and minuses that are easily overcome by a deliberate, informed wealth planner. For example, if you're considering a small-firm advisor, ask him or her whether they see their firm's small size as a limitation. If so, how do they overcome it? And ask what advantages they feel they have over an advisor in a bigger firm. You may find that the small-firm advisor has assembled a large network of colleagues who can be called on to consult on a plan. This may work in your favor because the advisor can choose the consultants that work best in each case—rather than having to always consult the same roster of partners and associates, as a planner in a big firm might. What's more, a firm's small size may help the advisor control overhead, and since the other specialists are only called as needed they don't have to be paid unless they're used.

Your advisor should not be so small, however, that they don't have professional office space where they can meet you. Whether this space is a lavish "class A" office in a ritzy part of town or simply a suite of rooms in an executive office park, their location will give you an idea of the professionalism of their operation and whether their values match yours. While there, you should be able to meet with their staff and have a look at their offices.

Ask a large-firm advisor if they are hoping to cross-sell other services offered at their firm. Find out how much they consult with their colleagues in helping make financial planning recommendations and decide if the cross-selling pressure, if any, is a sufficient trade-off for the added in-house expertise. Get an idea of the advisor's relationship with the firm. Have they been working there long? If he or she left the firm to launch an independent financial planning office, could you follow them to their new location, or would a non-compete agreement between the planner and the firm that employs him or her stand in the way? After all, your relationship is with the advisor, not the company they work for. And what is their caseload like? Do they feel they have time to give your wealth plan the attention it needs? After hearing their answer, do you believe them?

SSENTIALS Don't be afraid to ask questions about your advisor and the way they work with their clients. Not all planners will be able to spend time with you face-to-face on that initial introductory call, but they should at least make you feel welcome enough during a first phone call to encourage you to ask questions about them and their work.

As in most of investing, the best policy in selecting between large-firm or small-firm advice is to ask questions. Find out as much as you can about the advisor, the firm they work for—or own—and purchase financial advice just the way you make financial investments: deliberately and from a position of information.

Where to Find Advisors

Finding a good advisor can be a challenge. Where do you start your search?

Friends

The best way is to collect referrals from friends and colleagues. Touch base with friends who seem to have a financial situation similar to your own. Is their income about the same? Do they live in the same vicinity? Ask them what they like about their advisor and what they don't care for. Ask them how they first discovered their advisor and how long they've been working together. Collect a couple of names, then call the advisors and ask for information about their firms.

Referral Sources, Lists, and Associations

Many advisors will pay a subscription or membership fee to be listed on a variety of referral lists. Industry associations like the Financial Planners Association (*www.fpanet.org*) and the National Association of Personal Financial Advisors (*www.napfa.org*) both offer consumers a list of their members. This is also a good place to look for advisor candidates, because you can often search these lists by location or by specialty. You might not be able to find a friend who has the type of advisor you need, and in that case, a referral or association list might be another option. Remember, though, that having their name on one of these referral lists only means that the advisor is a member of the organization or that they paid for the listing.

Check out the referring organization, too. What are the membership requirements? Do they screen the advisors on their list? In many cases you may find that the organization does not vouch for the advisors on their lists—the screening process is still up to you.

Seminars, Books, and the Media

Any opportunity you have to see an advisor in action before hiring them is a plus. Many teach classes, offer seminars, write articles, or appear regularly in local or national media, presenting you with an opportunity to get to know them and understand their philosophy. This offers an excellent way to sort out the people on your referral list before making that initial interview call.

Once you have narrowed your list down to a few potential advisors, give each person a call to ask about the services they provide and the clients they work with. Most advisors will spend some time with you on the phone discussing your needs and their business and whether the two of you might be a good match. Some advisors will meet with you in person for this interview, but keep in mind that successful advisors are busy and you should expect to pay for such a face-to-face meeting. During this meeting, ask the questions we list in the Questions to Ask section below, and if you're satisfied with the answers, you can feel comfortable about finalizing your arrangements.

Compensation

There are four basic compensation models under which most advisors work: commission, fee-only, fee-based, and a combination. The price you pay for each of these different types of advisors may be very similar, so the choice between models is not necessarily a cost-saving one. The difficulty lies in understanding what you are paying for. Is your advisor being compensated exclusively by you, or are they also beholden to a financial product provider?

FACTS

Don't be shy about asking an advisor up front about his or her fees. If the advisor hesitates or gives an unclear answer, think about looking for a financial advisor elsewhere. You must be able to talk frankly with your advisor and if they are unclear about fees from the start, you may not ever build the type of relationship you want.

Commission

Commissioned advisors are working to sell the financial products offered by a financial services company. You don't pay them directly;

the company they represent signs their paycheck. Commissioned advisors are paid by the companies who offer the products you purchase from them. These products may have a sales charge that you pay upfront when you make an investment, or the advisors may charge a fee when you sell your securities. They may charge ongoing fees and they may charge differently based on the volume of assets and trading activity they conduct on your behalf. Advisors may earn more per sale if their customers buy more financial products from a particular company. They may receive an annual commission from the products that their clients continue to own year after year—regardless of whether they continue to provide the client service. They may receive an up-front fee from a financial services company when you buy a designated product, regardless of whether you paid a fee up-front or will pay a fee when you sell.

Fee-Only

Fee-only advisors charge you for their services, and receive no other compensation from their recommendations. Fee-only advisors will charge you for the time they spend with you and the time they spend working on your plan. Ask them ahead of time whether they charge per hour, per month, or per year, or whether they prefer to charge by the project. Identify exactly how much they charge for each segment of time. If they charge by the hour, ask how many hours they expect to spend on your plan. Ask the advisor to send you a bill each month, or partway through your plan, to avoid being surprised by a large bill at the end of the engagement.

Fee-Based

Fee-based advisors charge a fee that's calculated as a percentage of the amount of assets you place under their management. They're often focused on helping you invest your assets, and have a specific business focus on building investments for their clients.

Ask fee-based advisors to explain their fee as well. What percentage are they charging for their services—common rates are 1 to 2 percent of assets managed—and what assets do they intend to include in their fee? For example, are they basing their fee on your entire net worth, or only on the accounts that they are helping you to manage, or managing for you? Find out whether the advisor charges you in arrears—after the time period for managing the assets has passed—or in advance. Since the fee is based on the value of your investments, this can make a major difference. If you are investing in a shrinking market where investment values are generally going down, you will pay less if the advisor is billing you in arrears. Also, if you decide to fire your advisor, you will not be asking for a refund of fees if you have been paying them in arrears. You may owe them some money for the services you received, but at least you won't be waiting to receive a refund from an advisor you have fired.

Combination

Some advisors offer a mixture of these compensation plans that we'll call hybrids. The fees of hybrid advisors are probably a little tougher to understand than the other fee models because their charges may change depending on the project they are working on with you. They may charge an hourly or project rate for your financial plan, and then they may earn a commission for the insurance or investment product you purchase.

FACTS

Be absolutely sure you know when you are paying a fee and when you are paying a commission. You will probably need to frequently revisit the fee discussion with advisors who structure their fees this way to keep it clear between the two of you how much money you'll pay for their financial planning advice.

Conflicts of Interest

Conflicts of interest are inherent in many advisory relationships. You can avoid—or at least reduce—potential problems by being an informed consumer of financial advice, asking questions, and keeping an open line of communication with your advisor.

Commissioned advisors, or hybrid advisors selling on commission, are salespeople representing the companies whose products they represent.

Keep in mind that the sales quotas imposed on them by certain product providers may influence their recommendations. Ask about the relationship the advisor has with the provider of the product, and then thoroughly discuss with them the investment options that will make you richest, regardless of their sales motives. If you are using a salesperson as an advisor, remember that this conflict will always be a part of your relationship—the products and services you purchase from them will determine the size of their weekly paycheck or bonus.

Fee-only and fee-based advisors pride themselves on being free of the conflicts of interest that are inherent in the commissioned-sales relationship. But these advisors may have their own conflicts as well. For example, the fee-based advisor, whose income could depend on the amount of assets they manage on your behalf, may prefer that you leave your money invested rather than pay off a large debt like a mortgage, because retiring your mortgage with a single balloon payment could reduce their fee.

Even the fee-only advisor, who is generally the least beholden to outside interests, may collect a finder's fee or referral fees from other specialists they recommend to you. And the advisor may receive gifts or other incentives for using a particular holding company for your investments. Ask your advisor about the other relationships they have. These conflicts can be managed as long as you are aware of them.

Licensed or Not?

Advisors who work as salespeople must, in most cases, be licensed to sell the financial products they recommend. People selling investments are overseen by a broker/dealer and the National Association of Securities Dealers (NASD). They have to pass a series of examinations that covers the products they sell, and the licenses resulting from those examinations must be "hung" with a broker/dealer. Without a broker/dealer, the salesperson can't sell financial products. The broker/dealer may put pressure on the salesperson to sell specific products, so be sure you ask if this is the case with your advisor.

Financial planning, per se, is not regulated as are other professions such as law, tax preparation, public accounting, and insurance. There are no legal requirements to be a financial planner. (That's why it's important to ask about the credentials of your prospective advisor, their professional affiliations, and their continuing education.) Certified Financial Planners are held to a stringent code of ethics. They must pass a rigorous, two-day exam and must have three years of experience to earn their certification.

Investment advice is regulated. If the advisor is not a salesperson being overseen by a broker/dealer, then they must be regulated in another manner. The most common of these involves enrolling as a registered investment advisor. If your advisor is fee-only or fee-based, they are probably a registered investment advisor, or more specifically a registered investment advisor representative. Depending on the assets they oversee for their clients, they either register with the state in which they do business or with the federal government through the U.S. Securities and Exchange Commission. A registered investment advisor is required to pass a series of exams—often the same exams that salespeople must take—and must pay a registration fee and file a Form ADV. Part of this form is usually provided to the customer of the registered investment advisor at the beginning of their relationship. Read the form to discover how the advisor does their business and what their outside relationships are.

Questions to Ask

To summarize and supplement our recommendations for selecting a financial advisor, here is a list of questions you should ask a potential advisor:

1. What is your specialty?
2. How long have you been in business?
3. How many people are there in your firm, and what are their relationships to you?
4. Is your firm growing? What are your future plans for your business/practice?
5. What is your average client like?
6. What do you like about your business? Why did you choose it?
7. What don't you like, or do you like least, about your business?

8. How are you compensated?
9. How often do you send out bills?
10. Are there any other charges that I might have to pay?
11. Do you receive finder's fees or other compensation from other entities or advisors?
12. How do you think our relationship might proceed?
13. Have you dealt with my type of situation before? How often?
14. What types of conflicts of interest do you foresee in this relationship?
15. Will you keep everything we discuss confidential?

Firing an Advisor

Sometimes, the unfortunate will happen and you'll have to fire your advisor. In most cases, this is due to a lack of communication, a series of misunderstandings, or simply mismatched personalities. For the sake of good business practices, it's important not to make an enemy of your advisor. There may come a time in the future that the two of you might work together again.

Don't forget to ask for a copy of your file should you fire your advisor. Your advisor has extensive financial information about you that will take time for your new advisor to reconstruct. Expect a delay in getting the copies and, unless you've agreed otherwise in advance, expect to pay an administrative fee.

If you are having difficulty with your relationship with an advisor, don't let it stew. Express your concerns right away, and schedule time with the advisor to talk over the problem. You might even be able to work it out, and may have a stronger relationship for it.

If the difficulty remains, ask the advisor to stop work on your case, find another advisor, and ask them to transfer all files and information to either you or the new advisor.

Acting as Your Own Advisor

How much wealth planning you do yourself and the relationship you develop with your advisors (because, yes, unless you expect to make this a full-time occupation you will still need an advisor, at least occasionally) depends on your time, aptitude, and desire. The more you want to know about your plan and the more time you want to commit to it, the better. If you decide to take this on—take it seriously. You must study much of the same materials that the professionals in the industry do, and subscribe to many of their research tools and industry publications.

SSENTIALS

If you choose the do-it-yourself route to wealth, be certain you're not planning in a vacuum. Join—or start—an investment club or a financial planning club, take classes, and meet annually with an advisor for a second opinion. Build a support network of peers around you to discuss ideas and keep your ideas fresh.

Self-study guides can be purchased for the primary securities exam—called the "Series 7"—from a variety of sources (see Appendix A). This exam is required of salespeople and some registered investment advisors alike before giving investment advice to their clients. If you have decided to take on this part of your plan, you should complete these studies as well. (Unless you change careers in favor of financial services, you won't be able to take the exam because you have to be sponsored by a securities company to do so. But most study courses will provide self-exams to test your knowledge.) Insurance self-study courses are available, as well, with their own self-exams.

Some professional advisors started out as consumers who wanted to get informed. Maybe the same will happen to you!

If this track is a little too diehard for you, you may find that you want to split the planning duties pretty much fifty-fifty with your advisor. In this case, read everything you can get your hands on about wealth planning, investing, insurance, tax planning, estate planning, and retirement. You'll be able to bring more targeted questions to the table and you'll feel more in control of the progress of your plan.

CHAPTER 18
Personal Mergers

Sometimes, wealth building can reach into areas of our lives that people don't expect. After all, no one has a clear view into the future, even though they continue to race deeper into it every day. In this chapter, you'll look at your relationships with a significant other, your children, and your grandchildren, and you'll learn a bit about the logistics and psychological aspects of transferring and sharing wealth.

Yours and Theirs: Separate or Joint Accounts?

Managing a monthly household budget and sharing expenses is an important topic between adults in a household. But in addition to being a key part of bringing order to their lives and providing a foundation for building wealth, budgets and expenses can be a main source of disagreement and conflict.

Marriage or intimate relationships that involve combined housekeeping can create a broad matrix of potential problems and issues. Personalities alone can be a challenge in a new relationship without the financial baggage, behaviors, and hang-ups we all have when it comes to money. Different families handle these issues in different ways: Some choose to keep their finances separate, some keep separate accounts but pool household expenses, and others dive right in and pool their resources completely.

FACTS

The credit situation of your partner is an important consideration in deciding whether to combine assets or keep them separate. Virtually all assets in a person's name, whether held jointly or individually, are subject to the claims of bill collectors.

Whichever way you choose to manage money and the budgets in your family, communication is key. Decide ahead of time how financial duties and expenses will be divided up and plan a regular time to review your family's financial situation. Make time to discuss your feelings about money and the part it plays in your life. Talk about your short-term money concerns as well as your long-term financial goals. Everyone feels differently about their money. By understanding your own and your partner's relationship with money you will be able to build an even stronger relationship with each other.

It could be that your first try at managing the financial aspects of your relationship flops. Don't become discouraged: Several attempts and a few false starts might be needed before you find the perfect system that satisfies everyone. And, in the long run, discussions about money and financial control in a relationship can lead to a better understanding of each other and, ultimately, create a stronger bond between you and your life partner. Here are some guidelines to consider.

Separate Accounts and Monthly Contributions

In this arrangement, you keep your money in separate accounts and each partner makes a monthly contribution to the household expenses. This approach is often best for folks who have already been through a divorce or two, or who have lived on their own for many years and developed their own money habits before marrying or creating a household with a new partner. You may also consider keeping separate accounts if your partner has a poor credit history or spendthrift habits. Holding your assets separately could protect you—to a point—from these wealth-robbing problems. Talk to your financial, legal, or tax advisor about how to protect yourself in this type of situation.

SSENTIALS

Having a written record of what you and your partner agreed to when discussing how to manage household expenses can help avoid misunderstandings and arguments later. If you and your partner are uncomfortable writing down your plan, meet with a financial advisor to develop a plan and ask him or her to summarize in writing what you both agreed to.

If you agree to have each partner in the relationship pay a share of the household expenses, take special care that the division of household expenses is equitable. If both spouses bring in about the same monthly income, it may be fair to divide the expenses equally. But, if one spouse earns significantly more than the other, it might be better to establish a contribution that more closely matches each partner's earning power.

As part of the monthly household contribution, a special account should also be funded to cover both the expected and unexpected major expenses that life seems to constantly throw in our way. Things like vacations, home and automobile repairs, major purchases, and, especially, wealth building, need to be planned for in advance, particularly in a household that manages their money separately.

Pooled Resources

A more common approach is to simply pool the resources of both partners in joint accounts, from which you'll draw the money you need to meet your household budget. In this case, make especially certain that both you and your partner understand the family finances. Although one partner may not have the daily task of paying bills and managing the budget, both of you should be aware of how much money comes into the household and how much goes out.

How to Build Credit

If you and your spouse pool your assets and maintain most of your accounts in joint name, it's important to be sure that you both develop a personal credit rating. After all, it's not uncommon, even in today's enlightened age, for wives to be entirely left out of financial affairs as her husband takes out loans, buys cars, and even signs mortgages in his name alone. For that matter, wives sometime move into the house their husband owned when they were courting, leaving them entirely anonymous as far as the mortgage lender—and, in the event of her husband's death, various credit-granting agencies—are concerned.

Be aware of whose credit rating is affected by each of your family's accounts. For example, your personal credit rating can be ruined by a partner who, while in charge of the family bill paying, neglects to make payments to an account in your name.

Without a strong credit rating, a widowed spouse can find herself in the difficult position of not being able to open credit accounts, rent an apartment or a car, get a loan, or refinance a mortgage. Lack of a credit rating can even affect the widowed partner or spouse's auto insurance premiums! By simply opening some accounts with the spouse's name listed as the primary borrower under her social security number, she will create a credit rating for herself. In addition, each spouse should have at least one account in his or her name alone.

Transferring Wealth

Regardless of which approach you decide to take, special care should be taken with the following issues that could prove pivotal in managing your wealth after death.

Without a Plan

Accounts held individually are not readily available to other people in the household when the owner dies. Unless provisions are made, these accounts must pass through the legal process called probate to be distributed according to the owner's will or other estate instructions. If no will or estate plan exists, the owner is said to have died "intestate," and the money in the accounts pass according to the laws of the state. This could have the unintended effect of directing the funds away from the household and the people to whom the owner had hoped to pass his or her wealth. Married spouses are allowed provisions to capture part of the estate of their deceased spouse, even if the estate documents indicate otherwise. But, if you are unmarried and the lifestyle of your partner depends on your income or assets, it's important to take into consideration your partner's access to capital after your death. (There's more on wills later in this chapter.)

Transfer on Death Accounts

Individual accounts can often be designated as transfer on death, or TOD accounts, to facilitate the transfer of the accounts after the owner's death. Under this designation the individual named to receive the account has no power over it or its assets while the owner is alive. But when the owner dies, the account and its assets are transferred to the beneficiary without being subject to probate.

Joint Property

If you and your unmarried partner own property together, you should take special care in choosing how that ownership is structured—particularly if the property is something as valuable as your home. There are three basic types of property ownership: tenants in common, joint with rights of survivorship, and tenants in the entirety. Tenants in common and tenants in the entirety apply to home ownership. Joint with rights of survivorship can apply to other assets as well as homes.

If you own your home as "tenants in common," each of you has exclusive ownership of your share of the property. These shares don't necessarily need to be equal and they stay separate. If one partner-owner dies, their share passes into their estate to be distributed according to their directions.

If you own property "jointly with rights of survivorship," both partners or spouses own the complete property; their shares are not separate. If one partner-owner dies, the surviving partner-owner will inherit the deceased partner's share of the property.

Ownership as "tenants in the entirety" is only available to married couples, and means that each owns the property in whole. But, contrary to joint ownership, this type of ownership protects the ownership rights of one spouse against the claims of the other spouse's creditors as long as they continue to own the property and it remains their primary residence. Like joint property, if one spouse dies, the remaining spouse immediately inherits the entire property.

Transfers by Contracts

A relatively easy way to ensure the financial protection of your partner or spouse without giving up control of an asset while you're alive is through a process called "transfer by contracts." Life insurance, annuities, individual retirement accounts, and other personal retirement accounts like SEPs and SIMPLEs, 401(k)s, and 403(b)s can all be transferred outside of your will through transfers by contract. Each of these accounts remains under your control (in fact, most of these accounts must remain under the owner's sole control for tax purposes) and then transfer to your beneficiary according to the directions you have given the company holding the account.

Your employer offering the 401(k), 403(b), or pension account will let you list a primary beneficiary—to receive assets first—and a contingent beneficiary—to receive assets if the primary beneficiary dies before you do. The trustees holding your personal retirement accounts will also offer this opportunity, as will the insurance companies providing your life insurance and annuity accounts. Be sure to review and update your beneficiary designations on these accounts on a regular basis, and don't assume that they list whom you intend.

Purchasing extra life insurance can be a good way to ensure the support of a widowed partner in place of those employer benefits—pension, lifetime health benefits, educational benefits—that are offered to widowed spouses.

Sharing an Account with Kids

A common strategy used by retired parents who want to provide their kids with access to their money in an emergency is to add the kids' names to their bank and investment accounts. This can be very helpful in a pinch because the children do, in fact, have ownership rights to the funds in the account. But, they also have access during any other time, as well. And, if the account is owned jointly with rights of survivorship, so do the kids' creditors!

As you can see, putting your kids' names on your accounts—or as part owners of your house—can be fraught with problems. To avoid this there are other—albeit more complicated—ways to give them access to your assets in an emergency. Talk to your estate-planning lawyer about giving your kids power-of-attorney (under which they can act as your legal representative) and/or about creating a trust to hold the assets, and giving your children certain powers under the trust.

Marriage and Taxes: When to Say "I Do"

Deciding whether to marry the love of your life is seldom a financial decision. But, unfortunately for the romantics among us, there are important financial and legal decisions that should be considered.

In Sickness and in Health

In many cases, only immediate family members have access to a patient in a hospital or other similar facilities. If your soon-to-be-wed partner is sick, you don't want to be excluded from their sickbed or from important medical decisions merely because of an unreasonable hospital policy. If you are not yet married, talk to your lawyer about preparing a health-care proxy or other similar document giving your partner authority over your health decisions. This document should help your unmarried partner gain access to you if you're admitted to a hospital.

Employee Benefits and Pensions

Some of the more forward-thinking American companies are starting to offer employee insurance benefits and pension survivor coverage to the unmarried partners of their employees. This may or may not be the case with your own employer. If it is, you can apply for benefits as usual. If your employer has not yet provided this important benefit, and your lobbying efforts in your own behalf have failed, you'll need to take extra care in your plan to provide this needed coverage. If getting married is not an option, you will have to budget for extra private life insurance coverage to provide financial support or replace your pension if you die before your partner. You'll also have to buy health insurance privately if your partner isn't covered by their own employer's health benefits.

Sharing Assets with the Family

Transferring assets between people can be sticky business for a number of reasons: Once the assets are out of your control they can be used for purposes other than what you originally intended. The individual receiving your assets may not want to return them to you or purchase the care or other needs you were planning on when the transfer was first made. Also, transferred assets become exposed to the creditors of the recipient and could be lost in an unforeseen lawsuit, gambling debt, or simple overspending.

Good tax counsel is imperative when you decide to make a gift or other transfer of wealth. Check with your tax advisor about changes in federal and state tax laws that could sap your riches.

Whenever assets are transferred from one individual to another, Uncle Sam looks for his cut. In other words, if you give money or some other asset to someone or to some entity, whether you are living or dead, you may owe a tax. Fortunately, there are also certain exclusions to transfer taxes; understanding these exclusions, and when to use them, is important if you are going to build wealth and manage how you pass it along to your loved ones. For the sake of simplicity, think of transfer taxes as pooled together to cover all assets an individual transfers—while living or after death. We'll explain the exclusions as they come up.

The Vanishing Loophole

Transfer taxes are meant to target the transfer of wealth between generations. If they are being applied after death they are called estate taxes or death taxes. If they are applied during life, they are called gift taxes. That means, as you grow rich, you become an increasingly attractive target for Uncle Sam and his tax collectors. Currently, everyone is allowed to transfer a small amount during their lifetime which is exempt from federal tax. This exemption, sometimes called a unified credit, is provided as a tax credit to shelter a certain amount of transferred assets from tax. In 2002, this sheltered amount will be $1 million, meaning that an individual can transfer up to $1 million during their lifetime, or after death, without paying a federal transfer tax. Under new estate tax laws passed in 2001, this sheltered amount is slated to grow to the point that it will protect $3,500,000 in 2009, and in 2010 there is to be no federal estate tax charged against the assets of folks who die in that year.

But there are no guarantees after that. If Congress takes no further action, the new law "sunsets," meaning it will vanish from the books. Starting in 2011, the old laws will again be in effect, and the unified credit will return at its pre-law level, $1,000,000. This sunset provision adds an extra bit of uncertainty into planning asset transfers and estate planning. Also, since the attacks on the World Trade Center and the Pentagon on September 11, 2001, legislators are talking about changing the tax laws again to fund the war or terrorism. This uncertainty makes tax planning very difficult. Be sure to talk to your tax advisor before making any large gifts, creating joint accounts, or otherwise transferring money.

Spouses

You may transfer an unlimited amount of your wealth to your spouse whenever you choose, and without a tax. This so-called marital deduction not only protects assets transferred between spouses during their lifetimes, but it also shields the wealth after a spouse dies.

Giving Small Gifts

The gift-tax exclusion provides that assets transferred in small amounts—$10,000 or less per person per year—during your lifetime can be exempt from both transfer taxes, and also doesn't count against your unified credit. This exclusion means that you can give up to $10,000 per year to as many people you want without eating into your unified credit or triggering a gift tax.

The Invisible Charity

As far as the taxman is concerned, charities can lend a cloak of invisibility to your wealth. You can donate as much money as you want to a charitable organization during your lifetime, or even after death, without paying a gift tax or counting against your unified credit. In fact, in most cases, you get a tax deduction for this type of transfer!

Basic Estate Planning

A proper estate plan is best created by an attorney who is knowledgeable—and up-to-date—in the estate laws of your state. Here, by way of preparing you for your first estate-planning meetings with your lawyer, is some fundamental information about the basic strategies you and they might discuss. There are many nuances to the law that could be lost on the layperson and that could sabotage the plans of an unknowing do-it-yourselfer. Be sure to hire an attorney when you create an estate plan.

FACTS

If you would like to leave assets to a charity and give an inheritance to your children, you can set up a life insurance policy to expand the money in your estate. By paying some of your money now in the form of a premium, you may be able to purchase a life insurance policy that allows you to fund both your charitable and family support desires.

The realm of estate planning provides many tools for the distribution of your wealth after your passing. While in most cases, without a plan to indicate otherwise, your spouse would inherit most of your estate, special provisions must be made for the sake of your family members other than a spouse—your partner, if you're an unmarried couple, and your kids.

Your Will

Your will, the most basic estate document, is essentially a list of instructions to the probate court outlining how you'd like your wealth and your belongings handed out after you die. You might indicate that you want your partner to receive your share of the home you shared, your adult kids to receive some of your bank and other wealth accounts, and a museum to receive your works of art, for example. If you have children who are still young, your will may list a guardian for them. The proceedings of the probate court are public, and often take more than twelve months. Unless you've made provisions for other methods of bequeathing your wealth—most commonly through trusts, as we'll discuss in a moment—your heirs will be delayed in receiving the support they may need.

Other Estate Documents

Your lawyer may suggest other estate-planning documents besides a will, depending on your situation:

- A **health-care proxy** transfers power to another person to act in your behalf in making decisions about your medical care. The document outlines under what conditions the health-care proxy is activated and the amount of powers you want your designee to have. For instance, if you are unconscious, you will want a close friend or family member to act as your representative and provide direction to your doctor as to your course of care.

FACTS

Give a copy of your health-care proxy to your primary physician. Ask that they review it to be sure that it will be acceptable to them if the time comes to use it. They should keep it on file, in addition to the copy held by your lawyer and/or proxy, so that it is available when your proxy needs to invoke its powers.

- Your **power-of-attorney** document transfers decision-making power to another person whom you select to represent your legal affairs if you are unable to do it. Like the health-care proxy, this document outlines the parameters under which your representative is given these legal powers, what they can or cannot do for you, and when their powers are activated. A durable power of attorney is one that is in effect from the moment you sign the documents. A springing power of attorney comes into effect after other triggering events, including poor health or an accident.
- A **living will** is sometimes presented as part of the health-care proxy, though it can also be a separate document. The living will outlines your wishes on matters like life support and using mechanical means

to keep you alive. In most cases, your health-care proxy or family may be able to offer their own opinion as to what kind of medical care you should be receiving, as well as "resuscitate" and "do not resuscitate" instructions. But a living will adds your own voice when you cannot be heard from.

Trusts

Let's face it, your ability to truly dictate from the grave is limited. Trusts are tools that help you control the distribution of your estate after your death. A trust is a legal vehicle through which your assets can be managed according to instructions from you, whether or not you are around to oversee it. Trusts can either come into being while you're living—called a living trust—or it can be put into effect by your will—an intervivos trust. A trust can either be changeable by you during your lifetime—a revocable trust—or unchangeable—an irrevocable trust.

A trust is an entirely separate legal entity from you, and it can continue its legal life long after your physical life ends. Since the trust does not die, assets put into it can be distributed at some future date instead of immediately, as would happen through a will. When you—with the help of your lawyer—create a trust, you name a trustee who is in charge of following the instructions in the trust to distribute and manage your wealth. If you're creating a living trust, you may name yourself as the first trustee, then name other successor trustees to take over at your passing.

The laws regulating trusts are subject to change. Be sure to review these documents as well as the remainder of your estate plan every three to five years or whenever a life change occurs, such as a birth, death, or significant financial change.

A trust can be a useful wealth-management tool because it can control the distribution of your hard-earned assets to the next generation and—if prepared carefully—can help reduce estate taxes. If a trust is irrevocable, meaning that you cannot change it during your lifetime, the assets in the trust may not be subject to estate taxes. Like the assets given directly to your kids, the assets you put into the trust are out of your direct control. Therefore, once transferred, they are no longer part of your estate and are not taxed like other assets.

Trusts are complex entities that should only be created with help from an attorney specializing in trusts. There are also separate tax laws that are applied to trusts that are similar to those taxes applied to individuals. Certain trusts pay their own income taxes at rates that could be higher than the rate paid by the individual. So you'll have to take special care when creating a trust to account for the possible vagaries of the tax laws.

Trusts can be customized to fit your asset distribution needs as well—passing out your assets in phases to your heirs, limiting their access to the assets altogether, and providing them only income from the trust. This strategy could come in handy if you or your spouse or partner have children from a previous relationship. For example, you may wish to provide income for your spouse or partner after your death, but don't want to transfer assets directly into their control. At your widow's death, assets that are transferred to your widow without any conditions or control by a trust, could be channeled, without your consent, to your widow's children and away from your own children. But a trust could provide income to support your spouse during their lifetime, and then transfer sufficient assets to your kids after your spouse's death.

CHAPTER 19

Preserving Wealth During Divorce

N
o one enters into a relationship planning for its demise. We all hope that "this will be the one" and that we'll be with our partner forever. But if that doesn't happen, special care must be given to preserving wealth and moving forward. Divorce can turn a wealthy couple into a pair of unmarried, money-strapped people who must start from scratch to build their riches.

Preserving What's Yours

Most people don't consider the financial aspects of combining a household with another until they are forced to part. Dividing the household is expensive and difficult. Even amicably separated spouses must decide whose assets belong to whom, a process that costs money and time, money that could be spent building wealth and time that could be spent multiplying it. But a divorce or breakup, while a potential major setback to your wealth plan, doesn't rule out growing rich. Even if you're faced with this stressful life change, it's important that you continue to plan your wealth throughout the process. Too often, the spouse or partner who most wants the divorce process to come to a rapid end is the one who sacrifices their financial security for the sake of a quick ending.

Care and time must be given to understanding the divorce or separation negotiations and their effect on your future financial security. Taking a slow, deliberate approach to the matter could help you avoid mistakes and oversights that could cost you a true fortune.

FACTS

The assets you accumulated before your marriage may or may not be considered marital assets if they have been combined into joint accounts. Talk to your lawyer about these ramifications before you start dividing things up. The best option: to have been clear about these issues before you combined assets in the first place. (In the next chapter we'll tell you about prenuptial agreements.)

Gather Information About Assets

Divorce should not be a departure from your regular wealth planning process. It may not have been part of your plan in the beginning, but it is one of the unfortunate obstacles that you may find yourself facing. If you are already doing a good job of keeping track of your assets—balancing checking and investment accounts, tracking investments, reviewing goals, and rebalancing investments—you should have no problem making a current net-worth statement to list your family's assets and liabilities. If you are just learning to pull together your financial information and have not yet developed net-worth and cash-flow statements, you may want to review Chapters 3 and 4 before getting started. In those chapters we talk about gathering asset and liability information, assuming that all parties are joined in the effort of getting on the path to wealth. This is not always the case in a divorce. If you and your partner are in the process of separating, you may find it more difficult to gather information unless you have regularly been part of its management.

A L E R T

Don't rush through the information-gathering phase, no matter how badly you want the separation process over with. Take the time to carefully gather assets and discover their true value. Once the divorce is final, there's no going back.

Your first step should be to gather several previous months' checking account statements. These statements should show withdrawals for regular household expenses such as utilities, mortgage or rent, debt payments, investments, and savings. Bank statements should also show deposits of wages and withdrawals of cash. Use the statements to develop a summary of where your monthly income comes from and where it goes. If there are no deposits from employers or business income, search for the accounts that these monies have been deposited into. If these payments are being converted directly to cash, they will be harder to track. In this case, ask your soon-to-be ex or their attorney for records showing the income received and an accounting of what was done with the money.

Use the bank account statements and other cash information to develop a household budget. Separate the various cash inflows and outflows into a list with a total amount at the bottom. At a glance you'll be able to see a picture of what it costs to run the household, where money is coming from, and where it goes.

While performing this chore—which you would be wise to do on your own, separate from the influence of the person you are separating from— you may notice that things have changed over the past few months. Depending on your personal situation, your partner may have started redirecting cash some time ago to better position themselves for the breakup. Be wary of this possibility and be alert to learn the details of any changes you notice in the budget information, such as:

- **Cash.** More cash withdrawals without explanation
- **Income change.** Reduction in income from employer or money drawn on business interests, or lower deferred commission payments for salespeople
- **Investment changes.** Increased investment expenses into separate accounts—employee stock purchase plans, pension or deferred compensation plans, 401(k) and 403(b) plans, and the like
- **Gifts.** Increased spending on gifts or other hard-to-track items.
- **Collectibles.** Disappearance of valuable or hard-to-value items

In addition, make sure that insurance premiums continue to be paid. Don't let unpaid life or disability payments go unnoticed as you gather information about your assets. Health and homeowner's insurance must also be continued. Check past bank statements for information about the companies that provide these insurances and contact them directly to be sure policies are up-to-date.

FACTS

Some studies have predicted that today's divorced fifty-year-old woman will be tomorrow's working poor. If you find yourself going though divorce proceedings later in life after spending a lifetime raising your kids, don't be afraid to hire competent legal counsel to guard your interest, as well as a financial planner who can help you understand your future financial needs.

Adjust Your Investments

Your next step should be to review your current investment portfolio with an eye toward your new situation. Investments that have been made for the long term may not be suitable if you are now in a more precarious financial situation that may require a more conservative approach. Don't necessarily make changes immediately before reassessing your goals. But a quick review of your investments at this early point can be helpful as you continue to collect information and adjust your plan.

Account statements showing your investment accounts should be received regularly in the mail: monthly, quarterly, or annually. You can also review past tax returns for evidence of interest or dividend payments made from various accounts. If you can't find an account statement from an investment listed in your tax return, contact the company directly for account information.

Some life insurance policies and all annuities have cash value that doesn't necessarily show up on tax returns. Pay extra attention to your mail for annual statements and to your checking account for premium or income payments to find these elusive assets.

At this early point you should check your investment accounts for:

- **Aggressive investments.** Overly aggressive investments could experience wild volatility over the short term. If assets drop significantly in value during the divorce proceedings, you may find yourself with less to divide than you might have originally thought. This may force you to sell and divide more stable assets, whose values have not changed, even though you might not have had reason to sell them if the investments had maintained value.

- **Too much employer stock.** Continuing to buy company stock may not be prudent in the necessarily shorter investment horizon a divorce often creates. Most employer plans allow the employee to make deposits directly from their paycheck. Be aware of how much is being invested and what the company withdrawal or sale policies are so you can make an informed decision about whether to not to continue purchasing.

- **Accounts that have been moved to new institutions.** Tracking investments across a move is sometimes difficult and assets can be "lost" in the transfer. Be sure you have copies of the account statements from both the old and new accounts. Check investment share amounts on both ends of the transfer to be sure all assets are accounted for.

If you're facing divorce you should delay making big financial decisions. New investments to your portfolio, home-improvement projects, expensive vacations and other large purchases can wait until you have a clear financial horizon in front of you. If your spouse or partner needs a new place to live, or if you are leaving the family home, rent, don't buy. Projects, investments, and purchases undertaken when you are under stress are seldom the right decision for the long term and can sap wealth right when you need it most.

Establishing Your New Goals

Now that you've established your starting point—collecting your financial information and adjusting your investments, if necessary—you're ready to start building your new financial goals.

Reviewing Your Own Plan

The plan you had before separating from your partner may no longer reflect your goals—maybe it never did. Go back to the wealth journal we discussed in Chapter 8 and your wealth mission statement from Chapter 1 and write about your new goals. Your wealth journal will help you express your new ideas about financial security and the future and may help you avoid chasing quick changes that are unsatisfying and wealth robbing. Talk to your counselor about the financial changes you're undergoing and ideas for the future. Many folks let the financial part of divorce go undiscussed—but it was one of the most important parts of your life before the separation, and it should be after. Think about, talk about, and plan your financial future. Then, with a long-term perspective in mind, go to the negotiating table.

ESSENTIALS Regardless of how amicable your separation is, hire your own financial planner to help you understand your personal financial situation and plan financial negotiations. If you and your partner have been working with someone for a long time, talk about who will continue with them and who will hire a new advisor.

Adjusting Your Financial Goals

Go back over the goals that you had before your separation. Which ones are yours alone and which ones reflected the wishes of your partner? Do you still want a new house, to pay for college for the kids, to vacation in an expensive resort every year, to retire in Florida, to drive an expensive car? Don't worry if these answers don't come to you right away. Give yourself time to search for the new you and move ahead slowly with your new financial self. In the meantime, review your investment portfolio with an advisor who's practiced working with people facing divorce. Decide whether you should make changes or whether your current asset allocation still works in your new situation. Ask them for help planning for your new goals and ask them to act as a second opinion on your negotiating points. An experienced financial planner can be an invaluable resource to keep your wealth plan on track as you negotiate your divorce.

The Expense of Getting Divorced

Getting divorced is not cheap. The expense of the extra legal, financial, and tax advice you'll need is one of those financial roadblocks that we come across in life that can derail a plan. Don't overly depend on your advisors. You can think through many of the decisions that have to be made on your own, and then go to your advisors for a second opinion. Some things you might consider before talking to your advisors are:

- Do you want to keep the house yourself or sell it and split the proceeds with your partner? What would it cost to support the house? Can you afford to keep the house and still save for your other financial goals? How much could you get if you sell the house? How could you use that money? If you had that money today, would you buy the house again?
- How do you feel about funding your children's education? Splitting one household into two will be more expensive than maintaining the one. This extra expense may necessitate rethinking your college funding plans. What are your new goals for college saving?

- Are you going to change your work life? If you are currently not working, should you get a job? What would that job pay? Are there jobs in that field available in the area?

Consider the expense of setting up housekeeping in a new location if you are the one to leave the family home. New dishes, towels, furniture, lawn-care equipment, and the like can add up and could break your new budget if you don't include their cost in your negotiations.

The more thinking and planning you do yourself, the better off your pocketbook will be when the dust settles. By planning and reflecting on your finances ahead of time, collecting financial information well in advance, and preparing for each meeting with your advisors you can save valuable cash while still getting good advice. Use your meetings with your advisors wisely, but don't scrimp on professional advice. Remember too that your lawyer, financial planner, and accountant are not counselors. While they may be sympathetic to your situation, their primary function is to help safeguard your money and other interests. If you need to talk to someone about the pain you're feeling, see a counselor.

Negotiating Your Share of the Wealth

Once complete financial information has been gathered, most people do a good job of recognizing how to split the bank and investment accounts in half. But most don't realize the true value of pension plans and career earning potential.

Pension Plans: Money Now Is Better Than Money Later

As we've discussed in earlier chapters, a pension plan is a promise of retirement income. They are only offered by some employers, including the government, and are generally a payment based on the employee's tenure with the company and their salary at retirement. Some pension benefits completely disappear if the employee leaves the employer before a certain age or time (called a vesting schedule). Some benefits vest over a period of time so that even a short-term employee may be entitled to some benefits even if they leave their employment before retirement.

Many separation agreements will cause the pension benefit to be paid solely to one or the other of the partners (regardless of whose pension it is). Some will ignore the benefit altogether. Neither of these choices—like much of the separation agreement—is the best choice for either party. Before pursuing one or the other strategy, you should be informed about the pluses and minuses of each.

FACTS

If you are getting divorced, your ex-spouse's retirement plan can be transferred into your name without a tax penalty through a legal directive called a quadro. As part of the divorce agreement, the court can order that the account—or part of the account—be transferred into your name. Then you can use the account just as if it was yours all along.

Some pension benefits can be changed by the company and could disappear altogether if the company goes out of business. Money now is always better than money later. And money that you control yourself is best. If the pension is not due to be paid until some long-future date, many things could happen to reduce the benefit:

- The employee—or ex-employee—could die, triggering a reduced payment of benefit or no benefit to the employee's estate.
- The employee could leave the company, possibly reducing the benefit payable.
- The company could make a change in the pension plan that would make it less valuable an asset. This often happens when the company changes to a pension plan called a cash balance plan. In this case, participants are essentially "bought out of" their pension benefit with a cash payment equal to the present value of the pension benefit. Since

the assumptions used in determining this present value amount are not necessarily the same as those used to calculate the pension, the employee's account may be given less than expected as a payout.

Waiting for a future benefit based on the work history of an ex-partner or ex-spouse also keeps you linked to that partner longer than you might have intended. Being unable to make a clean break from each other can have psychological ramifications that go beyond the cash lost through an uninformed pension plan negotiation.

Earning Potential

The second major oversight committed in many separation agreements is the unequal future earning ability of each partner. If this difference is the result of different career tracks it may not seem equitable to penalize the higher-earning partner, but if the difference is the result of one partner being out of the workforce to raise the couple's children a discussion about support should be considered.

In most cases, the future value of a worker's earnings is so great the couple may not have assets enough to make a truly fair split. But, regardless of whether or not this is the case, an understanding of the true value of a partner's ability to earn a better living will help you to stand fast on other parts of the negotiation. Let's look at two examples (for help with these present value calculations, refer to the charts in Appendix B):

1. One couple aged forty-five has two teenage kids; one partner makes $85,000 per year, the other $42,000. Both partners are in business and would usually be expected to make a similar amount of money if not for the late start the lower-earning partner had into the workforce because she stayed home full-time to raise the kids.

   If both work until they are sixty-five, the present value of the higher-earning partner (using 4 percent inflation and no future raises) is $1.3 million. The present value of the lower-paid spouse under those same circumstances is $660,000. Should the higher-earning partner pay the lower the difference of $670,000? Maybe not, and they probably would not be able to even if they had the money, but other allowances should be made commensurate with the couple's circumstances. Maybe assets should be held back from the couple's estate to help the lower-paid partner with additional job training and support. Or the lower-earning partner should retain a larger portion of the couple's joint assets considering that the higher-earning partner is walking away with the greatest asset—their tenure in their job!

2. Another couple, aged fifty, have one child; one partner makes $150,000 per year as a doctor and the other partner receives $30,000 per year as an artist. Neither partner took time off from their careers to raise the one child. In fact, they both spent equal time caring for and nurturing their family. Up to this point the higher-earning partner has provided most of the family's support allowing the lower-paid partner to pursue other interests including that as an artist. Should the lower-paid partner be entitled to part of the difference between their two incomes of $1.3 million? Maybe not—after all, it was the high pay and career progress of the higher-paid partner that allowed the lower-earning partner to pursue their career dreams.

Your situation will almost certainly be different than these but hopefully these examples will help you to think along the lines of a fair division of assets with earning potential in mind.

Don't Argue over the Dishes

If possible, try to keep your separation negotiations from bogging down in the details of who gets what personal item. Arguments over simple household items with little or no sentimental value can be an immense wealth robber. Don't ask your attorney to spend hours arguing with the other side over who gets the good china and who gets the TV. And don't get drawn into these battles yourself, either. The legal fees, and subsequent therapy, you spend recovering from a dirty situation is not worth retaining the can opener and the ironing board. If your partner needs to keep the laundry basket—let 'em have it! You can set up a new household elsewhere after you've finished negotiations and gone on your way.

These examples may seem silly, but they are taken from real life. Stay focused on your goal of getting through the divorce with as much of your wealth and sanity intact as possible. Look ahead to re-establishing your wealth goals and getting back on track to financial security. If you're the one leaving the household and feel set-upon for the inconvenience, ask for a few extra thousand to pay for new dishes as part of the settlement but don't spend thousands more on legal fees when you don't have to.

To Mediate or Not to Mediate?

Mediation is becoming a popular alternative to the old-fashioned lawyer-driven divorce. The thought is that this process is less argumentative, less negative, and less expensive. A mediator acts as a impartial third party to help the two separating partners come to a mutual agreement on how to separate. Each partner can bring their own suggestions to each mediation session or they may each bring information in response to the mediator's questions.

Some couples work with a mediator for the sake of their children because they think the process will be less confrontational. This may or may not be the case. Before considering this route, look closely at your ability to negotiate and the status of both partners in the relationship.

Take the time to interview a couple of mediators before making a choice. Some mediators also work as attorneys and could be retained to represent you in your divorce as long as you haven't previously discussed mediation with them.

When It Works—and When It Doesn't

Mediation can work well when both parties are on relatively equal emotional and financial footing. Each is able to understand the proceedings and each is represented by separate legal counsel who is providing information about the legal ramifications of each decision. If you and your partner couldn't have a civil discussion about money or the kids while you were together, why would you think that your separation would allow you any greater civility? If both partners are equally involved and both feel equally empowered by the process, mediation can be a productive means to an end. But, if one person feels browbeaten, pushed into a decision, or simply grows too weary of the process to continue, the process will fail. In the worst case, the agreement reached will be inequitable. Or at least, the mediator will recognize the problem and send both partners to their respective attorneys.

How to Work with a Mediator

No matter what type of divorce you pursue, you must retain your own legal counsel. Even if your mediator is a lawyer, they will be unable to offer legal advice in your interest. As a mediator they must remain impartial and can only offer general advice. The court should avoid allowing an uneven judgment and, regardless of its equality, the final decree is unchangeable. Don't proceed with such an important decision without qualified legal counsel. Also, maintain a close relationship with your financial advisor throughout the mediation process. Talk to them about your progress and be sure that you are maintaining a strong position throughout the negotiations.

CHAPTER 20

Preserving Wealth When You're a Widow or Widower

Picking up the pieces after a loved one's death is seldom easy. That's even more the case if you've lost a partner or a spouse. Aside from the pain of losing a close friend, the financial recovery can be difficult, especially if your partner was the one handling the money. Making the family's financial information easy to understand should be a goal for every family member.

The Executor's Duty

Even after the death of a spouse or partner, the mundane daily financial matters with which we are all familiar must still be tended to. Bills fill up our mailbox; rents and mortgages must be paid each month. And the final salary check for wage-earning deceased loved ones still comes in, meaning we must decide how best to manage that income and income from other streams. Pulling all this information together and managing the closing of the estate of the deceased person is most often the duty of the executor. After being nominated by the probate court—which either follows the instructions left in a will or nominates a suitable person if no will was left by the deceased—the executor should get to work gathering the financial information and managing the remaining loose ends of the estate. These loose ends may include:

- Assessing the value of the estate
- Representing the estate before the probate court
- Selling real estate or other property in order to distribute assets to the heirs
- Managing the day-to-day affairs of the estate
- Making final distributions to the heirs

SSENTIALS It's prudent to create a summary of the state of things with a competent advisor before letting your affairs lie for a bit. There may be some pressing issues that need your immediate attention, and a competent advisor can help you decide if that's the case.

The probate process is—intentionally and necessarily—a slow process. If you are the widow or widower, and find yourself also in the role of the executor of a spouse's or partner's estate, it's very important that you understand a vital point that could save you wealth by encouraging you to seek professional advice: Few decisions need to be made quickly. (The lawyer handling the probate will advise you on any decisions that need to be made right away.)

For example, it may take a month or two for you to be formally named as the executor of the estate. Until then, you will have access to the funds in the accounts you and your spouse or partner held jointly. You can also review the estate and decide what to do with your spouse or partner's retirement accounts, pensions, and life insurance policies. Or you can wait and focus on emotional healing, and leave the money until you are able to deal with it reasonably.

Assessing the Estate: Finding Your Starting Point

The duties of an executor or trustee can be so varied that they can seem almost endless, particularly when a great deal of wealth and a broad spectrum of assets are at stake. Assume for the sake of this discussion that you have already tended to these many duties, or are not required to. We'll assume that you are simply trying to get your personal finances together, pick up the pieces, and move forward with your wealth plan. As you gather your financial information, you should summarize each account and policy on a list, depending on its type. When you're finished, you'll have an asset list, a liability list, an income list, and a monthly expense list. From there you'll be able to rework an existing wealth plan or create a new one. Before taking action with any of the accounts, be sure to talk to your financial, tax, or legal advisor about the ramifications of each decision.

Where and How to Find Information

Financial information is found in a variety of places. A bankbook or other record of bank transactions can act as a helpful guide in discovering where everything is. If your loved one didn't have a central place where he or she kept financial records, your best bet in collecting information is keeping a close eye on the mail. Account statements from various places are mailed on a fairly regular basis to keep the account owner aware of balances and transactions. Organize the accounts you find and jot down—on a note pad or in a computer file—notes about what needs to be done next with each of them.

Bank Accounts

Bank account statements are mailed every month. If you haven't already received one, look for a checkbook in the estate records and call the banks listed on the checks to find out about accounts there. Of course, banks will usually be reluctant to give account information to anyone other than the account owner. Find out what paperwork the bank needs to release information to you or to the executor, and mark it down on your list. Also list the name, address, and phone number of the bank, the account number, and the approximate account balance.

Brokerage Accounts and Other Investment Accounts

Brokerage account statements and statements from other investments are often sent monthly. Some accounts feature a checking option, so you may find a checkbook as well as account statements among the financial records. Following the same process you did with the bank account statement, collect the account information and list it on your asset list.

If the brokerage account statement suggests that the account may be a margin account or that there is a loan out against the assets in the account, talk to the broker or other investment advisor about whether or not this loan should be paid sooner rather than later. Value could be lost if the loan is left against assets in a declining market. If the assets lose value to such a degree that the loan is not covered by the value of the securities held in the brokerage account, the account could experience a "margin call" for more money to be deposited. This call could result in the automatic sale of assets—at depressed prices—to cover the loan.

Annuities and Life Insurance

Annuity and life insurance statements are sent annually or semi-annually, so these accounts may not be easily noticed. Look for the policies them-selves, which are usually thin booklets with the name of the insurance company and a policy description on them. Some policies may be folded and contained within plastic envelopes or other protective sleeves. Contact the insurance company to find out who the beneficiary or beneficiaries of the account are and ask for distribution paperwork. Ask about the distribution options; both life insurance and annuities can be paid out as a lump sum payment or a stream of income to the beneficiary. The insurance company may also offer to hold the proceeds in a money market account. You can then have access to this money, as you need it.

There may be tax implications to receiving some annuities, and even some—although this is unlikely—life insurance proceeds. At this point in the process, you should only be collecting the information about these accounts and listing them on your asset list. Decisions about their dissolution can be made after talking to your tax advisor.

Credit Cards and Liabilities

Most creditors send bills on a monthly basis. These bills will need to be one of your first priorities, and should be forwarded to the executor or trustee to be paid. The executor will be given an account he or she can dip into to make these payments—often the deceased person's bank account or other liquid assets that will be relisted in the estate's name for this very purpose.

If you're the executor, make sure all the liabilities of the estate—including estate and income taxes—are satisfied before distributing assets from the estate. As executor you could be liable if the estate distributes money before paying off its liabilities.

List the estate's liabilities on a separate piece of paper with the details of each account: creditor name, account number, balance, minimum payment, and interest rate. Add to the list of details whether the liability applies only to the estate—something like a personal credit card of the deceased—or whether it continues to be a liability to you, the survivor—such as a joint mortgage on a jointly owned home, for example. As part of the dissolution of the estate, the personal debts of the deceased will be paid, but you will have to plan to continue to pay your debts yourself. We'll talk about planning for this in a moment when we discuss cash flow and budgets.

Pension Benefits

Check with your loved one's employer and past employers to find out if they were eligible for a pension payment. A pension may have a survivorship provision that pays a lump sum or an income to you or another beneficiary. Talk to the human resources department about the details. They will be able to calculate the benefit and will give you paperwork to claim the benefit. If the pension will be paid to you as a regular income payment, start a new, separate list, and record the amount of the payment and how frequently payments will be made.

If you have income choices, list these instead, along with the deadline, if any, for you to make a decision. As part of the budgeting analysis, you can decide which income choice might be best for you and your family. And if the pension will be paid as a lump sum, list it on the assets list.

Some pension benefits expire with the death of the worker unless a spousal benefit election has been made prior to death. Take extra care to review your pension benefit to ascertain whether this is the case and to make adjustments.

Back Pay

As the spouse or partner of an employee, you may be entitled to back wages the employee earned before his or her death. These wages may be paid to the estate—and can be used to pay debts—or they may be payable to you. Talk to the human resources department at your spouse or partner's workplace to find out what is available to you or the estate. List this information on the asset list as money that is expected and not yet received, or—if you have received a check—talk to the executor about where to deposit the money. Then list it as part of the balance of that account.

Health Benefits

As the spouse of a deceased employee, you may be eligible for health benefits under a program called COBRA—short for the Consolidated Omnibus Reconciliation Act. Under this program—which also applies in most cases after leaving an employer or if you have divorced an employee—you are eligible for health benefits for up to thirty-six months. Talk to the human resources department about your eligibility and how to apply. You'll have to pay a premium for this benefit, and you'll need to add this cost to a new list of monthly expenses.

Before deciding whether COBRA is your best option for health coverage, talk to your own employer or an agent about other coverage available and their costs. COBRA insurance can be surprisingly expensive.

Retirement Benefits from the Employer

Your loved one's employer may have provided a retirement program that lists you as the account beneficiary. Such programs could be called savings programs, 401(k), or thrift plans. Talk to the human resources department about these accounts and gather the distribution paperwork from them. There are several choices available to you as the widowed spouse:

- Leave the account as it is and let it grow tax-deferred until you need it.
- Transfer the account to an individual retirement account in your name.
- Transfer the account to an individual retirement account in the decedent's name.

There are many tax and legal ramifications involved with each of these choices. Talk to your advisors to decide which is the best choice for you.

Social Security

You may be eligible for a social security benefit at retirement based on your deceased spouse's work record. When you decide to begin drawing social security retirement benefits—age sixty-two is the earliest age you can do this—talk to the Social Security Administration about this benefit. You will receive a retirement benefit based on either your own benefit or your share of your late spouse's benefit, whichever is higher. If you are eligible to begin receiving an income benefit from social security, list the benefit on your income list.

FACTS

If you are caring for the deceased's children, you may be eligible to receive a monthly income benefit from social security. This benefit is available until the children are eighteen—or longer, if they were disabled before that age. The benefit will be divided between both you and the children, and may be reduced, depending on household income. Check with the Social Security Administration for details.

Developing a Plan: Net Worth and Cash Flow

Now that you have gathered all the information about available assets and income and have either settled all liabilities or assumed responsibility for some of them yourself, you are ready to prepare a net worth statement and a cash flow statement. Take a look back at Chapters 3 and 4 for instruction on how to develop these two crucial worksheets.

Once you have completed your net worth statement, you will have an idea of your assets, which you can use in achieving your wealth goals, and your debts or liabilities. Your cash flow statement will tell you from which sources your income is coming and what expenses and wealth goals it gets applied to each month. Work with your expenses and income so that there's ample money each month to develop a savings plan towards your wealth goals.

Adjusting Your Wealth Goals

Being single again after the years spent planning and growing with your partner is a difficult adjustment. Don't feel hurried to make changes to your wealth plan right away. Often, for the first year or two, it suffices to continue putting savings aside into a well-balanced investment account until your head is clear enough to think about what you want to do next. Talk to your advisors about your desire to tread water for a little while, and count on them to help direct you. Don't make drastic changes to your plan without first checking it with a couple of advisors. And be wary of people who tell you to make quick adjustments to your investments or finances.

When the time comes to make changes, spend time thinking about your new goals and wealth objectives in light of your new financial situation. If your loved one had extensive medical bills or other final expenses, you may find yourself set back a bit financially and with a need to catch up if you want to reach your wealth target on time. If your partner was well insured, you may, thankfully, find yourself with many choices and the power to make decisions without the pressure of having to scramble to cover daily expenses. If your budget is tight, with income only barely covering expenses, consider the following options.

Getting a Job

Depending on your monthly shortfall, you may only need a part-time job to fill in the gaps. If you are more financially strapped, you may need to concentrate on finding full-time work that pays well.

Sometimes the routine of even a part-time job is enough to help you get your life moving forward again in a way that helps you see the past and the present, and plan for the future.

Selling the House

Often a large part of a family's wealth is in their home. You may find that it offers great peace of mind to move to a new environment and have the cash available from the sale of your home for income or for investing toward wealth. The lower expenses of a smaller home, and having more income than expenses, may also be welcome feelings.

Teaming Up

Being alone after many years of marriage or loving relationship can be a difficult transition, to say the least. Consider combining expenses with a friend or family member as a roommate. You may find the company—and extra income—most welcome.

Readjusting Your Estate Plan and Estate Documents

As we've mentioned, any significant life change should prompt a review of your estate plan. The loss of a spouse or partner is certainly one of these occasions. Get in touch with your estate-planning attorney—he or she may even be handling your spouse or partner's estate—and review your plan. Here are some things to think about before discussing your estate plan:

- Assigning a new executor or trustee for your own estate
- Assigning a new health-care proxy and power of attorney
- Making changes to health-care proxy or power-of-attorney documents if you wish to give different instruction to your new representatives
- Making changes to your will or trust documents to designate your assets to different beneficiaries
- Considering whether your new situation warrants keeping your life insurance and annuity plan, and if so, making beneficiary changes
- Making changes to asset ownership: Do you want to hold your assets individually, or should they be in trust or owned jointly with another?
- Clarifying any issues regarding your partner's estate with your own estate-planning attorney before receiving or disclaiming assets.

    It may be wiser, depending on your situation, not to receive some or any of the assets from your spouse's estate for tax purposes. If your own estate is already large enough to support you, it may be better to disclaim assets left to you by your spouse in favor of passing those assets to your children or other heirs. This is a complex legal and financial maneuver; be sure you have competent legal and tax guidance before attempting it.

Remarriage Safeguards

After this estate-plan update, the next occasion you might find to visit your lawyer might be if you remarry. Especially if either you or your new spouse has children from a previous marriage, you may consider ways to support the other, in the case of one's death, while still leaving your assets to your own children. Also, you may want to protect your wealth from your new spouse in the case of a divorce.

Some feel that prenuptial agreements or marriage contracts strip away some of the romance of an engagement and wedding, but these documents speak to the stark realities of our society. If you have worked hard to accumulate wealth before your marriage, it's wise to talk to a matrimonial attorney about an agreement to protect those assets.

SSENTIALS

If you're contemplating a prenuptial agreement, or if you're asked to sign one by your betrothed, be sure to consult an attorney well versed in matrimonial law. Contact the American Academy of Matrimonial Lawyers, *www.aaml.org*, for a list of professionals in your area.

A well-written prenuptial agreement can protect you from a legal concept that goes by an intriguing name: "fruit of the poisonous tree doctrine." This concept speaks to the problem of commingling assets in a marriage. The courts generally agree that those assets that are yours before the marriage continue to be yours after the marriage. That means if you maintain your assets in an account separate from your spouse, you may retain those assets even after a divorce. But if you give your spouse any access to those accounts, you risk commingling, and having the assets treated as joint assets under a law called the "equitable distribution statute." This aptly named rule states that assets of the marriage should be split fifty-fifty in the event of a divorce. Commingling can be very insidious, and may be taking place even when you're not aware of it. Even linking your spouse's checking account to your separate brokerage account could result in you losing half the account in a divorce.

A/B Trusts

As we discussed in Chapter 18, trusts can be designed to achieve a variety of estate-planning goals. They can be formed to leave money to a favorite charity, manage assets for small children, manage the cost of estate taxes, or, as we'll discuss here, they can direct your assets to your children while ensuring that your new spouse maintains his or her standard of living after your passing. Lawyers call this type of trust arrangement an A/B trust. This is how it works:

- After the asset owner dies, their assets are divided into two parts. Each part is deposited in a trust. One is called the A trust. One is called the B trust.
- The assets in the A trust are available to the spouse outright. He or she may withdraw them immediately; they may transfer the assets to their own account or give them away to their children.
- The assets in the B trust are not available to the widowed spouse except under special circumstances. These assets are managed within the trust, and the income is made available for the support of the widow. At the widow's death, the principal of the B trust and any unused interest are then distributed to the original asset owner's children. Trusts can be designed in a variety of different ways, depending on your desires and financial situation. A qualified estate-planning attorney will help you design a plan that is right for you.

APPENDIX A
Resources

Books

Downes, John, et al. *Dictionary of Finance and Investment Terms (Barron's Finance and Investment Handbook, 4th Ed).* Barron's Educational Series, 1998.

Hill, Napoleon. *Think and Grow Rich.* Fawcett Books, 1990.

Kiyosaki, Robert T., and Sharon L. Lechter. *Rich Dad, Poor Dad: What the Rich Teach Their Kids About Money—That the Poor and Middle Class Do Not!* Warner Books, 2000.

Kiyosaki, Robert T., and Sharon L. Lechter. *Rich Dad's Rich Kid, Smart Kid: Giving Your Children a Financial Headstart.* Warner Books, 2001.

Orman, Suze. *The Courage to Be Rich: Creating a Life of Material and Spiritual Abundance.* Riverhead Books, 1999.

Orman, Suze. *9 Steps to Financial Freedom: Practical and Spiritual Steps So You Can Stop Worrying.* Three Rivers Press, 2000.

Orman, Suze. *Road to Wealth: A Comprehensive Guide to Your Money—Everything You Need to Know in Good and Bad Times.* Riverhead Books, 2001.

Orman, Suze, and Linda Mead. *You've Earned It, Don't Lose It: Mistakes You Can't Afford to Make When You Retire.* Newmarket Press, 1997.

Sease, Douglas and John Prestbo. *Barron's Guide to Making Investment Decisions.* New York Institute of Finance, 1999.

Shapiro, Gail (ed.). *Money Order: The Money Management Guide for Women.* Simon & Schuster, 2001.

Siegel, Alan M., et al. *Wall Street Journal Guide to Planning Your Financial Future: The Easy-To-Read Guide to Planning for Retirement.* Fireside, 1998.

Stanley, Thomas J. *The Millionaire Mind.* Andrews McMeel Publishing, 2000.

Stanley, Thomas J., and William D. Danko. *The Millionaire Next Door: The Surprising Secrets of America's Wealthy.* Longstreet Press, 1996.

Series 7 Guides

Curley, Michael T., and Joseph A. Walker. *Barron's How to Prepare for the Stockbroker Exam: Series 7 (Barron's How to Prepare for the Stockbroker's Examination: Series 7, 2nd Ed).* Barron's Educational Series, 2000.

Meyers, Philip, et al. *Series 7 Stockbroker NASD Exam (5th Ed).* Arco Publishing, 1998.

Passtrak Series 7: General Securities Representative. Dearborn Trade, 2001.

Independent Rating Companies

A.M. Best Co., *www.ambest.com*

Moody's Investor Services, *www.moodys.com*

Morningstar, *www.morningstar.com*

Standard & Poor's, *www.standardandpoors.com*

Value Line, *www.valueline.com*

Investment Firms

Dreyfus, *www.dreyfus.com*

Eaton Vance Distributors, *www.eatonvance.com*

Fidelity Group, *www.fidelity.com*

John Hancock Funds, *www.johnhancock.com*

Putnam Investments, *www.putnaminv.com*

Vanguard Group, *www.vanguard.com*

Planners Association Web Sites

The Financial Planners Association, *www.fpanet.org*

National Association of Personal Financial Advisors, *www.napfa.org*

Appendix B
Charts

FUTURE VALUE FACTORS—CHART A

PERIODS	1%	2%	3%	4%	5%	6%	7%
1	1.0100	1.0200	1.0300	1.0400	1.0500	1.0600	1.0700
2	1.0201	1.0404	1.0609	1.0816	1.1025	1.1236	1.1449
3	1.0303	1.0612	1.0927	1.1249	1.1576	1.1910	1.2250
4	1.0406	1.0824	1.1255	1.1699	1.2155	1.2625	1.3108
5	1.0510	1.1041	1.1593	1.2167	1.2763	1.3382	1.4026
6	1.0615	1.1262	1.1941	1.2653	1.3401	1.4185	1.5007
7	1.0721	1.1487	1.2299	1.3159	1.4071	1.5036	1.6058
8	1.0829	1.1717	1.2668	1.3686	1.4775	1.5938	1.7182
9	1.0937	1.1951	1.3048	1.4233	1.5513	1.6895	1.8385
10	1.1046	1.2190	1.3439	1.4802	1.6289	1.7908	1.9672
11	1.1157	1.2434	1.3842	1.5395	1.7103	1.8983	2.1049
12	1.1268	1.2682	1.4258	1.6010	1.7959	2.0122	2.2522
13	1.1381	1.2936	1.4685	1.6651	1.8856	2.1329	2.4098
14	1.1495	1.3195	1.5126	1.7317	1.9799	2.2609	2.5785
15	1.1610	1.3459	1.5580	1.8009	2.0789	2.3966	2.7590
16	1.1726	1.3728	1.6047	1.8730	2.1829	2.5404	2.9522
17	1.1843	1.4002	1.6528	1.9479	2.2920	2.6928	3.1588
18	1.1961	1.4282	1.7024	2.0258	2.4066	2.8543	3.3799
19	1.2081	1.4568	1.7535	2.1068	2.5270	3.0256	3.6165
20	1.2202	1.4859	1.8061	2.1911	2.6533	3.2071	3.8697
21	1.2324	1.5157	1.8603	2.2788	2.7860	3.3996	4.1406
22	1.2447	1.5460	1.9161	2.3699	2.9253	3.6035	4.4304
23	1.2572	1.5769	1.9736	2.4647	3.0715	3.8197	4.7405
24	1.2697	1.6084	2.0328	2.5633	3.2251	4.0489	5.0724
25	1.2824	1.6406	2.0938	2.6658	3.3864	4.2919	5.4274
26	1.2953	1.6734	2.1566	2.7725	3.5557	4.5494	5.8074
27	1.3082	1.7069	2.2213	2.8834	3.7335	4.8223	6.2139
28	1.3213	1.7410	2.2879	2.9987	3.9201	5.1117	6.6488
29	1.3345	1.7758	2.3566	3.1187	4.1161	5.4184	7.1143
30	1.3478	1.8114	2.4273	3.2434	4.3219	5.7435	7.6123
31	1.3613	1.8476	2.5001	3.3731	4.5380	6.0881	8.1451
32	1.3749	1.8845	2.5751	3.5081	4.7649	6.4534	8.7153
33	1.3887	1.9222	2.6523	3.6484	5.0032	6.8406	9.3253
34	1.4026	1.9607	2.7319	3.7943	5.2533	7.2510	9.9781
35	1.4166	1.9999	2.8139	3.9461	5.5160	7.6861	10.6766
36	1.4308	2.0399	2.8983	4.1039	5.7918	8.1473	11.4239
37	1.4451	2.0807	2.9852	4.2681	6.0814	8.6361	12.2236
38	1.4595	2.1223	3.0748	4.4388	6.3855	9.1543	13.0793
39	1.4741	2.1647	3.1670	4.6164	6.7048	9.7035	13.9948
40	1.4889	2.2080	3.2620	4.8010	7.0400	10.2857	14.9745
41	1.5038	2.2522	3.3599	4.9931	7.3920	10.9029	16.0227
42	1.5188	2.2972	3.4607	5.1928	7.7616	11.5570	17.1443
43	1.5340	2.3432	3.5645	5.4005	8.1497	12.2505	18.3444
44	1.5493	2.3901	3.6715	5.6165	8.5572	12.9855	19.6285
45	1.5648	2.4379	3.7816	5.8412	8.9850	13.7646	21.0025
46	1.5805	2.4866	3.8950	6.0748	9.4343	14.5905	22.4726
47	1.5963	2.5363	4.0119	6.3178	9.9060	15.4659	24.0457
48	1.6122	2.5871	4.1323	6.5705	10.4013	16.3939	25.7289
49	1.6283	2.6388	4.2562	6.8333	10.9213	17.3775	27.5299
50	1.6446	2.6916	4.3839	7.1067	11.4674	18.4202	29.4570

FUTURE VALUE FACTORS—CHART A

PERIODS	8%	9%	10%	11%	12%	13%	14%
1	1.0000	1.0000	1.0000	1.0000	1.0000	1.0000	1.0000
2	2.0800	2.0900	2.1000	2.1100	2.1200	2.1300	2.1400
3	3.2464	3.2781	3.3100	3.3421	3.3744	3.4069	3.4396
4	4.5061	4.5731	4.6410	4.7097	4.7793	4.8498	4.9211
5	5.8666	5.9847	6.1051	6.2278	6.3528	6.4803	6.6101
6	7.3359	7.5233	7.7156	7.9129	8.1152	8.3227	8.5355
7	8.9228	9.2004	9.4872	9.7833	10.0890	10.4047	10.7305
8	10.6366	11.0285	11.4359	11.8594	12.2997	12.7573	13.2328
9	12.4876	13.0210	13.5795	14.1640	14.7757	15.4157	16.0853
10	14.4866	15.1929	15.9374	16.7220	17.5487	18.4197	19.3373
11	16.6455	17.5603	18.5312	19.5614	20.6546	21.8143	23.0445
12	18.9771	20.1407	21.3843	22.7132	24.1331	25.6502	27.2707
13	21.4953	22.9534	24.5227	26.2116	28.0291	29.9847	32.0887
14	24.2149	26.0192	27.9750	30.0949	32.3926	34.8827	37.5811
15	27.1521	29.3609	31.7725	34.4054	37.2797	40.4175	43.8424
16	30.3243	33.0034	35.9497	39.1899	42.7533	46.6717	50.9804
17	33.7502	36.9737	40.5447	44.5008	48.8837	53.7391	59.1176
18	37.4502	41.3013	45.5992	50.3959	55.7497	61.7251	68.3941
19	41.4463	46.0185	51.1591	56.9395	63.4397	70.7494	78.9692
20	45.7620	51.1601	57.2750	64.2028	72.0524	80.9468	91.0249
21	50.4229	56.7645	64.0025	72.2651	81.6987	92.4699	104.7684
22	55.4568	62.8733	71.4027	81.2143	92.5026	105.4910	120.4360
23	60.8933	69.5319	79.5430	91.1479	104.6029	120.2048	138.2970
24	66.7648	76.7898	88.4973	102.1742	118.1552	136.8315	158.6586
25	73.1059	84.7009	98.3471	114.4133	133.3339	155.6196	181.8708
26	79.9544	93.3240	109.1818	127.9988	150.3339	176.8501	208.3327
27	87.3508	102.7231	121.0999	143.0786	169.3740	200.8406	238.4993
28	95.3388	112.9682	134.2099	159.8173	190.6989	227.9499	272.8892
29	103.9659	124.1354	148.6309	178.3972	214.5828	258.5834	312.0937
30	113.2832	136.3075	164.4940	199.0209	241.3327	293.1992	356.7868
31	123.3459	149.5752	181.9434	221.9132	271.2926	332.3151	407.7370
32	134.2135	164.0370	201.1378	247.3236	304.8477	376.5161	465.8202
33	145.9506	179.8003	222.2515	275.5292	342.4294	426.4632	532.0350
34	158.6267	196.9823	245.4767	306.8374	384.5210	482.9034	607.5199
35	172.3168	215.7108	271.0244	341.5896	431.6635	546.6808	693.5727
36	187.1021	236.1247	299.1268	380.1644	484.4631	618.7493	791.6729
37	203.0703	258.3759	330.0395	422.9825	543.5987	700.1867	903.5071
38	220.3159	282.6298	364.0434	470.5106	609.8305	792.2110	1,030.9981
39	238.9412	309.0665	401.4478	523.2667	684.0102	896.1984	1,176.3378
40	259.0565	337.8824	442.5926	581.8261	767.0914	1,013.7042	1,342.0251
41	280.7810	369.2919	487.8518	646.8269	860.1424	1,146.4858	1,530.9086
42	304.2435	403.5281	537.6370	718.9779	964.3595	1,296.5289	1,746.2358
43	329.5830	440.8457	592.4007	799.0655	1,081.0826	1,466.0777	1,991.7088
44	356.9496	481.5218	652.6408	887.9627	1,211.8125	1,657.6678	2,271.5481
45	386.5056	525.8587	718.9048	986.6386	1,358.2300	1,874.1646	2,590.5648
46	418.4261	574.1860	791.7953	1,096.1688	1,522.2176	2,118.8060	2,954.2439
47	452.9002	626.8628	871.9749	1,217.7474	1,705.8838	2,395.2508	3,368.8380
48	490.1322	684.2804	960.1723	1,352.6996	1,911.5898	2,707.6334	3,841.4753
49	530.3427	746.8656	1,057.1896	1,502.4965	2,141.9806	3,060.6258	4,380.2819
50	573.7702	815.0836	1,163.9085	1,668.7712	2,400.0182	3,459.5071	4,994.5213

PRESENT VALUE OF ANNUITY FACTORS—CHART B

PERIODS	1%	2%	3%	4%	5%	6%	7%
1	0.9901	0.9804	0.9709	0.9615	0.9524	0.9434	0.9346
2	1.9704	1.9416	1.9135	1.8861	1.8594	1.8334	1.8080
3	2.9410	2.8839	2.8286	2.7751	2.7232	2.6730	2.6243
4	3.9020	3.8077	3.7171	3.6299	3.5460	3.4651	3.3872
5	4.8534	4.7135	4.5797	4.4518	4.3295	4.2124	4.1002
6	5.7955	5.6014	5.4172	5.2421	5.0757	4.9173	4.7665
7	6.7282	6.4720	6.2303	6.0021	5.7864	5.5824	5.3893
8	7.6517	7.3255	7.0197	6.7327	6.4632	6.2098	5.9713
9	8.5660	8.1622	7.7861	7.4353	7.1078	6.8017	6.5152
10	9.4713	8.9826	8.5302	8.1109	7.7217	7.3601	7.0236
11	10.3676	9.7868	9.2526	8.7605	8.3064	7.8869	7.4987
12	11.2551	10.5753	9.9540	9.3851	8.8633	8.3838	7.9427
13	12.1337	11.3484	10.6350	9.9856	9.3936	8.8527	8.3577
14	13.0037	12.1062	11.2961	10.5631	9.8986	9.2950	8.7455
15	13.8651	12.8493	11.9379	11.1184	10.3797	9.7122	9.1079
16	14.7179	13.5777	12.5611	11.6523	10.8378	10.1059	9.4466
17	15.5623	14.2919	13.1661	12.1657	11.2741	10.4773	9.7632
18	16.3983	14.9920	13.7535	12.6593	11.6896	10.8276	10.0591
19	17.2260	15.6785	14.3238	13.1339	12.0853	11.1581	10.3356
20	18.0456	16.3514	14.8775	13.5903	12.4622	11.4699	10.5940
21	18.8570	17.0112	15.4150	14.0292	12.8212	11.7641	10.8355
22	19.6604	17.6580	15.9369	14.4511	13.1630	12.0416	11.0612
23	20.4558	18.2922	16.4436	14.8568	13.4886	12.3034	11.2722
24	21.2434	18.9139	16.9355	15.2470	13.7986	12.5504	11.4693
25	22.0232	19.5235	17.4131	15.6221	14.0939	12.7834	11.6536
26	22.7952	20.1210	17.8768	15.9828	14.3752	13.0032	11.8258
27	23.5596	20.7069	18.3270	16.3296	14.6430	13.2105	11.9867
28	24.3164	21.2813	18.7641	16.6631	14.8981	13.4062	12.1371
29	25.0658	21.8444	19.1885	16.9837	15.1411	13.5907	12.2777
30	25.8077	22.3965	19.6004	17.2920	15.3725	13.7648	12.4090
31	26.5423	22.9377	20.0004	17.5885	15.5928	13.9291	12.5318
32	27.2696	23.4683	20.3888	17.8736	15.8027	14.0840	12.6466
33	27.9897	23.9886	20.7658	18.1476	16.0025	14.2302	12.7538
34	28.7027	24.4986	21.1318	18.4112	16.1929	14.3681	12.8540
35	29.4086	24.9986	21.4872	18.6646	16.3742	14.4982	12.9477
36	30.1075	25.4888	21.8323	18.9083	16.5469	14.6210	13.0352
37	30.7995	25.9695	22.1672	19.1426	16.7113	14.7368	13.1170
38	31.4847	26.4406	22.4925	19.3679	16.8679	14.8460	13.1935
39	32.1630	26.9026	22.8082	19.5845	17.0170	14.9491	13.2649
40	32.8347	27.3555	23.1148	19.7928	17.1591	15.0463	13.3317
41	33.4997	27.7995	23.4124	19.9931	17.2944	15.1380	13.3941
42	34.1581	28.2348	23.7014	20.1856	17.4232	15.2245	13.4524
43	34.8100	28.6616	23.9819	20.3708	17.5459	15.3062	13.5070
44	35.4555	29.0800	24.2543	20.5488	17.6628	15.3832	13.5579
45	36.0945	29.4902	24.5187	20.7200	17.7741	15.4558	13.6055
46	36.7272	29.8923	24.7754	20.8847	17.8801	15.5244	13.6500
47	37.3537	30.2866	25.0247	21.0429	17.9810	15.5890	13.6916
48	37.9740	30.6731	25.2667	21.1951	18.0772	15.6500	13.7305
49	38.5881	31.0521	25.5017	21.3415	18.1687	15.7076	13.7668
50	39.1961	31.4236	25.7298	21.4822	18.2559	15.7619	13.8007

PRESENT VALUE OF ANNUITY FACTORS—CHART B

PERIODS	8%	9%	10%	11%	12%	13%	14%
1	0.9259	0.9174	0.9091	0.9009	0.8929	0.8850	0.8772
2	1.7833	1.7591	1.7355	1.7125	1.6901	1.6681	1.6467
3	2.5771	2.5313	2.4869	2.4437	2.4018	2.3612	2.3216
4	3.3121	3.2397	3.1699	3.1024	3.0373	2.9745	2.9137
5	3.9927	3.8897	3.7908	3.6959	3.6048	3.5172	3.4331
6	4.6229	4.4859	4.3553	4.2305	4.1114	3.9975	3.8887
7	5.2064	5.0330	4.8684	4.7122	4.5638	4.4226	4.2883
8	5.7466	5.5348	5.3349	5.1461	4.9676	4.7988	4.6389
9	6.2469	5.9952	5.7590	5.5370	5.3282	5.1317	4.9464
10	6.7101	6.4177	6.1446	5.8892	5.6502	5.4262	5.2161
11	7.1390	6.8052	6.4951	6.2065	5.9377	5.6869	5.4527
12	7.5361	7.1607	6.8137	6.4924	6.1944	5.9176	5.6603
13	7.9038	7.4869	7.1034	6.7499	6.4235	6.1218	5.8424
14	8.2442	7.7862	7.3667	6.9819	6.6282	6.3025	6.0021
15	8.5595	8.0607	7.6061	7.1909	6.8109	6.4624	6.1422
16	8.8514	8.3126	7.8237	7.3792	6.9740	6.6039	6.2651
17	9.1216	8.5436	8.0216	7.5488	7.1196	6.7291	6.3729
18	9.3719	8.7556	8.2014	7.7016	7.2497	6.8399	6.4674
19	9.6036	8.9501	8.3649	7.8393	7.3658	6.9380	6.5504
20	9.8181	9.1285	8.5136	7.9633	7.4694	7.0248	6.6231
21	10.0168	9.2922	8.6487	8.0751	7.5620	7.1016	6.6870
22	10.2007	9.4424	8.7715	8.1757	7.6446	7.1695	6.7429
23	10.3711	9.5802	8.8832	8.2664	7.7184	7.2297	6.7921
24	10.5288	9.7066	8.9847	8.3481	7.7843	7.2829	6.8351
25	10.6748	9.8226	9.0770	8.4217	7.8431	7.3300	6.8729
26	10.8100	9.9290	9.1609	8.4881	7.8957	7.3717	6.9061
27	10.9352	10.0266	9.2372	8.5478	7.9426	7.4086	6.9352
28	11.0511	10.1161	9.3066	8.6016	7.9844	7.4412	6.9607
29	11.1584	10.1983	9.3696	8.6501	8.0218	7.4701	6.9830
30	11.2578	10.2737	9.4269	8.6938	8.0552	7.4957	7.0027
31	11.3498	10.3428	9.4790	8.7331	8.0850	7.5183	7.0199
32	11.4350	10.4062	9.5264	8.7686	8.1116	7.5383	7.0350
33	11.5139	10.4644	9.5694	8.8005	8.1354	7.5560	7.0482
34	11.5869	10.5178	9.6086	8.8293	8.1566	7.5717	7.0599
35	11.6546	10.5668	9.6442	8.8552	8.1755	7.5856	7.0700
36	11.7172	10.6118	9.6765	8.8786	8.1924	7.5979	7.0790
37	11.7752	10.6530	9.7059	8.8996	8.2075	7.6087	7.0868
38	11.8289	10.6908	9.7327	8.9186	8.2210	7.6183	7.0937
39	11.8786	10.7255	9.7570	8.9357	8.2330	7.6268	7.0997
40	11.9246	10.7574	9.7791	8.9511	8.2438	7.6344	7.1050
41	11.9672	10.7866	9.7991	8.9649	8.2534	7.6410	7.1097
42	12.0067	10.8134	9.8174	8.9774	8.2619	7.6469	7.1138
43	12.0432	10.8380	9.8340	8.9886	8.2696	7.6522	7.1173
44	12.0771	10.8605	9.8491	8.9988	8.2764	7.6568	7.1205
45	12.1084	10.8812	9.8628	9.0079	8.2825	7.6609	7.1232
46	12.1374	10.9002	9.8753	9.0161	8.2880	7.6645	7.1256
47	12.1643	10.9176	9.8866	9.0235	8.2928	7.6677	7.1277
48	12.1891	10.9336	9.8969	9.0302	8.2972	7.6705	7.1296
49	12.2122	10.9482	9.9063	9.0362	8.3010	7.6730	7.1312
50	12.2335	10.9617	9.9148	9.0417	8.3045	7.6752	7.1327

FUTURE VALUE OF ANNUITY FACTORS—CHART C

PERIODS	1%	2%	3%	4%	5%	6%	7%
1	1.0000	1.0000	1.0000	1.0000	1.0000	1.0000	1.0000
2	2.0100	2.0200	2.0300	2.0400	2.0500	2.0600	2.0700
3	3.0301	3.0604	3.0909	3.1216	3.1525	3.1836	3.2149
4	4.0604	4.1216	4.1836	4.2465	4.3101	4.3746	4.4399
5	5.1010	5.2040	5.3091	5.4163	5.5256	5.6371	5.7507
6	6.1520	6.3081	6.4684	6.6330	6.8019	6.9753	7.1533
7	7.2135	7.4343	7.6625	7.8983	8.1420	8.3938	8.6540
8	8.2857	8.5830	8.8923	9.2142	9.5491	9.8975	10.2598
9	9.3685	9.7546	10.1591	10.5828	11.0266	11.4913	11.9780
10	10.4622	10.9497	11.4639	12.0061	12.5779	13.1808	13.8164
11	11.5668	12.1687	12.8078	13.4864	14.2068	14.9716	15.7836
12	12.6825	13.4121	14.1920	15.0258	15.9171	16.8699	17.8885
13	13.8093	14.6803	15.6178	16.6268	17.7130	18.8821	20.1406
14	14.9474	15.9739	17.0863	18.2919	19.5986	21.0151	22.5505
15	16.0969	17.2934	18.5989	20.0236	21.5786	23.2760	25.1290
16	17.2579	18.6393	20.1569	21.8245	23.6575	25.6725	27.8881
17	18.4304	20.0121	21.7616	23.6975	25.8404	28.2129	30.8402
18	19.6147	21.4123	23.4144	25.6454	28.1324	30.9057	33.9990
19	20.8109	22.8406	25.1169	27.6712	30.5390	33.7600	37.3790
20	22.0190	24.2974	26.8704	29.7781	33.0660	36.7856	40.9955
21	23.2392	25.7833	28.6765	31.9692	35.7193	39.9927	44.8652
22	24.4716	27.2990	30.5368	34.2480	38.5052	43.3923	49.0057
23	25.7163	28.8450	32.4529	36.6179	41.4305	46.9958	53.4361
24	26.9735	30.4219	34.4265	39.0826	44.5020	50.8156	58.1767
25	28.2432	32.0303	36.4593	41.6459	47.7271	54.8645	63.2490
26	29.5256	33.6709	38.5530	44.3117	51.1135	59.1564	68.6765
27	30.8209	35.3443	40.7096	47.0842	54.6691	63.7058	74.4838
28	32.1291	37.0512	42.9309	49.9676	58.4026	68.5281	80.6977
29	33.4504	38.7922	45.2189	52.9663	62.3227	73.6398	87.3465
30	34.7849	40.5681	47.5754	56.0849	66.4388	79.0582	94.4608
31	36.1327	42.3794	50.0027	59.3283	70.7608	84.8017	102.0730
32	37.4941	44.2270	52.5028	62.7015	75.2988	90.8898	110.2182
33	38.8690	46.1116	55.0778	66.2095	80.0638	97.3432	118.9334
34	40.2577	48.0338	57.7302	69.8579	85.0670	104.1838	128.2588
35	41.6603	49.9945	60.4621	73.6522	90.3203	111.4348	138.2369
36	43.0769	51.9944	63.2759	77.5983	95.8363	119.1209	148.9135
37	44.5076	54.0343	66.1742	81.7022	101.6281	127.2681	160.3374
38	45.9527	56.1149	69.1594	85.9703	107.7095	135.9042	172.5610
39	47.4123	58.2372	72.2342	90.4091	114.0950	145.0585	185.6403
40	48.8864	60.4020	75.4013	95.0255	120.7998	154.7620	199.6351
41	50.3752	62.6100	78.6633	99.8265	127.8398	165.0477	214.6096
42	51.8790	64.8622	82.0232	104.8196	135.2318	175.9505	230.6322
43	53.3978	67.1595	85.4839	110.0124	142.9933	187.5076	247.7765
44	54.9318	69.5027	89.0484	115.4129	151.1430	199.7580	266.1209
45	56.4811	71.8927	92.7199	121.0294	159.7002	212.7435	285.7493
46	58.0459	74.3306	96.5015	126.8706	168.6852	226.5081	306.7518
47	59.6263	76.8172	100.3965	132.9454	178.1194	241.0986	329.2244
48	61.2226	79.3535	104.4084	139.2632	188.0254	256.5645	353.2701
49	62.8348	81.9406	108.5406	145.8337	198.4267	272.9584	378.9990
50	64.4632	84.5794	112.7969	152.6671	209.3480	290.3359	406.5289

FUTURE VALUE OF ANNUITY FACTORS—CHART C

PERIODS	8%	9%	10%	11%	12%	13%	14%
1	1.0000	1.0000	1.0000	1.0000	1.0000	1.0000	1.0000
2	2.0800	2.0900	2.1000	2.1100	2.1200	2.1300	2.1400
3	3.2464	3.2781	3.3100	3.3421	3.3744	3.4069	3.4396
4	4.5061	4.5731	4.6410	4.7097	4.7793	4.8498	4.9211
5	5.8666	5.9847	6.1051	6.2278	6.3528	6.4803	6.6101
6	7.3359	7.5233	7.7156	7.9129	8.1152	8.3227	8.5355
7	8.9228	9.2004	9.4872	9.7833	10.0890	10.4047	10.7305
8	10.6366	11.0285	11.4359	11.8594	12.2997	12.7573	13.2328
9	12.4876	13.0210	13.5795	14.1640	14.7757	15.4157	16.0853
10	14.4866	15.1929	15.9374	16.7220	17.5487	18.4197	19.3373
11	16.6455	17.5603	18.5312	19.5614	20.6546	21.8143	23.0445
12	18.9771	20.1407	21.3843	22.7132	24.1331	25.6502	27.2707
13	21.4953	22.9534	24.5227	26.2116	28.0291	29.9847	32.0887
14	24.2149	26.0192	27.9750	30.0949	32.3926	34.8827	37.5811
15	27.1521	29.3609	31.7725	34.4054	37.2797	40.4175	43.8424
16	30.3243	33.0034	35.9497	39.1899	42.7533	46.6717	50.9804
17	33.7502	36.9737	40.5447	44.5008	48.8837	53.7391	59.1176
18	37.4502	41.3013	45.5992	50.3959	55.7497	61.7251	68.3941
19	41.4463	46.0185	51.1591	56.9395	63.4397	70.7494	78.9692
20	45.7620	51.1601	57.2750	64.2028	72.0524	80.9468	91.0249
21	50.4229	56.7645	64.0025	72.2651	81.6987	92.4699	104.7684
22	55.4568	62.8733	71.4027	81.2143	92.5026	105.4910	120.4360
23	60.8933	69.5319	79.5430	91.1479	104.6029	120.2048	138.2970
24	66.7648	76.7898	88.4973	102.1742	118.1552	136.8315	158.6586
25	73.1059	84.7009	98.3471	114.4133	133.3339	155.6196	181.8708
26	79.9544	93.3240	109.1818	127.9988	150.3339	176.8501	208.3327
27	87.3508	102.7231	121.0999	143.0786	169.3740	200.8406	238.4993
28	95.3388	112.9682	134.2099	159.8173	190.6989	227.9499	272.8892
29	103.9659	124.1354	148.6309	178.3972	214.5828	258.5834	312.0937
30	113.2832	136.3075	164.4940	199.0209	241.3327	293.1992	356.7868
31	123.3459	149.5752	181.9434	221.9132	271.2926	332.3151	407.7370
32	134.2135	164.0370	201.1378	247.3236	304.8477	376.5161	465.8202
33	145.9506	179.8003	222.2515	275.5292	342.4294	426.4632	532.0350
34	158.6267	196.9823	245.4767	306.8374	384.5210	482.9034	607.5199
35	172.3168	215.7108	271.0244	341.5896	431.6635	546.6808	693.5727
36	187.1021	236.1247	299.1268	380.1644	484.4631	618.7493	791.6729
37	203.0703	258.3759	330.0395	422.9825	543.5987	700.1867	903.5071
38	220.3159	282.6298	364.0434	470.5106	609.8305	792.2110	1,030.9981
39	238.9412	309.0665	401.4478	523.2667	684.0102	896.1984	1,176.3378
40	259.0565	337.8824	442.5926	581.8261	767.0914	1,013.7042	1,342.0251
41	280.7810	369.2919	487.8518	646.8269	860.1424	1,146.4858	1,530.9086
42	304.2435	403.5281	537.6370	718.9779	964.3595	1,296.5289	1,746.2358
43	329.5830	440.8457	592.4007	799.0655	1,081.0826	1,466.0777	1,991.7088
44	356.9496	481.5218	652.6408	887.9627	1,211.8125	1,657.6678	2,271.5481
45	386.5056	525.8587	718.9048	986.6386	1,358.2300	1,874.1646	2,590.5648
46	418.4261	574.1860	791.7953	1,096.1688	1,522.2176	2,118.8060	2,954.2439
47	452.9002	626.8628	871.9749	1,217.7474	1,705.8838	2,395.2508	3,368.8380
48	490.1322	684.2804	960.1723	1,352.6996	1,911.5898	2,707.6334	3,841.4753
49	530.3427	746.8656	1,057.1896	1,502.4965	2,141.9806	3,060.6258	4,380.2819
50	573.7702	815.0836	1,163.9085	1,668.7712	2,400.0182	3,459.5071	4,994.5213

Index

A

A/B trusts, 288
Accountants, 146
Actively managed fund, 154
Active managed accounts, 147
    passive accounts versus, 150
Activities of daily living (ADL) in
    ong-term care insurance, 94
Actuarial tables, 71
Actuaries, 70, 71
Adjusted gross income, 229
Advisors
    commissioned, 241–42, 243–44
    fee-based, 242–43, 244
    fee-only, 242, 244
    hiring financial, 16
    wealth, 235–47
Aggressive allocation, 111
Aggressive investments, 267
All-risk policy, 74
A.M. Best, 146
American Academy of Matrimonial
    Lawyers, 287
American Stock Exchange, 160
Annuities
    future value of annuity factors,
        296–97
    present value of annuity factors,
        294–95
    in settling estate, 280–81
    variable, 161–62
Appraisals, 44
Asset allocation, 108–14, 156
    analyzing investment portfolio for,
        117–20
Asset correlation, 204
Assets
    bonds as, 40–41
    fixed, 40–41
    gathering information about,
        in divorce, 264–66
    insuring, 80
    invested, 37, 39
    leaving, to charity, 259
    on net worth statement,
        37–44

sharing, with family, 256–57
    use, 38, 40
A trust, 288
Attitudes toward money, 2–8
Auto insurance
    collision/comprehensive, 79
    liability coverage, 78
    medical payments, 78–79
    uninsured/underinsured, 78–79
Average cost per share, 48

B

Back-end loads, 153
Back pay in settling estate, 282
Balanced allocation, 111
Bank accounts
    in settling estate, 280
    sharing, with children, 255
Bank account statements, 265
    in tracking money, 57
Benefit amount
    in disability insurance, 92
    in long-term care insurance, 94
Benefit period
    in disability insurance, 91
    in long-term care insurance, 94
Berkshire Hathaway, 131
Bonds, 136–38
    as asset in net worth statement, 37
    buying, 129–30
    convertible, 128
    credit ratings, 145–46
    diversifying your risk in, 127–28
    EE, 128
    face value of, 40
    foreign, 128
    government, 127
    high-yield, 128
    inflation, 128, 201, 234
    interest rates on, 138, 199
    in investment portfolio,
        114, 127–28
    junk, 145
    municipal, 128, 233–34
    retirement and, 203–4
    treasury, 127–28, 200, 233–34
    U.S. savings, 128

Bonuses, investing, in building wealth,
    17–18
Brokerage accounts, 47–48
    cash in, 48
    self-directed, 18
    in settling estate, 280
Brokerage firms
    discount, 108
    full-service, 108, 132
B trust, 288
Budgeting, 62–68, 194
    cash flow and, 60–61
    hitting your targets, 61–62
Buffet, Warren, 131
Business owners, income taxes
    for, 226–27

C

Cable television, saving money on, 67
Cancellation in disability insurance, 92
Capital gains, 148, 231
Capital gains taxes, 49, 148, 232
Cash-balance plan, 211
Cash/cash equivalents in net worth
    statement, 37, 40, 48
Cash flow statements, 53–68, 265
    budgeting and, 62–68
    cash flow and, 59–60, 60–61
    divorce and, 265
    hitting your budgeting targets, 61–62
    sample, 63
    tallying income, 58–59
    tracking your expenses, 54–58
    for widow/widower, 194–95
Cash in investment portfolio, 114, 128
Cash issues, 50
Cash savings, 128
Cash value, 82
    of traditional life insurance, 37
Cash value coverage, 74
    replacement cost versus, 74
Certificates
    redeeming, 130
    safeguarding, 130
Certificates of deposit (CDs), 41, 128
Certified Financial Planners, 245
Certified Insurance Counselor (CIC), 72

We Have EVERYTHING!

Everything® **After College Book**
$12.95, 1-55850-847-3

Everything® **American History Book**
$12.95, 1-58062-531-2

Everything® **Angels Book**
$12.95, 1-58062-398-0

Everything® **Anti-Aging Book**
$12.95, 1-58062-565-7

Everything® **Astrology Book**
$12.95, 1-58062-062-0

Everything® **Baby Names Book**
$12.95, 1-55850-655-1

Everything® **Baby Shower Book**
$12.95, 1-58062-305-0

Everything® **Baby's First Food Book**
$12.95, 1-58062-512-6

Everything® **Baby's First Year Book**
$12.95, 1-58062-581-9

Everything® **Barbeque Cookbook**
$12.95, 1-58062-316-6

Everything® **Bartender's Book**
$9.95, 1-55850-536-9

Everything® **Bedtime Story Book**
$12.95, 1-58062-147-3

Everything® **Bicycle Book**
$12.00, 1-55850-706-X

Everything® **Breastfeeding Book**
$12.95, 1-58062-582-7

Everything® **Build Your Own Home Page**
$12.95, 1-58062-339-5

Everything® **Business Planning Book**
$12.95, 1-58062-491-X

Everything® **Candlemaking Book**
$12.95, 1-58062-623-8

Everything® **Casino Gambling Book**
$12.95, 1-55850-762-0

Everything® **Cat Book**
$12.95, 1-55850-710-8

Everything® **Chocolate Cookbook**
$12.95, 1-58062-405-7

Everything® **Christmas Book**
$15.00, 1-55850-697-7

Everything® **Civil War Book**
$12.95, 1-58062-366-2

Everything® **Classical Mythology Book**
$12.95, 1-58062-653-X

Everything® **Collectibles Book**
$12.95, 1-58062-645-9

Everything® **College Survival Book**
$12.95, 1-55850-720-5

Everything® **Computer Book**
$12.95, 1-58062-401-4

Everything® **Cookbook**
$14.95, 1-58062-400-6

Everything® **Cover Letter Book**
$12.95, 1-58062-312-3

Everything® **Creative Writing Book**
$12.95, 1-58062-647-5

Everything® **Crossword and Puzzle Book**
$12.95, 1-55850-764-7

Everything® **Dating Book**
$12.95, 1-58062-185-6

Everything® **Dessert Book**
$12.95, 1-55850-717-5

Everything® **Digital Photography Book**
$12.95, 1-58062-574-6

Everything® **Dog Book**
$12.95, 1-58062-144-9

Everything® **Dreams Book**
$12.95, 1-55850-806-6

Everything® **Etiquette Book**
$12.95, 1-55850-807-4

Everything® **Fairy Tales Book**
$12.95, 1-58062-546-0

Everything® **Family Tree Book**
$12.95, 1-55850-763-9

Everything® **Feng Shui Book**
$12.95, 1-58062-587-8

Everything® **Fly-Fishing Book**
$12.95, 1-58062-148-1

Everything® **Games Book**
$12.95, 1-55850-643-8

Everything® **Get-A-Job Book**
$12.95, 1-58062-223-2

Everything® **Get Out of Debt Book**
$12.95, 1-58062-588-6

Everything® **Get Published Book**
$12.95, 1-58062-315-8

Everything® **Get Ready for Baby Book**
$12.95, 1-55850-844-9

Everything® **Get Rich Book**
$12.95, 1-58062-670-X

Everything® **Ghost Book**
$12.95, 1-58062-533-9

Everything® **Golf Book**
$12.95, 1-55850-814-7

Everything® **Grammar and Style Book**
$12.95, 1-58062-573-8

Everything® **Guide to Las Vegas**
$12.95, 1-58062-438-3

Everything® **Guide to New England**
$12.95, 1-58062-589-4

Everything® **Guide to New York City**
$12.95, 1-58062-314-X

Everything® **Guide to Walt Disney World®,**
Universal Studios®, and
Greater Orlando, 2nd Edition
$12.95, 1-58062-404-9

Everything® **Guide to Washington D.C.**
$12.95, 1-58062-313-1

Everything® **Guitar Book**
$12.95, 1-58062-555-X

Everything® **Herbal Remedies Book**
$12.95, 1-58062-331-X

Available wherever books are sold!
To order, call 800-872-5627, or visit everything.com
Adams Media Corporation, 57 Littlefield Street, Avon, MA 02322. U.S.A.

Everything® **Home-Based Business Book**
$12.95, 1-58062-364-6

Everything® **Homebuying Book**
$12.95, 1-58062-074-4

Everything® **Homeselling Book**
$12.95, 1-58062-304-2

Everything® **Horse Book**
$12.95, 1-58062-564-9

Everything® **Hot Careers Book**
$12.95, 1-58062-486-3

Everything® **Internet Book**
$12.95, 1-58062-073-6

Everything® **Investing Book**
$12.95, 1-58062-149-X

Everything® **Jewish Wedding Book**
$12.95, 1-55850-801-5

Everything® **Job Interview Book**
$12.95, 1-58062-493-6

Everything® **Lawn Care Book**
$12.95, 1-58062-487-1

Everything® **Leadership Book**
$12.95, 1-58062-513-4

Everything® **Learning French Book**
$12.95, 1-58062-649-1

Everything® **Learning Spanish Book**
$12.95, 1-58062-575-4

Everything® **Low-Fat High-Flavor Cookbook**
$12.95, 1-55850-802-3

Everything® **Magic Book**
$12.95, 1-58062-418-9

Everything® **Managing People Book**
$12.95, 1-58062-577-0

Everything® **Microsoft® Word 2000 Book**
$12.95, 1-58062-306-9

Everything® **Money Book**
$12.95, 1-58062-145-7

Everything® **Mother Goose Book**
$12.95, 1-58062-490-1

Everything® **Motorcycle Book**
$12.95, 1-58062-554-1

Everything® **Mutual Funds Book**
$12.95, 1-58062-419-7

Everything® **One-Pot Cookbook**
$12.95, 1-58062-186-4

Everything® **Online Business Book**
$12.95, 1-58062-320-4

Everything® **Online Genealogy Book**
$12.95, 1-58062-402-2

Everything® **Online Investing Book**
$12.95, 1-58062-338-7

Everything® **Online Job Search Book**
$12.95, 1-58062-365-4

Everything® **Organize Your Home Book**
$12.95, 1-58062-617-3

Everything® **Pasta Book**
$12.95, 1-55850-719-1

Everything® **Philosophy Book**
$12.95, 1-58062-644-0

Everything® **Playing Piano and Keyboards Book**
$12.95, 1-58062-651-3

Everything® **Pregnancy Book**
$12.95, 1-58062-146-5

Everything® **Pregnancy Organizer**
$15.00, 1-58062-336-0

Everything® **Project Management Book**
$12.95, 1-58062-583-5

Everything® **Puppy Book**
$12.95, 1-58062-576-2

Everything® **Quick Meals Cookbook**
$12.95, 1-58062-488-X

Everything® **Resume Book**
$12.95, 1-58062-311-5

Everything® **Romance Book**
$12.95, 1-58062-566-5

Everything® **Running Book**
$12.95, 1-58062-618-1

Everything® **Sailing Book, 2nd Edition**
$12.95, 1-58062-671-8

Everything® **Saints Book**
$12.95, 1-58062-534-7

Everything® **Selling Book**
$12.95, 1-58062-319-0

Everything® **Shakespeare Book**
$12.95, 1-58062-591-6

Everything® **Spells and Charms Book**
$12.95, 1-58062-532-0

Everything® **Start Your Own Business Book**
$12.95, 1-58062-650-5

Everything® **Stress Management Book**
$12.95, 1-58062-578-9

Everything® **Study Book**
$12.95, 1-55850-615-2

Everything® **Tai Chi and QiGong Book**
$12.95, 1-58062-646-7

Everything® **Tall Tales, Legends, and Outrageous Lies Book**
$12.95, 1-58062-514-2

Everything® **Tarot Book**
$12.95, 1-58062-191-0

Everything® **Time Management Book**
$12.95, 1-58062-492-8

Everything® **Toasts Book**
$12.95, 1-58062-189-9

Everything® **Toddler Book**
$12.95, 1-58062-592-4

Everything® **Total Fitness Book**
$12.95, 1-58062-318-2

Everything® **Trivia Book**
$12.95, 1-58062-143-0

Everything® **Tropical Fish Book**
$12.95, 1-58062-343-3

Everything® **Vegetarian Cookbook**
$12.95, 1-58062-640-8

Everything® **Vitamins, Minerals, and Nutritional Supplements Book**
$12.95, 1-58062-496-0

Everything® **Wedding Book, 2nd Edition**
$12.95, 1-58062-190-2

Everything® **Wedding Checklist**
$7.95, 1-58062-456-1

Everything® **Wedding Etiquette Book**
$7.95, 1-58062-454-5

Everything® **Wedding Organizer**
$15.00, 1-55850-828-7

Everything® **Wedding Shower Book**
$7.95, 1-58062-188-0

Everything® **Wedding Vows Book**
$7.95, 1-58062-455-3

Everything® **Weight Training Book**
$12.95, 1-58062-593-2

Everything® **Wine Book**
$12.95, 1-55850-808-2

Everything® **World War II Book**
$12.95, 1-58062-572-X

Everything® **World's Religions Book**
$12.95, 1-58062-648-3

Everything® **Yoga Book**
$12.95, 1-58062-594-0

Visit us at everything.com

Everything® is a registered trademark of Adams Media Corporation.